Britain's Withdrawal
From the Middle East, 1947-1971:
The Economic and Strategic Imperatives

By

Jacob Abadi

1982

Announcing the Kingston Press Series:

LEADERS, POLITICS AND SOCIAL CHANGE

IN THE ISLAMIC WORLD

General Editor: Carl Max Kortepeter

*Jacob Abadi, BRITAIN'S WITHDRAWAL FROM THE MIDDLE
   EAST: THE ECONOMIC AND STRATEGIC IMPERATIVES

Charles Issawi and Ihsan Abbas, ed. and tr., Ra'if
   Khuri's CHANNELS OF THE FRENCH REVOLUTION TO
   THE ARAB EAST

Taysir Jbara, HAJJ AMIN AL-HUSAYNI, MUFTI OF
   JERUSALEM AND PALESTINIAN LEADER

Carl M. Kortepeter, THE UNITED STATES AND THE
   MIDDLE EAST: THE FLAWED FOUNDATIONS,
   1776-1976

Taysir Nashif, ATOMIC WEAPONS IN THE MIDDLE EAST

* Robert Olson, THE BA'ATH IN SYRIA, 1947-1982

Günsel Renda and C.M. Kortepeter, eds., ATATÜRK
   AND THE TRANSFORMATION OF TURKISH CULTURE

* Available in 1982, the other items, June, 1983.

Britain's Withdrawal
From the Middle East, 1947-1971:
The Economic and Strategic Imperatives

By

Jacob Abadi

The Kingston Press, Inc.
P.O. Box 1456
Princeton, New Jersey 08540

1982

Acknowledgements

I wish to express my gratitude to all those individuals who helped me in the preparation of this study. First and foremost I would like to thank Professors Carl M. Kortepeter and Robert J. Scally of New York University. Their thoughtful comments helped me to substantially improve the quality of this study. I would also like to express my thanks to Professor Albert U. Romasco for his helpful suggestions. I am indebted to Professor Peter J. Chelkowski from the Department of Near Eastern Languages and Literatures at New York University for arranging access to the services of the Firestone Library at Princeton University.

I would like to express my great appreciation for the assistance and cooperation of the following institutions where most of the research on this study has been conducted: the U. S. Military Academy at West Point, N.Y. and the U. S. National War College at Washington, D.C. Special thanks also goes to the staff members of the Nimitz Library at the U. S. Naval Academy, Annapolis, Maryland, for their full cooperation and kind assistance. I would also like to thank the staff members of the library of Nuffield College of Oxford University for providing me with some of the material which was essential for the completion of this study. Special thanks also to the staff members of the Bobst Library and especially to Ms. Deborah Rossi. In addition I would like to thank Ms. Sara Steinmetz of the Politics Department of New York University.

Above all I wish to thank my wife, Chaia, for the understanding and full support that I enjoyed during the years of research and writing.

December, 1982   Jacob Abadi

TABLE OF CONTENTS

Acknowledgements............................. v

Map.......................................viii

Preface.................................... ix

Introduction..............................xiii

CHAPTER   I   Palestine: Economic Crisis and
               Withdrawal..................... 1

CHAPTER   II The Strategists and Their
               Influence..................... 38

CHAPTER   III The Quest for the New Security
               Arrangements and Alternative
               Bases......................... 56

CHAPTER   IV Air Power and Strategic
               Deployment................... 116

CHAPTER   V   Suez and the Hydrogen Bomb..... 149

CHAPTER   VI The Royal Navy and the
               Mobile Base Policy............ 173

CHAPTER   VII Imperial Remnants: Aden and
               the Persian Gulf.............. 196

CONCLUSION................................. 219

BIBLIOGRAPHY............................... 227

INDEX...................................... 267

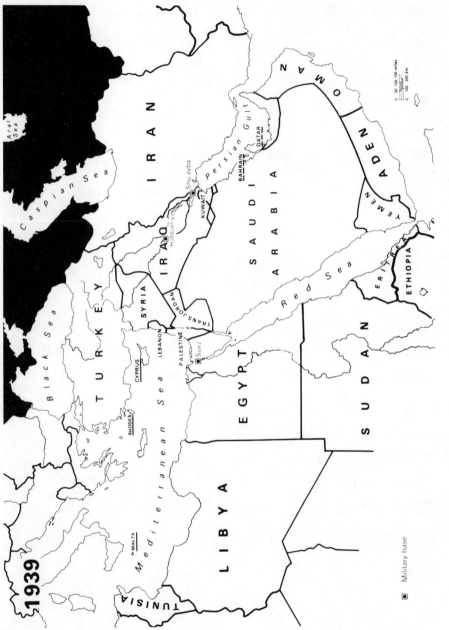

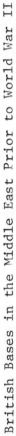

1939

Aral Sea

Caspian Sea

Black Sea

IRAN

TURKEY

Mediterranean Sea

CYPRUS

RHODES

MALTA

SYRIA

LEBANON

PALESTINE

TRANSJORDAN

IRAQ

Habbaniya

Shu'ayba

KUWAIT

Persian Gulf

BAHRAIN

QATAR

SAUDI ARABIA

OMAN

ADEN

YEMEN

Suez

EGYPT

LIBYA

TUNISIA

Red Sea

SUDAN

ERITREA

ETHIOPIA

0 50 100 150 miles
0   100   200 km

■ Military base

Britsh Bases in the Middle East Prior to World War II

viii

PREFACE

Overseas bases were regarded by the British as indispensible in safeguarding the life-line of the British Empire. Yet, in the years which followed the Second World War, doubts concerning the usefulness of those bases emerged in Britain. Consequently, they were evacuated. The aim of this study is to examine the domestic and global factors which were responsible for Britain's retreat from the traditionally most crucial of the imperial areas: Palestine, Egypt with its huge base in the Suez Canal Zone, Aden and the Persian Gulf.

Britain's withdrawal from the Middle East has been widely discussed by historians. They, however, dealt with this phenomenon in an external rather than in a domestic context. Excessive emphasis had been laid on the role of Arab and Jewish revolutionary nationalism as the instruments compelling the British to retreat from the Middle East. But British strongholds in the Middle East, like other imperial bases stretching from the home island to Singapore and Hong Kong, had become less important due to the rise of a new set of domestic restraints. These restraints derived chiefly from the traumatic experience of the Second World War and from the revolution in technology which introduced air power and atomic weapons into strategic thinking.

This study highlights the process of readjustment in British defense policy produced in the first instance by crucial domestic pressures. For this purpose analyses of the views of the civil and military elites are presented throughout the study. The basic argument of the study is that forces of nationalism alone were never adequate to cause the retreat of an imperial power. As George Woodcock noted, "Never had the will or the action of a subject people, however heroic or persistent, been alone sufficient to destroy an imperial power."

Since the British economy nearly collapsed in the aftermath of the Second World War, the contribution which the weak economy made to the process of readjustment is discussed extensively at the beginning of the study. British policy toward overseas bases is also examined against the background of cold war diplomacy. The changes in the strategic deployment of British defense forces are followed closely in light of the revolution in technology which made air power a decisive factor in warfare, gave rise to atomic weapons, and caused confusion regarding the role of the Royal Navy and the bases.

The study focuses on major events in British defense policy during the period between 1945 and 1971: the decision to evacuate Palestine made in 1947, the Anglo-Egyptian Agreement of 1954 terminating the presence of the British garrison in the Suez Canal Zone and the withdrawal of British forces from Aden (1962) and the Persian Gulf (1971).

The conviction that domestic constraints are no less crucial in the making of foreign and defense policy than the changes in the external environment is derived from the theses of prominent scholars such as Arno J. Mayer, James N. Rosenau, Hans J. Morgenthau and others who emphasize that foreign and defense policies must be seen and treated in relation to domestic constraints.

Some historians have already explained the decline of the British Empire as a result of domestic weaknesses. For example, Carlo M. Cippola thought that economic weakness was the main cause for the decline of empires. E. J. Hobsbawm explained the decline of Britain in the same way. George Dangerfield attributed the death of Liberal England to a set od domestic factors, the most important of which was the English working class unrest, the rise of the suffragettes' movement, and the Irish problem. Using an approach reflecting these positions, the main domestic pressures in Britain are examined. The economic weakness, the technological innovations, and the power of pressure groups and public opinion are extensively discussed.

The source material consulted for the investigation of the British attitude toward Middle Eastern bases include the following: Minutes of Cabinet meetings, debates in the House of Commons and the House of Lords and memoranda of instructions by those who were most intimately associated with the making of defense policy, i.e., Cabinet members, ministers, chiefs of staff and civil servants. Also, the author has drawn heavily on military periodicals dealing with defense and military issues such as: Brassey's Annual and the Journal of the Royal United Service Institution because they contain the views of the military elite of the three services. Such views were crucial in the formulation of defense policy. Other periodicals such as Air Power, Army Quarterly, Military Review, Round Table, Fortnightly Review and many others proved quite valuable. Also important were weekly magazines such as The Economist, New Statesman and Nation, and Time and Tide. London dailies also elucidated many problems, particularly the London Times and The Daily Telegraph.

Finally, the author has attached great importance to the studies of military professionals and theoreticians of war, the most prominent of whom were A. T. Mahan, B. H. Liddell Hart, Major General J. F. C. Fuller, Admiral Lord Louis Mountbatten, Marshal of the R. A. F. John Slessor, Air Vice Marshal E. Y. Kingston-McCloughrey and others. In addition, many pieces of unpublished material have contributed significantly to the preparation of this study. Such items as the unpublished dissertations of Lieutenant Colonel (U.S. Army) DeWitt C. Armstrong, "The Changing Strategy of British Bases" and Commander (U.S. Navy) William J.Croeve, "The Policy Roots of the Modern Royal Navy 1946-1963" were found to contain invaluable

information.   These   sources   and   commentary
together   with   numerous books reflecting different
opinions   about this important subject inspired the
author to present a new synthesis.

J. A.

HISTORICAL INTRODUCTION

This balanced and challenging study, written
by Dr. Jacob Abadi, an important contemporary
military historian, deals with a topic of great
importance for the economic and military planner
and Middle East specialists. Just over two
hundred years ago, after the Seven Years War
(1756-1763) or the French and Indian War, as it
was known in North America, the British, by
defeating the French in North America and India,
began to assert their dominance in world affairs.
This dominance was based upon a new and incredibly
productive economic system derived from the
control of essential raw materials and their
processing by machines in factories into refined
and mass produced items of trade which could be
sold at a price far below a comparable item
produced purely by hand labor. The British
government, in turn, taxed these items and the
wage earners producing them to sustain an enormous
network of trading posts, missionary stations and
military bases. Many of these extensions of
Britain in Africa, Asia and on islands in the
major oceans evolved into British colonies or
protectorates in the nineteenth century as British
strategists, government personnel and overseas
agents began to trace the grand design of British
world dominance. Lord Palmerston, as British
Foreign Minister, State Secretary for Internal
Affairs and then Prime Minister between 1830 and
1865, was a key individual in shaping British
Imperial policy. The "Eastern Question" became a
catch phrase in his day and referred to strain on
the international system which the sudden
dismemberment of the Ottoman Empire would cause.
Even in the nineteenth century, the Ottoman Empire
included within its borders a major portion of
North Africa, the Near East and the Balkan
Peninsula, in short, most of the Middle East in
today's parlance except for Iran and Afganistan.
By the early nineteenth century, India had become
the gem of the British imperial system, not only
its anchor and training ground in the east, but
also a source of colonial manpower and a large

colonial marketplace. Palmerston and his successors, Disraeli, Gladstone, Salisbury, Grey, Balfour, Lloyd-George, MacDonald and many others guarded jealously the lifeline to India which passed through the Mediterranean and then overland either through Syria and Iraq or Egypt. The 'lifeline' of course became even more clearly defined with the completion of the Suez Canal in 1869.

With the decline of Ottoman economic and military power, Imperial Russia, often allied with the Habsburgs of Austro-Hungary, became eager to seize Ottoman territory in the Balkan Peninsula, the Ukraine and the Caucasus. Essentially, with British and Imperial German moral and material assistance, the Ottomans fought a rearguard defense of its northern territories against Russia throughout the nineteenth century.

Britain had faced a dangerous challenge by France under Napoleon (1798-1814), but in Palmerston's time it became clear that Russia was the power to watch in the Middle East. Britain wisely recognized that it was more important to foster Ottoman reform and constitutionalism as a check on Russian expansion, rather than to consider garrisoning the entire communications link with India across the Middle East. In time this system underwent two modifications. First of all when it became apparent that Balkan national states such as Greece, Rumania and Bulgaria, would provide a stronger bulwark to Russian expansion than Ottoman troops, the British shifted its support to Balkan nationalism. Only toward the end of the nineteenth century did Britain regard the formation of permanent bases in the Middle East as essential. This new policy evolved out of perceived threats to the British lifeline to India deriving from French and German imperial interests in parts of the Ottoman Empire and the annexation by Russia of large chunks of territory in the Caucasus and Central Asia. The French, blocked by Britain elsewhere and dominated by Prussia on the European Continent after 1870, had augmented its hold on Algeria by annexing Tunisia in 1881, thus pushing perilessly close to British concerns in Egypt. Britain had received Cyprus at the Congress of Berlin in 1878 where Bismarck had also given the nod for France to sieze Tunisia. Austria also picked up Bosnia and Herzegovina thus further blocking Serbian expansion to the Dalmatian coast. Britain had precipitated a crisis in Egypt in 1879 with the ouster of Khedive Ismail because Egypt had defaulted on loan payments. This highhandedness produced a national reaction in 1881-82 led by Urabi Pasha, Minister of Defense. The insolvence, the anti-foreign nature of the Egyptian revolt, but particularly the perceived threat to the 'lifeline', led to Britain's annexation of Egypt and the ushering in of the second phase of European imperialism. The first phase had developed in the penetration of cheap manufactured goods which threatened the local craft guilds with extinction. The second phase, outright annexation, was often connected with two new developments: the incredible advances in military technology making conquest 'inexpensive', in terms of western manpower; and secondly, the realization that insolvence in economically dependent areas such as the Middle East, could threaten the banking and financial institutions of European patron states.

Alarm over the growing power of Imperial Germany began to materialize after the Franco-Prussian War in 1870 but only with the conception of the Berlin-Baghdad Railroad in the 1890's did Germany stir deeper concern. This project was virtually neutralized as a German plan when British and French banking interests bought heavily into the enterprise.

Doubtless the German decision to build a strong navy in the first decade of the twentieth century, as a counter weight to Britain's dominance of the high seas and colonial markets, heightened the British desire for overseas bases and garrisons. The British navy, more than any other institution, had become the glue holding together and protecting British trade and imperial interests. But a large military establishment, such as Britain had fostered, required a healthy imperial economy. Unfortunately, investment in Britain in the late nineteenth century had largely shifted to the financing of colonial ventures or to the underwriting of governments such as Egypt or the Ottoman Empire where usurious interest rates were paid. But not enough re-investment had taken place in the home isles to maintain competition against the challenges from Germany, the U.S. and Japan.

The history that unfolds under the careful analysis of Dr. Abadi is one first of all of British financial crisis after World War II. While it is true that this crisis was long in developing because of the burden of two world wars and uncertain economic conditions between the wars, it is also true that the United States precipitated the crisis in 1945 by cutting off lend lease aid the very day of victory in Europe. Was this stinginess and small mindedness on the part of the United States or were other forces at work? On the one hand, one might note that the concept of the British Empire had always been so well advertised in the United States that many officials may have felt that Britain no longer required support. It is more likely, however, given the tendency of American foreign policy to be entangled with domestic ethnic issues, that Britain had its lend lease cut off so abruptly because American Zionists had pressured Henry Morgenthau, Secretary of the Treasury, and also President Truman. The Zionists had not forgotten the British White Paper of 1939 which restricted Jewish immigration into Palestine after the war.

As Dr. Abadi indicates, the financial crisis forced both the Labor and Conservative governments to review all colonial policy because many colonies and dependencies had ceased to pay their own way and had thus became a direct burden on the British budget. The maintenance of overseas bases after the war also proved to be a critical waste of manpower at a time when industry and mining was desperately short of hands.

While groping for new imperial and strategic concepts, the postwar leadership turned to an influencial circle of strategists who were busy absorbing the new strategic concepts based upon the weapons and military experience of World War II. In their eyes, rapid deployment by aircraft of home-based troops appeared more desirable than relying upon bases situated in hostile colonial territory. The appearance of accurate atomic weaponry also tended to discourage the maintenance of overseas bases. In the eyes of some strategists, aircraft had become a formidable weapon; consequently, the Royal Navy lost its role and purpose. Only by demonstrating the value of aircraft carriers did the navy maintain any kind of major role for itself.

Thus Dr. Abadi demonstrates that through the intermediary and interpretive role of the strategists, government officials were able to adopt the unpopular position that overseas bases were no longer useful. As many were to argue, a base was only useful if the people round about wanted it to be there. Even the argument that Middle Eastern bases were necessary for the protection of oil fields and oil supplies was proven unsound by Dr. Abadi. By 1971 Britain had withdrawn formally from all of its commitments in the Middle East to the east of Suez.

I take great pleasure in recommending this study, the second in the Kingston Press Series, to your interest and attention.

Carl M. Kortepeter
New York University
December, 1982

CHAPTER I

PALESTINE: ECONOMIC CRISIS AND WITHDRAWAL

The strategic value of Palestine and the Suez
Canal Zone was recognized by the British long
before they assumed responsibility for the mandate
entrusted to them by the League of Nations in
1921. Since the opening of the Suez Canal in 1869
the Middle East was regarded as a vital bridge to
British possessions in India and the Far East, and
as a highway for British trade. The Middle East
played a major role in imperial defense during the
First and Second World Wars. In the postwar era,
the region remained strategically important to the
Western countries because of its vast oil resources and the fear that they might be captured
by the Soviet Union. Despite the abundance of
Middle-Eastern oil, the retreat had already begun
in the interwar period. Iraq had become a const-
itutional monarchy in 1930 and had entered a
treaty relationship with Britain, which afforded
the latter control of the airfields, military
installations and means of communication for an
indefinite period. Transjordan was granted similar independence in 1946 with British subsidies
and military assistance. Egypt, which had been
nominally independent since 1922, became fully
sovereign, except in cases of national emergency,
by a treaty of friendship signed in 1936 when the
British forces withdrew to the Suez Canal Zone.
The smaller sheikdoms of the Arabian Peninsula and
the Persian Gulf, except for Saudi Arabia, remained tied to Britain by defense treaties.
Palestine was among the last territories to
be evacuated by the British, due to the hostility
between Jews and Arabs. The British government
was under obligation to support the establishment
of a Jewish National Home in Palestine as stipu-

lated in the Balfour Declaration of 1917. Simul-
taneously the British government was committed to
the establishment of an independent Arab rule in
Palestine, according to the promises given to
Sherif Hussein by Sir Henry McMahon during the
First World War.[1]

Throughout the 1930s Jews immigrated to
Palestine in large numbers and Arab objections
intensified. An Arab revolt had erupted in 1936
and lasted for three years. British attempts to
set limits on Jewish immigration and on the sale
of land to Jews had failed. Several attempts to
impose partition plans on both parties were also
doomed to failure. Following the Second World
War, Jewish nationalism had become violent as
well. By then, the British economy was faltering
and the government found it increasingly difficult
to finance the occupation.

Most historians attribute the British withdrawal from Palestine mainly to the inability of
the British government to suppress the forces of
nationalism. Nevertheless, a review of the factors that led to British retreat from the Middle
East and from Palestine in particular, reveals
that the most important factor determining British
policy in the critical years 1945-1948 was the
weakness of the British economy. The economic
weakness of Britain was not conducive to an aggressive foreign policy.[2] C. M. Woodhouse wrote
that: "Britain's postwar economy even at its most
prosperous. . . could not afford the defense bill
of an entirely independent power."[3] Economic
stagnation prevented Britain from playing a major
role in world affairs.[4]

In postwar Britain, the defense problem was
acute because economic growth was limited and the
rate of production was slow due to a severe lack
of manpower. Domestic demand soared while foreign
commitments became very costly. British statesmen

found that decisions affecting foreign policy were becoming increasingly dependent upon conditions of domestic finance. The retreat from Palestine in 1948 had demonstrated the strength of the economic constraint as much as any other political move of postwar Britain.

What reason had the Labour Government to abandon Palestine in 1948 other than economic? The argument that Arab and Jewish nationalism was the major cause for retreat seems inadequate as George Woodcock explained: "Never had the will or the action of a subject people, however heroic or persistent been alone sufficient to destroy an imperial power."[5]

Arab nationalism had become extremely vocal and militant during the Palestinian revolt between 1936-1939, yet the British did not withdraw at that time. Successive British governments undertook the unpleasant task of reconciling Arabs and Jews. They endeavored to prevent Jewish immigrants from landing in Palestine in order not to antagonize the Arabs and thus lose their grip on the area which they considered vital for the protection of the Suez Canal, the lifeline of the Empire. Oil became increasingly important for the British economy, especially following the Second World War. Nevertheless, the new Labour Government under Clement Attlee did not have the means to finance the postwar reconstruction.[6]

Britain's ability to import had depended heavily on earnings from investments overseas. Between 1939 and 1945 over 1.200 billion pounds sterling of capital invested abroad was liquidated in order to pay for the expenses of the war. During the war, the national debt increased by 14.800 billion pounds, or almost exactly twice the increase incurred in the First World War. Annual government expenditures far exceeded the total national income of any prewar year. British national income in 1938 had been 4,671 million pounds. In each of the fiscal years from the year ending March 31, 1940, to March 31, 1946, the government spent an average of 4,734 million pounds.

Between 1940 and 1945, the total annual consumption of goods and services in Britain, both personal and governmental, exceeded the total production each year by an average of 13 percent. This meant that for each 100 pounds of goods and services, British citizens and their government used 113 pounds. During the war, markets in Asia, Latin America and other places were deliberately abandoned so that factories which served these markets could be used to manufacture arms and munitions. In 1945 the British Government estimated that there was a need for a 50 percent increase in exports in order to finance a volume of imports no greater than the prewar level. Only then would Britain avoid upsetting the current balance of payments.[7]

Postwar Britain was in a severe economic crisis, although the subsequent economic growth was remarkable. The trading mechanism by which Britain earned her livelihood had been shattered. The British economy became increasingly dominated by the United States. The United States forced Britain to sell one billion pounds of her securities in order to pay for supplies at the beginning of the war.[8] By the end of the war, Britain had spent about 16.9 billion pounds abroad, and had earned only about 6.9 billion pounds, or about 40 percent of her imports in the period between September 1939 and December 1945. The rest had been financed by the sale of 1.2 billion pounds of capital invested abroad, by grants and by Lend Lease from the United States and Canada which amounted to 5.4 billion pounds.[9]

Britain became a debtor to many of her domin-

ions. Her debit balance to the United States on
the Lend Lease Account amounted to 4.2 billion
pounds. Britain's internal debt had reached dimensions undreamed of in her history. She came
out of the Second World War with a debt of 26
billion pounds after the United States had wiped
out her debt on the Lend Lease Account. Consider-
ing that the national debt in 1914 was only 800
million pounds, the increase was staggering.[10]

Britain had paid half of the cost of the war
by raising taxes and borrowing. She began the war
with 21 million tons of merchant shipping which
earned her 150 million pounds a year. Her export
trade had shrunk to 29 percent of what it had been
in 1939. Britain was always heavily dependent on
foreign trade. She imported 50 percent of her
food and raw material. Consequently, a considerable increase of exports was needed. In most
cases Britain had to pay either in dollars or in
gold. Gold and dollar reserves had dropped from
864 million pounds to 453 million pounds during
the war years. The economies of other European
countries were faltering and all of them depended
heavily upon assistance from the United States.

The Commonwealth countries were in economic
troubles of their own. Overseas commitments became heavier than ever. Countries such as Palestine, Greece, Egypt, Malaya and Cyprus, demanded
heavy expenditures. British control in distant
areas could be maintained only by large armies,
due to the need to purge the administration of
anti-British elements and to replace them with
British personnel. Britain had neither the will,
nor the resources for such aggressive policy.
British soldiers were impatient to return home.
The economy underwent a transition from wartime
needs to peacetime production. The war was responsible for direct shortages of capital and food
items. It disrupted the labor market by drawing

many workers away from the mines and the textile industries. Consequently, their return to these industries became extremely difficult.[11]

The most crucial element in the decline of the British economy was the loss of foreign investments as Attlee explained in one of his broadcasted speeches on the need for increased production.[12]

Foreign trade was adversely affected. In addition to the loss of income from foreign investment and markets, Britain was hindered by the fact that industrial machinery had become outworn. Buildings were demolished and a housing shortage caused a great hardship.[13] In 1945 three million houses, one third of the total, were over eighty years old. German bombing had destroyed nearly one third of the English homes. There was a loss of a half million units, whereas during the war years, the population had increased by nearly two million people.

The war was by no means solely responsible for the decline which occurred between the middle of the nineteenth century and the 1890s.[14] However, Britain of 1945 was significantly more impoverished than in 1938. The problems were immense. As Elizabeth Monroe explained:

> The first job for the cabinet was to organize British economic survival at a tolerable living standard, and the next to save Europe from famine and anarchy.[15]

After 1945 the unfavorable balance of payments worsened. In 1946 and 1947 the balance of trade reached 298 million pounds and 443 million pounds respectively. Bread and potatoes were added to the list of rationed items for the first time. These shortages were caused by the war, the

bad weather and the wet harvest of 1946.[16]   In his
article in the Soviet weekly magazine New Times,
the Soviet commentator E. Varga also blamed the
Labour Government for these difficulties. He attributed this situation to the determination of
Britain's ruling classes to continue the old imperialist policy regardless of the economic implications.[17]

In addition to food rationing, imports from
dollar areas were tightly controlled and tourist
spending from the sterling area was substantially
reduced. Thus, the demands made upon British citizens became heavier than they had been during the
war.[18] Taxation remained very high, and the rate
of house building remained low. There was an urgent need to increase exports, and since exports
had to be given the first priority, the Government
was compelled to cut the defense bill.[19]

British troops were still stationed in Germany, Austria, Japan, the Far East, Southeast
Asia, Venezia Gulia, Palestine, India and other
areas. The heaviest commitments were Palestine
and Germany. The cost of maintaining British
troops in Palestine was 100 million pounds a year
and 80 million pounds was needed every year to
maintain the British zone in Germany.[20] American
food supplies sent to India were debited to the
British account. The Minister of Food, Ben Smith,
expressed the fear of an imminent disaster.[21] A
radical change in defense policy became inevitable. Nothing short of quick disengagement could
have been the answer.[22]

As a percentage of its population, Britain
had almost as many men in the army as the United
States at a time when the economy prohibited substantial expenditure on defense.[23] Palestine had
three or four times as many British troops as had
India. Twenty thousand British troops were stationed there between 1936 and 1939 when the Pales-

tinian revolt erupted.[24] It became increasingly
obvious to the British leaders that the British
economy could no longer sustain the heavy expenditures in the Middle East, and in Palestine in particular, regardless of its strategic importance.
J.C. Hurewitz explained how the postwar weakness
of the British economy affected Britain's influence in the Middle East:

> The War had left the British economy in
> a state of near prostration. The United
> Kingdom therefore could not undertake
> costly ventures in the Arab East as vi-
> tal as the area was. Besides, the war
> had changed the United Kingdom's rela-
> tionship to Egypt, Palestine and Iraq
> from a creditor to a debtor nation,
> thereby further diluting British author-
> ity.[25]

Since Britain could not hope to occupy Egypt
indefinitely, Palestine was regarded as a convenient outpost from which the supply of petroleum
badly needed for domestic needs, could be guaranteed. Also, Palestine was important in securing
markets for British goods. Nevertheless, the economic weakness compelled the British to withdraw.
The military establishment in the Middle East
was costly, and British war debts to Egypt and
Iraq amounted to more than 2 billion dollars.[26]
By the end of the war, the expenditures became
even heavier in Palestine. The British authorities failed to subdue local resistance without imposing censorship. Curfews, arrests, and martial
law, became the usual methods of dealing with the
noncooperative population. These coercive methods
demanded a steady increase in the number of troops
and in funds. Whereas the number of the troops in
1939 was only 20,000, the number increased to

80,000 by the end of 1946. There were several
units of the Transjordan Arab Legion, and 16,000
British and local police. British manpower in
Palestine was nearly one-tenth of the total [27]
strength of the British army at the time. The
British taxpayer spent about $222.4 million for
the maintenance of the forces during the Labour
Government's year and a half in office, and the
Palestine Government at least another $20 million.
During the same period the cost of occupying all
overseas territories amounted to 300 million
pounds. According to Emanuel Shinwell, occupation
of overseas territories amounted to 200 million
pounds a year. [28] The total deficit in Britain's
balance of payments in 1946 was 450 million
pounds. The sum spent on overseas territories was
almost one half of the total deficit. [29]

Palestine's cost was so high because there
were extensive army camps, including about sixty
police structures, some as large as city blocks.
These structures were built between 1940 and 1944
to billet the policy and the Government offices.
They were equipped with the most modern police and
military facilities. [30]

In August 1945, the Lend-Lease program came
to an abrupt end. [31] At that time Britain was getting 25 percent of her imports from the United
States and 20 percent from Canada, but she was
selling less than 5 percent of her exports to the
United States, and even less than that to Canada.
The Government was unable to pay for imports.
Gold and dollar reserves were dropping below the
2,000 million pounds considered a safe minimum.

The termination of Lend Lease constituted not
only an economic blow, but also a psychological
one. There was a feeling of impending economic
disaster which undoubtedly compelled the British
Government to contemplate a drastic reduction of
overseas commitments.

The cessation of Lend Lease was regarded as a severe economic blow because it affected Britain's ability to pay for imported food.[32]   For the Labour Government, the announcement of the end of the Lend Lease was the blackest hour.[33]   Lord Keynes called it a "Financial Dunkirk."[34]   Prime Minister Attlee said in his memoirs:

> We were closely integrated with the United States economy through the opera- tion of Lend Lease, and this had meant we had not had to worry about our sup- plies of food and raw materials, nor about overseas payments.... We were faced once more with an acute crisis.[35]

Hugh Dalton, the Labour Chancellor of the Exchequer wrote: "...We now face not war anymore, only total economic ruin,"[36]   Emanuel Shin- well, the Minister of Fuel and Power reflected this same mood in his memoirs.[37]

The Labour Government's ability to remain in control of the Middle East was adversely affected by the American attitude toward Britain, not only as an imperial power, but one depicted in the American press as oppressing Jews in the Holy Land.[38]   Nevertheless, the British Government con- tinued to occupy Palestine until 1948 because British statesmen were still convinced that Bri- tain was a great power. Moreover, the magnitude of the economic crisis was inadequately assessed. The leaders of the Labour Party were aware of the link between foreign policy and the internal eco- nomic situation. The conduct of foreign policy was in the hands of Ernest Bevin, an extremely capable statesman.[39]   Bevin realized that Britain would soon be compelled to disengage from many overseas commitments because economic weakness made withdrawal inevitable. In the words of Lord

Strang: "Relative weakness imposes some measure
of disengagement in order to bring obligations
into line with material strength...."[40] Of
course, conservatives were also aware of these
problems.[41] Bevin disengaged in Palestine as he
did in Greece. He even tried to reach a disengagement agreement with the Egyptian Prime Minis-
ster Ismail Sidky in 1946.[42] The urgent need for
manpower made it impossible to keep troops in
Palestine or any other area, as the military historian C.J. Barlett explains: "What strategic
bases could be held through the world in the face
of such nationalism and Britain's weakened economy?"

In 1946, Attlee, in an attempt to withdraw
from overseas commitments, wanted to help Australia develop as an industrial and military power so
that she would be able to assume a portion of
Britain's responsibility in the Far East. The
White Paper on Defense from 1948 stated: "...the
first essential is a strong and sound economy with
a flourishing industry from which to draw the
strength to defend our rights and fulfill our obligations."[43]

British defense had to be reviewed in light
of the nation's economic difficulties.[44] The defense expenditure for 1946 was 1.73 billion
pounds, or one-fifth of the Gross National Product. The Government's main problem was to feed
its people and to supply its factories with raw
materials.[45] There was an urgent need for a loan.
In the summer of 1946 a loan of 3.75 billion dollars was drawn from the United States and another
loan of 1.25 billion dollars was taken from
Canada. According to the terms of the loan agreement signed with the United States, Britain assumed the following obligations: to abolish the
sterling bloc, to allow free exchange of pounds
for dollars by July 15, 1947 -- a year from the

date of the agreement; to pay her dominions and colonies all the debts in dollars; to purchase from the United States the same amount of goods as before; and to lower the preferential tariffs between Britain and her dominions. Britain had received less money than she asked for on harsher terms.[46]

The convertibility of the pound was suspended several months later by Hugh Dalton. In the last week prior to the suspension of the dollar convertibility (on August 20, 1947), Britain lost 237 million dollars. By September 1947, of the 3.75 billion dollars of the loan, only 400 million dollars remained undrawn.[47] The Labour leaders realized that they could not pursue the same policy indefinitely.[48]

As early as September 3, 1945, Attlee recognized that maintaining troops in the Middle East constituted a heavy burden on the British economy and suggested a regional defense arrangement under the auspices of the United Nations Organization. Some Britons believed that the U.N. could be relied upon.[49] Bevin had a distrust in it from the beginning.[50] The chiefs of the army, and especially the Chief of the Imperial General Staff, Lord Allanbrooke, also distrusted the U.N. and raised objection to such a scheme.[51]

The quest for a defense arrangement which would not require stationing of troops in the Middle East was repeated during the fifties. The Baghdad Pact of 1955 was the result of these efforts.[52] In the early postwar years, however, the British did not think in terms of major alliances or comprehensive defense arrangements. Bevin believed that Palestine could be abandoned and that an alternative base should be built in Kenya following the evacuation of Egypt.[53] Attlee wished to abandon the Mediterranean and the Middle East, and to safeguard the Cape route for imperial

communication to the Far East.[54]   A memorandum by
the strategist, B. H. Liddell Hart, from 1946, had
considerable influence on Attlee.   The memorandum
mentioned the possibility of shifting the defense
line of the empire away from the Middle East.[55]

The above-mentioned proposals were meant to
alleviate the economic pressure on the Government.
On November 22, 1947 a political document of the
Labour Party was quoted in the New York Times:
"Before 1914 the people (of Britain) were owed by
the rest of the world a debt equal to 100
pounds (each).   Today each of us...owes the rest of
the world 100 pounds." The Labour Government had
striven to minimize the expenses on defense, especially in overseas territories. Attlee tried to
convince the military authorities to find an alternative line of defense in Africa from Lagos to
Kenya.[56]   Dalton supported this plan, and even
threatened to resign should the Government fail to
do so. He said: "Among the payments which if we
were to win must be cut hard and quickly, were...
particularly for forces stationed abroad."[57]   The
attempts to eliminate the need for stationing
forces in Palestine continued until 1948 but were
unsuccessful. Dalton more than any other British
statesmen realized that a failure to reduce foreign commitments would be disastrous to the Brit-
tish economy. Discussing the need for drastic
cuts in the national defense budget, he argued in
his memoirs: "What shall it profit Britain to
have even 1.500.000 men in the Forces and supply
and to be spending nearly 1.000 million pounds a
year on them if we come an economic and financial
cropper two years hence?"[58]

Dalton at the Exchequer and Cripps at the
Board of Trade insisted on changes in defense
plans, mainly those pertaining to reduction of
troops overseas. Bevin said about the pressures
exerted by Dalton:

> Week by week and day by day, he had to
> come to the Cabinet to report on the
> dollar position...it became perfectly
> clear with the rise in prices, that
> sooner or later, an enormous change in
> our whole position would have to be
> faced.[59]

The loans taken from the United States and Canada
were quickly depleting. Dalton argued that the
huge expenditure of manpower and money on defense
was making nonsense of the economy and the public
finance.[60]

In May 1947, at a Labour Party Conference,
Ian Mikardo and Richard Crossman (two members of
the "Keep Left" group within the Party) argued
that the British troops in the Middle East must be
withdrawn because they constituted an invisible
import and a burden on the balance of payments,
while oil from Iraq and cotton from Egypt should
be in any case available to Britain through commercial channels.[61]   Even Bevin, who was deeply
concerned about the defense of the British Empire,
was too committed to the welfare of the British
working class to pursue an aggressive foreign policy involving large expenditures.[62]

The Labour Government's commitment to the
welfare of British society required substantial
funds for welfare and other social projects. It
was a period of Labour rule and therefore the
needs of the working class were deemed most important. In the words of Pauline Gregg:

> There had been landlord rule, middle
> class rule, and now there was Labour
> rule. In each epoch an economically
> powerful class was enabled to control
> the legislature and fashioned it for its
> own advantage.[63]

The magnitude of the "Welfare State" project reveals the extent of the economic pressure exerted on the Labour Government. The project included various measures passed by the government to abolish poverty. These measures became so popular that even those who objected to them could not demand reduction of benefits for the poor, but only for the lower middle class.[64]

The following table shows the increase in the main items of the "Welfare State" project:[65]

	1938-9	1947-8
	(In million pounds)	
Social Security Services	310.5	559.8
Education	111.8	222.8
Health	74.4	174.7
Housing	23.7	55.8
Total	520.4	1013.1

These vast amounts of money had to be provided somehow. Since the loans were depleting, only two possibilities remained: additional taxation, or reduction of military expenditures. The first alternative had to be discarded because taxes were already high. Reduction of military expenses was the only alternative and that meant withdrawal from overseas bases.

The British leaders still wished to maintain the empire; however, they were not indifferent to economic problems. There was a general view that imperial defense was an economic necessity. On May 14, 1947 Bevin said in the House of Commons: "The British interests in the Middle East contribute substantially not only to the prosperity of the people there, but also to the wage packet of the workers of this country."[66]

When a Labour MP advocated cuts in defense expenditures, he was told by the War Minister, Field Marshal H. Alexander, "We shall not achieve final economic recovery unless we can maintain security for those working for us in the areas of the world upon which we depend for our economic recovery."[67] Moreover, Britain became increasingly dependent on oil from the Middle East. In 1939 its oil production amounted to less than one-twentieth of the world's output. In 1948, the figure was one-eighth.[68] Britain became heavily dependent on oil due to the postwar shortage of coal. A correspondent of The Economist wrote on May 17, 1947, "America needs Middle East oil, but Britain absolutely depends on it."[69] The Middle East remained important because financial resources were not available for constructing new refineries or new pipelines. Pipelines were needed to enable the oil to flow directly from the Persian Gulf to the Mediterranean without paying the required dues for passing through the Suez Canal.[70] One cannot argue therefore, that the desire to maintain the imperial possessions in the Middle East stemmed from a traditional obsession of the British leaders. However, although oil was considered an essential commodity, there was no assurance in the minds of the British leaders that there must be military control to insure its flow. Furthermore, oil had become an excuse for maintaining forces in the Middle East.[71]

Arguments for withdrawal became more frequently heard despite the dependence on oil in the
Middle East. When the balance of payments crisis
hit Britain after the introduction of sterling
convertibility, there was mounting pressure on the
part of many MP's to reduce military expenditure
in places such as Germany and Palestine.[72]
Towards the end of the 1940s, the Labour Government was weakening. There was a conflict between
two groups, one of which consisted of moderate
socialists with a trade union background, and the
other included members with a middle class background. The latter were more conservative and
more pacifist in foreign policy. Among the members of this group were Michael Foot, editor of
the Tribune, which offered a platform to the
Bevanites, Jennie Lee, wife of Aneurin Bevan,
Barbara Castle and Hugh Delargy. This group favored rapprochement with the Soviet Union. They
were not organized nor led by a prominent leader
until the beginning of the 1950s, when they were
led by Aneurin Bevan. Nevertheless, they were
quite vocal within the Labour Party.

The Government's decision to reduce the
number of all troops to 1,087,000 in March 1948
did not satisfy the Bevanites. Members of the
Defense Committee and a considerable part of the
trade unionists criticized the services' manpower
figure as detrimental to the national economy.
The Bevanites proposed that the services should
have only 750,000 men, thereby releasing a quarter
of a million productive workers without jeopardizing British defense commitments, instead of the
reduction of 340,000 from the December 1946 level
of 1,427,000.

Labour MP's who opposed the Government's
defense policy often attacked Bevin and his supporters.[73] Crossman thought that Britain must
quickly pursue a foreign policy commensurate with

her resources, for in trying to hold on to everything she might lose everything.[74]

The Bevanites continued their attacks on the
Conservative Government more vigorously. The
Bevanite pamphlet, One Way Only, argued that British society could afford for defense purposes only 100 million pounds and not 400 million pounds.

The pressures to withdraw came not only from
Labour MP's, but from the Conservatives as well.
Churchill, the leader of the opposition, urged the
the Government to concentrate on domestic recovery, on reconversion of the industries from wartime production to that of peace, on the provision
of houses, and the drastic curtailment of the national expenditure.[75] In a speech delivered at the
House of Commons on January 31, 1947 Churchill,
attacking Labour's policy in Palestine as most
detrimental to the British economy, stated:

> The responsibility for stopping a
> civil war in Palestine between Jews and
> Arabs ought to be borne by the United
> Nations and not by this poor, overbur-
> dened and heavily injured country....
>
> Unless the U.S. comes to take a
> half and half share of the bloodshed,
> odium, trouble, expense and worry, we
> will lay our Mandate at the feet of the
> United Nations Organization.[76]

Churchill repeated these arguments numerous
times, his views could not be ignored by the Labour Government. This head of the previous victorious coalition Government had a tremendous influence on the British public. On March 3, 1947 he
told the Colonial Secretary, Mr. Creech Jones,
that the occupation must come to an end at once.[77]

Churchill's opinions reflected the stand of

the Conservative Party towards the Palestinian
problem. The Conservatives tried to gain political profit by demonstrating the incompetence of
the Labour Government in handling the situation
and it is by no means definite that had they been
in power they would have evacuated Palestine immediately. The Conservatives usually favored the
retention of bases; nevertheless, in the case of
the Palestine mandate, they had demonstrated exceptional understanding of the inability of Britain to continue the occupation of the country.
Quintin Hogg Hailsham wrote: "It is no longer
possible for us to govern. The outside aid is not
forthcoming and the mandate and with it our material and moral power in Palestine may well be
lost."[78]

The press frequently voiced its opinion on
this matter. A correspondent of The Economist
wrote:

Financial as well as manpower difficulties arise from imperial commitments
from the need to keep forces in the
eastern Mediterranean, the Middle East
and the Indian ocean: therefore, an
attempt to solve them should take account of imperial resources.[79]

The press maintained that the mandate was an
obstacle to economic recovery.[80] Expenses on
troops abroad meant not only unproductive expenditure and shortage of men in the factories, but
also the inability to solve the balance of payments problem by increasing exports.[81] Manpower
had to be released from services and brought back
home. Consequently, there had to be a drastic
cutting down of responsibilities.[82]

Military experts expressed the opinion that
Britain's military efforts were in disproportion

to the country's economic capacity. Britain, with
a population of only 45 million, maintained nearly
800,000 men in the armed forces, and in addition
to that, 250,000 civilians were working for the
army and its ministries, and 320,000 were working
on production and equipment needed by the army. A
total of 1,350,000 men were occupied in the military effort. Liddell Hart argued that this figure represented a very heavy loss to Britain.
Therefore, he recommended that British troops
should stay mainly in Europe.[83]

British industry had an urgent need for a
larger labour force. Coal output fell drastically
due to a shortage of new entrants in that industry, while 250,000 soldiers were stationed in the
Middle East.[84] The argument that the British were
compelled to withdraw from Palestine mainly due to
economic difficulties can be proved also by the
fact that cabinet members who were directly involved in the economic rehabilitation of Britain[85]
exerted strong pressure on Bevin to withdraw.

James P. Warburg attributed the withdrawal
from Palestine to the "unexpected decline of British military and economic power."[86] It was not a
mere coincidence that the British Government announced, in March 1947, that she would surrender
the mandate into the hands of the United Nations.
In 1947 the economic difficulties were far more
severe than in the previous years. The loans
taken from the United States and Canada were
quickly diminishing. In the nine months from July
1946 to April 1947, the Government used 1,300 million dollars of the total credit of 3,750 million
dollars. Gold and dollar reserves were also depleting rapidly. By the second quarter of 1947,
the average drain on Britain's dollar reserves
amounted to 75 million dollars per week.[87] Dalton
described 1947 as a black year.[88] The pressure on
the Government to release more manpower was con-

stantly increasing. There was an urgent need for young men in the coal mines and the factories. Dalton insisted on the immediate release of these men because they were in the prime of their life-- not children leaving school, nor young ladies.[89] He demanded an immediate cut of 10 percent in defense expenditure in order to save 80 million pounds for the following year.[90]

According to the White Paper of January, the biggest problem of the economy was the shortage of manpower, especially in the coal mines, and in heavy industry. Half a million men were needed immediately. From August 1947 to January 1948, the services were under heavy pressure from Cripps, Dalton and other ministers to reduce expenses, and release manpower. "Here we come to the critical question," said Attlee in his speech on the need for increased production on March 3 and March 23, 1946: "Just as in the war, we shall have to reinforce with female labour. We shall have to use the older and less fit sections of our population."[91]

Undoubtedly, manpower and economic resources were needed for the Labour's social reform projects. To make things worse yet, the winter of 1946-1947 was so severe that industry was virtually at a standstill.[92] The number of the unemployed rose within two weeks from 350,000 to 2,300,000 or 15.5 percent of the work force.[93] This grim reality also must have prompted the British to relinquish their imperial responsibilities in 1947. Professor Fitzsimons wrote that: "As the difficult winter of 1946-1947 added to Britain's economic difficulties and compounded foreign policy problems, Secretary Bevin moved from a grimly studied optimism about the international scene to an urgent, almost desperate firmness."[94] Norman and Helen Bentwich in their book, Mandate Memories: 1918-1948, wrote that Britain abandoned Palestine in 1947 because the English people suffered heavily in that winter. In their opinion, the physical trial which found expression in a severe cold and shortages of every kind had a softening effect on the British attitude towards the creation of the new State of Israel and their final withdrawal.[95]

In February 1947 there was a drastic lack of coal, and the supply of electricity had to be cut. The shortage and depression were felt more heavily than in any other year. There is no wonder there- fore, that 1947 was a year of partial reappraisal of British world interests. Anthony Eden said that in that winter the British people experienced "the gravest domestic industrial crisis...in the last twenty years."[96]

The deficit in the balance of payments amounted in the same year to 600 million pounds. There was a chronic deficit in British trade with dollar areas. British imports from these areas were about three times its exports to them. Bri- tish exports to the United States were enough to cover no more than the cost of tobacco bought there. The rise in American prices erased many of the benefits which the American loan had given. By 1947 prices of imports from the United States were forty percent higher than the prices of De- cember 1945. This change in the terms of trade against Britain added 329 million pounds to the import bill.

On February 21, 1947, Britain announced that due to economic difficulties she could not contin- ue to aid Greece and Turkey. In March 1947 Bri- tain announced her decision to surrender the Pa- lestine mandate to the United Nations.

The year 1947 witnessed the beginning of the decline of the British Empire in the Middle East. India was granted independence in this year, because Britain of 1947, propped up by foreign

loans, could not afford the cost of maintaining
the country by force against Indian hostility.[97]
With the loss of India, Palestine lost its <u>raison
d'etre</u>. Britain failed in her attempts to recon-
cile Arabs and Jews. Besides, a military base in
Palestine or in the Suez Canal Zone was by no
means a guarantee that oil reserves would be protected.[98] The Suez Canal had never been a particularly good waterway in wartime, and the idea of
the Mediterranean as a kind of covered passage for
Britain had also been exploded.[99] In Palestine,
Egypt, Aden, Cyprus and Malta, they still guarded
the communications of the vanished Indian Empire.
Large garrisons and expensive installations became
purposeless.

It was painful for British statesmen whose
entire lives had been shaped by the idea of British imperial grandeur, to realize that weakness
and bankruptcy lay behind the imperial facade.[100]
Despite their socialist beliefs, neither Attlee
nor Bevin wished to be identified with withdrawal,
for withdrawal was still a stigma. Also, it is
likely that Bevin was impressed by Britain's victory in the Second World War to such an extent
that he failed to see that the war had produced
two super powers and that Britain became virtually
bankrupt.[101]

The British people were unwilling to rule
distant colonies. Also, they were overly taxed.
Between 1939 and 1949 there was a fourfold increase in taxation. Whereas in 1938-39 there were
7,000 persons who had net incomes of over 6,000
pounds per annum, in 1947-48 there were only
70.[102] Anthony Eden wrote: "The British economy
is already fully stretched with a higher level of
taxation than any other country in the world...men
and women are unwilling to do this [to pay additional taxes] even in conditions of crisis short
of actual war."[103]

In 1947 Britain's war debts to Iraq and Egypt amounted to 70 million pounds and 400 million pounds respectively. She could not offer goods because she had barely turned over to peacetime production and its dollars were in short supply. Furthermore, Britain could not offer armaments in the amounts requested by Arab leaders.

By mid-August 1947 the economic crisis reached another peak. The bill for Palestine between January 1945 and November 1947 was 100 million pounds. The bulk of the money spent in Palestine went for the preservation of peace and not for its development. Speaking on May 20, 1947, the Assistant Secretary for Economic Affairs in the Palestine Administration said that the expenditure on security had risen from 4.5 million pounds in 1945 to 8 million pounds for 1947.[104] This money was taken from the budget of the Palestine Administration and was not included in the 100 million pounds spent by the British Government in the same period.

The postwar period witnessed a gradual reduction in military expenditure due to economic problems. In 1946, 1667 million pounds were spent on defense. In 1947 the amount was reduced to 899 million pounds. The military manpower was reduced from a total of over two million in early 1946 to approximately 1.3 million in March 1947. The 1946 White Paper on Defense was described by Eden as "a progress on demobilization."[105]

The 1948 Statement Relating to Defense published during the severe winter of 1947-8 stated "It is both inevitable and right that the rehabilitation of the civil economy should increasingly absorb the country's effort and resources to the diminution of activities in the defence field."[106]

In January 1948, the War Office was warned that the strength of the army must be reduced to 305,000 by 1950. At the end of 1947 there were only 91 active infantry battalions, 50 fewer than in 1939. The economic pressures threatened the existence of the last armored divisions.[107]

The Chiefs of Staff required a budget of 825 million pounds for 1948 but had to settle for less than 700 million pounds.

In February 1947 when the dollar deficit rose over $200 million, the impact of the economic crisis upon defense planning became decisive.[108] Thereupon, the Government made the decision to abandon the costly mandate in Palestine. In July 1947, an acceleration in demobilization was ordered, and on August 30, Attlee announced a further cut which would reduce the number of troops to 1,007,000 by March 31, 1948. In December 1947 came another order to reduce this number to 937,000 by the same date.[109]

In October 1947 the government decided that 600 million pounds would be the limit of expenses and in January 1948, it sought to reduce the army share of 700 million pounds to 222 million pounds. This meant reducing the number of men in the services to 185,000 and spending less money for the purchase of armaments and replacement of outworn military equipment.[110]

The feeling that Britain had done its share during the war and deserved some relaxation influenced the British attitude towards overseas commitments. It became impossible to ask the British people to live on rations while the Government was spending money for imperial purposes. The British citizens were more concerned about their livelihood than about the maintenance of the empire. When the fresh meat ration was cut, British housewives protested. Rose Wood, a Cheshire housewife, sent her bacon and cooking fat allotment to John Strachey, the Food Minister, with the question: "Don't you think it is an insult to give us this amount to eat?"[111] The crisis created an atmosphere of depression. "The psychological effect of the crisis," said the correspondent of The Economist on February 22, 1947, "...has been profoundly depressing."[112]

Between March 1946 and January 1948, the Government failed to negotiate new treaties with Arab countries, because it could not offer anything even to Jordan - the poorest country in the Middle East.[113] Britain's economic weakness could by no means encourage the Arabs to acquiesce to her rule.[114]

In April 1946, an Anglo-American Committee recommended the entry of 100,000 Jews into Palestine. Bevin's refusal to allow the entry of additional Jews was financially motivated. He estimated that it would cost Britain as much as 200 million pounds as well as the quartering of another army division in Palestine.[115] According to the British commanding officer in Palestine, General K. D'arcy, to enforce an Arab solution to the Palestine issue, Britain would have needed three army divisions, and from four to six months to impose order.[116] Knowing the weakness of the British economy, Bevin could not impose a solution on either side. Commenting about the issue of the 100,000 Jews, the correspondent of The Economist wrote:

> It would be reasonable in this case to call on American military support in Palestine, for much more is involved in effecting the entry of the Jews than the President's offer of money and ships to assist their transfer from Europe. But there is no logic in the American attitude, and the British will almost certainly be left to carry the military burden alone.[117]

Attlee demanded that the United States pay not only the cost of transportation and maintenance of the 100,000 immigrants, but also additional money to bridge the gap between Jewish and Arab standards of living, and to finance other military commitments needed for the purpose of imposing this solution on the Arabs.[118]

The American leadership, however, was preoccupied with domestic politics. American public opinion objected to involvement in British affairs. Furthermore, there was resentment over Britain's imperialist aims in the Middle East.[119] Some Americans refused to believe that Britain was in serious economic trouble and thought that she must be concealing a hidden wealth. Admiral William Leahy, Truman's Chief of Staff in 1945, thought, for example, that Britain was not worth helping anymore.[120] Bevin's refusal to allow the entry of the Jews had created pressure on the part of American Jewry not to help Britain economically.[121]

The British leaders realized that a continuance of the mandate would mean, in the words of the correspondent of The Economist, to "...continue the conditions of the twenty years under which Jew and Arab, and American call the tune, while Britain pays the piper."[122] It was only natural for the Foreign Secretary Bevin to be more concerned about British defense and Britain's status as a world power than Dalton or Cripps who were mainly concerned about the financial aspect of Britain's foreign policy. Nevertheless, Bevin realized that withdrawal could not be delayed indefinitely. This remarkable foreign secretary understood ..."full well what the consequences of the war had been in altering permanently the old balance of power in Europe and how overstrained British resources were."[123]

Ruling Palestine meant not only stationing

forces there, but also heavy losses in human lives
and property. The correspondent of The Economist
said on July 6, 1946:

> It is surprising to learn that the
> damage done by Jewish rebels to British
> life and property over the last few
> months is to cost the large sum of 4
> million pounds. As the damage is
> largely to the army and the R.A.F.
> property, the burden will (presumably)
> fall on the British taxpayer.[124]

The occupation of Palestine demanded heavy
investments and grants due to the fact that many
Jewish settlers needed financial assistance, and
Arab farmers had to be compensated for their land.
A vast amount of money was needed to save Palestine from a great depression, especially when the
military expenditure was about to be reduced. The
military administration in Palestine absorbed
about one-fifth of the national output and paid
for it from funds provided by the British Exchequer. British commitments to the Arabs were already heavy. On May 20, 1947 Lyall Wilkes said in
the House of Commons:

> Every tank and airplane now being used
> by the Arabs has been supplied from the
> United Kingdom. The British air mission
> is still functioning in Iraq. The Bri-
> tish missions are now working, training
> and reequipping Arab armies in Saudi-
> Arabia and Iraq. Between 1945 and 1947
> we supplied Egypt alone with 40 military
> planes, 38 scout cars, and 298 carriers
> apart from a great quantity of small
> arms and light equipment. The Arab
> Legion is now waging war that is wholly

subsidized by us with 2 million pounds a
year and is commanded by 38 British
officers.[125]

The British taxpayer could no longer be convinced that higher taxes were essential for the
maintenance of foreign commitments. Recognizing
the bankruptcy of his policy which cost a substantial amount of money and a great loss of British
lives, Bevin called upon the United Nations to
provide a solution.[126]

An American offer of comprehensive aid to
Europe was made by the U.S. Secretary of State
General Marshall on June 5, 1947. Under this
plan, Britain received 700 million pounds. Consequently, 1948 was the first year to show a favor-
able balance of trade for Britain. The huge
deficit of trade with dollar countries was some-
what reduced, and imports from the sterling area
increased. However, the prewar level of production was surpassed only in 1949 and the target for
exports which had been set at 175 percent of the
prewar level in 1946, was achieved not earlier
than 1950.

On May 14, 1948, the British Government
issued a statement on the termination of the
mandate. The statement justified British withdrawal from Palestine in the following manner:

Eighty-four thousand troops, who received no cooperation from the Jewish
community had proved insufficient to
maintain law and order in the face of
the campaign of terrorism waged by highly organized Jewish forces equipped with
all the weapons of the modern infantry-
man. Since the war 388 British subjects
had been killed in Palestine while the
military forces there had cost the Bri-

tish taxpayer 100 million pounds.   The
further loss of British lives was inevitable.   The continued presence there of
British troops could no longer be justified.[127]

FOOTNOTES

CHAPTER I

1. Sherif Hussein of Mecca had been given a pro-
    mise by the British High Commissioner of
    Egypt, that if the Arabs would support the
    British forces against the Ottoman Empire,
    Britain would recognize Arab rule in all the
    areas liberated by the Arabs. The British
    argued later that Palestine was excluded from
    this pledge. Nevertheless, the Arabs re-
    mained convinced that the British failed to
    fulfill their obligation.
2. Francis Williams, Socialist Britain(New York,
    1949), p. 17.
3. C. M. Woodhouse, British Foreign Policy Since
    the Second World War(New York, 1962), p. 110.
4. Harold and Margaret Sprout, "Retreat from
    World Power: Process and Consequences of
    Readjustment," World Politics, 15/4 (July
    1963), p. 687.
5. George Woodcock, Who Killed the British
    Empire? An Inquest(New York,1974), p. 7.
6. C. R. Attlee, Purpose and Policy: Selected
    Speeches(New York, 1947), p. 60.
7. John and Anne-Marie Hacket, The British
    Economy: Problems and Prospects(London,
    1967), p. 58.
8. Eric Esotric, Stafford Cripps: Master
    Statesman(New York, 1949), p. 301.
9. Bentley B. Gilbert, Britain Since 1918(New
    York, 1949), p. 301.
10. Esotric, loc. cit.
11. Barbara Ward, "Despite Austerity Britain
    Still Faces a Crisis," in John F. Naylor,
    ed., Britain 1919-1970(Chicago, 1971), p.
    131.
12. Attlee, Purpose..., p. 70.
13. Gilbert, Britain p. 160. See also Sidney

Pollard, The Development of the British Economy 1914-1967 (London, 1969), p. 402.

14. E. J. Hobsbawm, Industry and Empire (Suffolk 1975), pp. 178-94.

15. Elizabeth Monroe, Britain's Moment in the Middle East: 1914-1956 (London, 1963), p. 152.

16. E. Varga, "The Marshall Plan and the British Economic Crisis," New Times, No. 42, 1947, p. 3.

17. Ibid., p. 4.

18. Gilbert, Britain p. 164.

19. W.N. Medlicott, British Foreign Policy Since Versailles 1919-1963 (London, 1968), p. 278.

20. R. N. Rosecrance, Defense of the Realm; British Strategy in the Nuclear Epoch (New York, 1968), p. 30.

21. Herbert Morrison, An Autobiography (London, 1960), p. 256.

22. Sprout, loc. cit. pp. 674-675.

23. Rosecrance, Defense p. 36.

24. Thornton, The Imperial Idea and Its Enemies (London, 1959) p. 328.

25. J. C. Hurewitz, The Struggle for Palestine (New York, 1968), p. 227.

26. Ibid., p. 276.

27. Palestine: Termination of the Mandate May 15 1948 (London, 1948), p. 10.

28. Emanuel Shinwell, The Labour Story (London, 1963), p. 178.

29. Varga, loc. cit. p. 4.

30. Hurewitz, Struggle p. 280. See also: "The Cost for Britain," National Jewish Monthly, 61/9 (May 1947), p. 306.

31. The American Lend-Lease program to Britain originated on Dec. 7, 1940. This was President Franklin D. Roosevelt's calculated step to intervene on behalf of the British war effort without in any way antagonizing those

American isolationists who were dominant at that time in the Republican Party. Moreover, Roosevelt was in no position to antagonize the influential isolationists within the Democratic Party, the most vocal of whom were Senator David I. Walsh, chairman of the Naval Affairs Committee, Joe Kennedy, the American Ambassador to London and Senators Burton Wheeler and Charles Lindbergh.

32. Leon D. Epstein, Britain's Uneasy Ally(Chicago, 1954), p. 36.
33. Williams, Socialist Britain p. 143.
34. Woodhouse, British Foreign Policy p. 122.
35. Attlee, As It Happened, pp. 150-1.
36. Hugh Dalton, High Tide and After: Memoirs 1945-1960(London, 1962), p. 68.
37. Shinwell, The Labour Story, passim.
38. G. Kolko, The Politics of War: Allied Diplomacy and the World Crisis of 1943-1945, (London, 1969), p. 313.
39. Attlee, As It Happened, p. 170. See also J. McDermott, A Lost Leader, p. 27.
40. Lord Strang, Home and Abroad(London, 1956), p. 291.
41. Woodhouse, British Foreign Policy p.111.
42. Strang, loc. cit.
43. "Statement Relating to Defence 1948," Cmd. 7327.
44. Barlett, C.J. The Long Retreat: A History of British Defense Policy 1940-1970(New York, 1972), p. 11.
45. Michael Foot, Aneurin Bevan: A Biography (London, 1973), p. 52.
46. Ibid., p. 54.
47. Gilbert, Britain p. 163.
48. Esotric, Cripps p. 319.
49. Beloff, Max The Future of British Foreign Policy(London, 1969), p. 8.
50. Geoffry L. Goodwin, Britain and the United

Nations(New York, 1959), p. 383.

51. A. Bryant, Triumph in the West(New York, 1959), p. 383.

52. See Chapter Three for details.

53. Bryant, Triumph p. 383, 406.

54. Dalton, High Tide p. 101.

55. B. H. Liddell Hart, Defense of the West, London; 1950, pp. 249-55. See also Chapter Three.

56. Dalton, High Tide, p. 105.

57. Ibid., p. 193.

58. Ibid., p. 197.

59. "Bevin to the Labour Party Conference." Scarborough, May 20, 1945. As cited in: Monroe, Britain's Moment, p. 158.

60. Dalton, High Tide, p. 198.

61. Report of the Annual Conference of the Labour Party 1947, pp. 141, 152.

62. S. P. Gupta, Imperialism and British Labour Government(New York, 1975), p. 290.

63. Pauline Gregg, Modern Britain: A Social and Economic History Since 1760(New York 1965), p. 449.

64. Pollard, British Economy, p. 398.

65. Based on the Monthly Digest of Statistics; also see, John Vaizy, The Cost of Social Services, Fabian Research Series, No. 166, 1954.

66. H. C. Debates, Vol. 437, col. 1946 (16 May 1947).

67. H. C. Debates, Vol. 468, col. 1399 (26 October 1949).

68. Monroe, Britain's Moment, p. 95.

69. "Palestine Parley," The Economist 152/5412 (May 17, 1947), p. 754.

70. R. S. Crossman, "The Role Britain Hopes to Play," Commentary (June, 1948), p. 496.

71. A. Hartley, A State of England(New York, 1963), p. 61. See also: Frankel, p. 301;

Jacob Abadi, "Oil Protection in Britain's Middle Eastern Defense Policy--A Rationalization or a Necessity?" The American Journal for the Study of Middle Eastern Civilization, Vol. 1, No. 1 (Spring, 1980), pp. 10-21.

72. Gupta, Imperialism p. 314.

73. H. C. Debates. Vol. 448, Col. 53 (1 March 1948).

74. R. S. Crossman, Palestine Mission: A Personal Record (New York, 1947), p. 55.

75. J. T. Murphy, Labour's Big Three (London, 1948), p. 253.

76. "Blood and Shame: Palestine" in R.R. James ed., in Winston S. Churchill, His Complete Speeches 1897-1963, Vol. VII (New York, 1974), pp. 7421-7425.

77. "Foreign Affairs," The Contemporary Review, Vol. 171 (April, 1947), p. 247.

78. Q. H. Hailsham, The Case for Conservatism, (London, 1948), p. 241.

79. "Defence in Two Worlds," The Economist 152/5398 (Feb., 1947), p. 227.

80. M. A. Fitzsimons, Empire by Treaty (Indiana, 1946), p. 59.

81. Elizabeth Barker, Britain in a Divided Europe: 1945-1970 (London, 1971), p. 54.

82. Ibid.

83. Liddell Hart, Defense..., Chapter XXI.

84. John Kimche, Seven Fallen Pillars (New York, 1976), p. 68.

85. Benjamin Shwadran, "The Beginning of the End," Palestine Affairs, 4/1 (Jan. 1949), p. 1-7.

86. J. P. Warburg, Crosscurrents in the Middle East (New York, 1948), p. 136.

87. Gilbert, Britain, loc. cit.

88. Dalton, High Tide p. 5.

89. Ibid., p. 196.

90. Ibid., p. 198.
91. Attlee, Purpose..., pp. 71-77.
92. Emanuel Shinwell, I've Lived Through It All, (London 1973), p. 40.
93. "Britain: God Save the People," Newsweek (April 28, 1947), p. 40.
94. Fitzsimons, Empire, p. 64.
95. Norman and Helen Bentwich, Mandate Memories: 1918-1948 (New York, 1965), p. 178.
96. "Britain: Blitz by General Winter," Newsweek (Feb. 17, 1947), p. 36.
97. Correli Barnet, Britain and her Army: 1509-1970 (New York, 1970), p. 480.
98. Woodhouse, British Foreign Policy, p. 174. See also: Hartley, Ibid., and also R.H.S. Crossman and Ian Mikardo's remark about oil, p. 32.
99. Francis Williams, Twilight of Empire: Memoirs of Prime Minister Clement Attlee (New York, 1962), p. 178.
100. Barnet, loc. cit.
101. Shinwell, The Labour Story, p. 183.
102. Arthur Marwick, Britain in the Century of Total War (Boston, 1968), p. 359.
103. Anthony Eden, "Britain in World Strategy," Foreign Affairs 29/3 (April 1951), p. 340.
104. "The Palestine Problem," The World Today 3/3 (Oct. 10, 1947), pp. 458-459.
105. H. C. Debates, Vol. 420, col. 239 (5 March 1946).
106. "Statement Relating to Defense 1946" Cmd 6743.
107. Bartlett, British Defense Policy, p. 24.
108. Rosecrance, Defense, pp. 61-62.
109. Herbert Nicholas, Britain and the U.S. (London, 1963), p. 43.
110. Viscount Montgomery of Alamein, The Memoirs of Field Marshal the Viscount Montgomery (New York, 1958), pp. 480-2.

111. "Britain: There'll Always Be a Headache,"
     Newsweek (Feb. 3, 1947), p. 29.
112. "Crisis as Usual," The Economist 152/5400
     (Feb. 22, 1947), p. 305.
113. Monroe, Middle East p. 156.
114. F. G. Northedge, British Foreign Policy: The
     Process of Readjustment, 1945-1961(London,
     1962), p. 183.
115. Ibid., p. 109. See also: Christopher Sykes,
     Crossroads to Israel(Ohio, 1955), p. 299.
116. Joseph J. Zasloff, Great Britain and
     Palestine: A Study of the Problem before the
     United Nations(Muenchen 1952), p. 46.
117. "Rebellion in Palestine," The Economist
     151/5367 (July 6, 1946) p. 8.
118. Francis Williams, Twilight...., p. 196.
119. Barker, loc. cit.
120. Ibid., p. 75.
121. The Zionists succeeded in having pro-Zionist
     planks inserted in the electoral platform of
     both parties in the United States already in
     1944 [See: Walter Laqueur, A History of
     Zionism(New York, 1972), p. 555].
122. The Economist, July 6, 1946.
123. Francis Williams, Ernest Bevin: Portrait of
     an Englishman(London, 1952), p. 242.
124. The Economist, July 6, 1946.
125. "Britain and Zionism: Jewish War Recorded,"
     London Times(May 22, 1948) 5:5.
126. "The Partition of Palestine," Ibid. (Jan.
     1948), p. 8.
127. "British Rule in Palestine: The Striving for
     Reconciliation," London Times(May 14, 1948)
     4:6. Also; "British Renew Bid of Palestine
     Aid," New York Times (May 14, 1948) 1:6, and
     "British Renew Offer to Palestine of Aid
     Short of Imposing Solution," New York Times
     (May 14, 1948) 4:4.

CHAPTER II

THE STRATEGISTS AND THEIR INFLUENCE

British thinking about overseas bases underwent a fundamental change in the postwar era. Until the Second World War, only a few questioned
the necessity of maintaining territories overseas.
A change of attitude developed, however, as a result of the constant pressure of the deteriorating
economy, the emergence of the Cold War and the
rise of nationalism in the Middle East. One cannot ignore the contention of many historians that
nationalism played an essential part in the process of disengagement. Nevertheless, it seems
that the inherent value of bases had changed
drastically after the Second World War. British
leaders, and Churchill in particular, no longer
attached great importance to them. In fact,
Churchill, the arch-imperialist was the one who
demanded withdrawal from Palestine in 1947 while
he was the leader of the Opposition, and it was he
who initiated the 1954 Agreement to evacuate the
Suez Canal Zone.

This change of policy developed mainly
because a great deal of thought had gone into
defense policy since 1945, perhaps more than in
any previous period except the years which preceded the First World War.[1] This process of
change can be properly assessed only if one under-
stands the domestic pressures in the United Kingdom. These pressures profoundly affected the military debate of the postwar period. Max Beloff
explained their nature in the following words:

> The most influential military thought of
> the period was opposed to the idea that
> Britain should ever fight a war of
> massed land armies. A belief in economy
> and the prevalence of near pacifist sen-

timent in the public mind, provided
further impulses in the same direction.
Foreign policy was for a long time con-
ditioned by these factors.[2]

One cannot underestimate the impact of these
factors because they were bound to affect the
British attitude towards the Middle East. The
decision to withdraw from Middle Eastern bases was
a clear political choice which reflected the
Labour Government's priorities for public spending. Withdrawal could not have been carried out
without the persistent effect of the domestic
needs.[3]

The economic factor continued to play its
restraining effect on defense policy. Throughout
the entire period between 1945 and 1971, British
statesmen, whether they were members of the ruling
party or of the opposition, argued that economic
crises could be avoided only if defense commitments were drastically reduced.[4]

Familiarity with the government's apparatus
and the key politicians who dealt with defense
matters will give the reader further insight and
understanding into the process of change in defense policy. The Prime Minister, the Defense
Minister, the Foreign Secretary, and the Chancellor of the Exchequer were those who officially
dealt with defense matters. Military matters,
however, were not just the government's business.
The government had to rely on the opinion of the
strategists. It is difficult to determine to what
extent these people whom we call "strategists" influenced the government's policy on defense, not
only because influence is difficult to measure,
but also because of the paucity of material
available on this period.[5]

A strategist is a person who deals with
strategic questions. Strategy, as defined in Jane's

Dictionary of Military Terms, is: "The plans for conducting a war in the widest sense, including diplomatic, political, and economic considerations as well as those of a purely military nature." According to Armstrong's definition, a strategist is "a person who takes a recurring interest in the way British forces are deployed, and who expresses his judgments in such a fashion that they enter the environment of the persons who decide questions of national strategy."[6]

Almost all men who could be called strategists were to be found in a few closely related occupational groups. These were: political leaders, senior civil servants, military officers of the three services and scholars. The latter were defined by Higham as "military intellectuals." Armstrong called them the "commentators group."[7] Journalists were also included in this category. All of these groups had a certain degree of influence on the framing of military and defense policies, including the deployment of British forces in Europe, and in other overseas territories.

In Britain, major strategic decisions are usually made by the Cabinet and its Defense Committee. The latter has its subcommittees and advisers. Some of the advisers are from outside the government altogether. In addition to the Prime Minister, Defense Minister, Foreign Secretary and Chancellor of the Exchequer, the Chiefs of Staff of the three services usually attended the meetings of the Defense Committee. The function of the Chiefs of Staff was advisory, yet, their voice was heard and they exerted influence over a long period of time.

Nearly all of the strategists had been brought up as members of the leadership group whether as civil servants, political leaders, military officers, scholars or journalists. The term "leadership group" does not necessarily mean aristocracy or a ruling class, but rather upper-middle class. The leadership group is constantly expanding down the socioeconomic ladder. It is a group which includes all the persons who have authority and influence over matters affecting national security. In the late forties and early fifties this group already included a substantial number of middle-class people. British society is homogeneous especially at the upper levels, and this led to a feeling of identification and responsibility towards the nation. Consequently, the professional strategists, who constantly demonstrated interest and concern for the nation's fate, were always in a preferred position and generally supported by the members of the leadership group.

Most strategists had relatives in the leadership group. An army officer would usually have a brother who was a member of Parliament. A commentator might have had an uncle who was an admiral. The MP could also have had a relative who was a senior member of the diplomatic service. A remarkable example of this is the fact that the Minister of Defense, the Secretary of State for the Army, and the Undersecretary of the Colonial Office were all sons-in-law of Prime Ministers.[8] The result of these contacts was that the strategist was exposed to matters of public concern and was able to influence other persons from the leadership group who might have access to the leaders.

Most strategists spend ample time in London where they meet other members of the leadership group who are engaged in occupations affecting national security. The majority of the strategists belong to one or more of the fifteen or twenty social clubs which are adjacent to Whitehall. Even military clubs include usually civilian members such as MP's, civil servants and businessmen. The United Service Club serves as a good example of this. Members of the Oxford and Cambridge Clubs were not only scholars, but also air marshals and other officers. In these clubs, problems of national defense were informally discussed despite the persistence of a myth that a British official never talks business over lunch.[9]

The most influential strategists were those who were known to be keeping abreast of matters affecting national defense and who enjoyed free access to fresh information. Men such as Sir John Slessor, Marshal of the Royal Air Force, or Rear Admiral Sir Anthony Buzzard remained highly influential even after their retirement because they continued to study defense matters.

The strategists of the services could be highly influential particularly when they held high ranks. They could be, and sometimes were, a part of the domestic political scene and could influence political decisions by their personal action. Field Marshal B. L. Montgomery is only one example of a high ranking officer who addressed audiences on many occasions. Vice Admiral Earle L. Mountbatten and other high ranking officers such as Slessor or Air Vice Marshal E. J. Kingston-McCloughry gave frequent speeches on strategic issues. Montgomery, although usually depicted by historians as a mediocre strategist enjoyed direct access to policy makers in the War Office. His influence and that of the other Chiefs of Staff on Emanuel Shinwell, the Secretary of State for War in Attlee's Ministry, was well known.[10]

The function of the Chiefs of Staff was advisory. Nevertheless, opposition by these men or other important military figures found wide expression in the press. If an important military officer threatened the government with resignation, his threat had wide political repercussions, because the leadership group, and especially the members of the party in opposition, would ponder over the cause of the resignation and its impact on defense policy. If a Chief of Staff expressed an opinion which might be considered sound in the eyes of the educated public, and especially members of the opposition, it was usually difficult for the Minister of Defense or the Cabinet members to ignore his views. Strategists could convince the government in any matter affecting national defense if their arguments were supported by a majority of the leadership group. Strategists, whether from the services, or any other group, frequently wrote articles in the leading newspapers and periodicals including military periodicals. They wrote letters to the editors and gave interviews to other members of the leadership group, in addition to their speeches in conferences and conventions. They sat in study groups of the Royal Institute of International Affairs.[11]

Military matters could never be separated from economic or political matters. There was always a budgetary and political bipartisan aspect to them. Any opinion about the increase of men in the armed forces or about the purchase of new arms and equipment had to take into consideration Britain's financial situation and the desire of the ruling party to gain the confidence of the British voters and remain in power. All these considerations which are involved in defense policy formulation are called "grand strategy."[12] Grand strategy is the direction and coordination of all resources of a nation towards the attainment of a political objective. While pure strategy is the art of the generals and concerns itself only with the need to achieve immediate objectives in a given war, grand strategy is the realm of statesmen.[13] Therefore, in Britain the statesmen must

rely on the opinions of the officers in the
services, the civil servants and other groups.
Military men are involved in politics and vice
versa as Armstrong has noted:

> The soldier, sailor and the airman must
> accept the fact that they now operate in
> a semi-political atmosphere and must
> adjust to it; so must the politicians.[14]

Robin Higham regarded the military intellectuals as an important and influential segment of
the British ruling class.[15]   Higham divided the
military intellectuals in Britain into two groups:
the official thinkers on the staffs and in the
military graduate colleges on the one hand, and
the unofficial military intellectuals on the
other. Both groups were influential. Studies
which were made by the intellectuals of the official group, especially in the Imperial Defense
College (which opened its doors in 1927 and included many bright personnel), had an important
effect on the formulation of defense policy over a
long period of time. Some of the students of the
I.D.C. attained positions of considerable influence.

The I.D.C. was opened with the intention of
training officers and civilian officials in
Imperial strategy. This school turned into a
meeting place for the British leadership. Officers, government ministers, civil servants and
industrialists, scientists, trade union leaders
and experts of all kinds met there. The Institute
often sponsored organized visits to defense and
civil institutions both in Britain, and abroad.
Its members also visited research centers, colleges and factories. These men were influenced by
each other and together formulated a general policy on defense which was eventually adopted by the

government.[16]

A new elite of young officers began to take shape after 1945 especially in the army. They were determined not to let the politicians interfere with military affairs as they had done in the era of the First World War. This new elite was represented by Field Marshals Earle A. P. Wavell and Lord F. Alanbrook. It concerned itself with developing an ability to communicate with the political leadership on equal terms. According to Higham, they wanted "to restrike what they considered a desirable balance between the makers and the executors of military as well as national policy."[17]

The politicians were not in a position to challenge these professional advisers on military issues because they were not well versed in military affairs, except for Churchill and a few others, they needed perhaps, as Higham stated "to be sent to the Institute for Strategic Studies."[18]

The unofficial military intellectuals included Vice-Admiral Sir Herbert Richmond, Major General J.F.C. Fuller, Captain B. H. Liddell Hart, Major General Sir Frederick Sykes, and Marshal of the Royal Air Force, Viscount Hugh Trenchard. With the exception of Liddell Hart, who was only twenty-three in 1918, all were in their forties when the First World War ended. These men had held positions of considerable power and influence. The most important position was held by Trenchard who became the Chief of the Air Staff and controlled the newly born Royal Air Force. Trenchard enjoyed power and influence for nearly 15 years, first as a general officer commanding the Royal Flying Corps in France and then as Chief of the Air Staff.

Second to him was Liddell Hart with his memoranda which included recommendations for thorough-going reforms in the services and which

were submitted to the Secretary of State, Sir
Leslie Hore Belisha on the eve of the Second World
War. Richmond was nominated as First Sea Lord,
Fuller was seriously considered for Chief of the
Imperial General Staff, and Liddell Hart had been
a candidate for the high position of Secretary of
the Committee of Imperial Defense.

To the list of the most important unofficial
intellectuals mentioned above one might add sever-
al less important figures such as Captain H. G.
Thursfield, the editor of Brassey's Annual, Sir
Archibald Hurd from the editorial staff of the
Daily Telegraph and the maritime journalist Hector
C. Bywater.

Most of these men wrote articles in the in-
fluential military periodical The Journal of the
Royal United Service Institution (JRUSI). The
Naval Review was the magazine of the Royal Navy.
The Royal Air Force also had a magazine of its
own, The Journal of the Royal Air Force College.
Other periodicals which published military arti-
cles were The Nineteen Century and After (called
The Twentieth Century from Dec. 1950), The Fort-
nightly Review and the Saturday Review.

The military intellectuals were influential
because of their activities in familiarizing
politicians with military problems. They could,
in Higham's words "draw the broad lessons and conclusions and could master the mysteries of the
military professions and explain them clearly to
the public."[19]

Their influence can be measured not only by
the eloquence of their ideas, but also by their
strenuous attempts to pressure the military and
the civil authorities into applying their theories. Trenchard made it his business to convince
the successive Secretaries of State for Air of the
validity of the deterrent counter-strike force
concept. This concept dictated that air power

must be developed to such an extent that it would constitute an effective deterrent and that if the deterrent failed, the air force must be in a position to strike back at the enemy. Liddell Hart and Fuller attempted to convert the War Office to the idea of mobility and mechanized power, first through the Chief of the Imperial Staff, Field Marshal Lord George Milne, and later with better success through the Secretary of War, Hore Belisha (May 1937-January 1940).

The opinions of other people who occasionally wrote articles and letters to the editors in various newspapers and periodicals were also influential though to a much lesser extent than the military intellectuals. The judgment of experts inside the government did not differ radically from the strong convictions of those on the outside.[20]

Besides the military periodicals mentioned earlier, articles dealing with defense matters were also published by the daily newspapers such as The Times, Manchester Guardian, Daily Telegraph and many others. Weekly magazines were especially important. The most distinguished among them was The Economist. Francis Williams, the best known commentator on the British press said:

> Nor when one talks of the Press and its influence must one overlook the weekly reviews such as the New Statesman, The Spectator, The Economist, and Time and Tide, to which I would add Tribune, which, although it appeals to a somewhat different public, has excellent qualities of its own. The serious weekly reviews exercise a political influence far beyond their circulations because they are read by men and women interested in reasoned argument and also

by many who are in a position to make
important decisions or to influence
large numbers of other people.[21]

The Economist was read by most of the leadership group who did any serious reading, and those
who wrote in it were either professional journalists or scholars.[22]

The press provided a useful instrument
through which commentators and people outside the
government could exert influence on the decision-
making process. At least a portion of the press
reflected the opinion of critics and decision-
makers alike. It seems unlikely that comments in
the press could have been constantly ignored by
the decision makers. Opinions in the press were
usually not bound to cause an immediate change in
policy. In the long run, however, comments which
appeared frequently exerted influence.

It is essential to examine the influence of
the press on defense policy formulation because
other sources, primary or otherwise, are limited.
The most important men who contributed to these
newspapers and periodicals were Liddell Hart and
J.F.C. Fuller, the leading propagandists of mobile
warfare. They developed the theory of dynamic
defense after the First World War. Trenchard,
Sykes and Grove belonged to the air power school
of thought and will be discussed in a later
chapter.[23]

Fuller and Liddell Hart had influence mainly
due to their contacts with their own Service.
Fuller was less influential than Liddell Hart
though he was an extremely prolific writer. Some
of his ideas affected British military thinking on
deployment of forces overseas. Fuller thought
that air power could be the main instrument of
imperial defense, and that the main object of land
forces was to establish protected air bases

throughout the imperial possessions. Thus, he
thought that surface forces of any kind could be
abolished. He was convinced that no power would
be foolish enough to bomb London out of existence
if it meant that "the whole aerial might of the
Empire would be turned against it in an overwhelming reprisal."[24]

Liddell Hart was most influential thanks to
his writing ability. He was able to use his
access to the seats of power and to compel people
to think about his ideas. His association with
Hore Belisha resulted in extensive military
reforms and in an actual purge in the military
command. In May 1937 the Minister for the Coordination of Defense, Sir Thomas Inskip, had asked
him to write a memorandum on army organization.
Liddell Hart's recommendations to double the
number of guns in the four anti-aircraft divisions
were accepted by the General Staff at the War
Office in 1938.

Liddell Hart's reputation had declined in the
early forties, but it rose again slowly in the
fifties. It is extremely important to emphasize
the stature and influence of Liddell Hart; for
this remarkable man was the pioneer propagandist
of every idea which affected British thinking and
attitudes toward bases and made the government
more willing to release its hold on bases in the
Middle East.

Liddell Hart was influential insofar as he
attempted to create a defense philosophy which
blended new military ideas with traditional British disinterest in armed forces in peacetime.[25]
His ideas about withdrawal from empire and the
creation of a strategic reserve at home were welcomed because they happened to come at the moment
when there was an urgent need for retrenchment and
disengagement. Some of his ideas constituted the
basis of the White Paper on Defense from 1957.[26]

Liddell Hart gained wide influence not only as a military correspondent for The Times and the Daily Telegraph, but also through his circulation of private memoranda. His influence and reputation gave him access to policy makers. Higham said that: "perhaps more than any other of the interwar pundits he had something like access to decision-makers...."[27] Liddell Hart was among the theorists who retained his influence in the postwar period. His ideas about the superiority of air power, the impact of the atomic weaponry, the need to shift the lines of communication from the eastern Mediterranean westward, the importance of "flexibility" and "mobility" as opposed to static bases and the need to create a "strategic reserve" were all accepted by the leaders of the postwar period. Brian Bond who was closely associated with Liddell Hart and who served in the Royal Artillery from 1954 to 1959 and became a lecturer in history in the University of Liverpool once said, "It would be entirely mistaken to see his original thinking on contemporary defense problems as being confined to the interwar years.[28] A.J.P. Taylor evaluated Liddell Hart as "the most formidable military writer of the age."[29] Ronald Lewin, a famous military historian said of Liddell Hart:

> It was fortunate in fact, that during the crucial years when his mind was most active and his energies most abundant he was not entirely rebuffed by the British Army--or by Whitehall and Westminster.[30]

It was thanks to Liddell Hart that the Air Ministry was given a scientific staff in the late 1930s. A research department was created in the War Office and many other changes were made under

his influence. The generals were influenced by
his ideas. General Sir Frederick Pile, who was
the General Officer and Commander-in-Chief of the
Anti-Aircraft Command and who was responsible for
the defense of Britain against air attack during
the Second World War, admitted that he was totally
imbued with Liddel Hart's ideas, and had decided
to train his brigade according to them. Trying to
evaluate Liddell Hart's influence he said:

> Liddell   Hart's   influence   on   German
> military thought is well known, but his
> influence on the British Army was ten
> times greater...for most of the time
> between the wars he was the sole
> prophet.[31]

Foreign generals were also highly influenced
by Liddell Hart's ideas. The German encyclopedia
Der Grosse Brockhaus quoted General Heinz Guderian
as saying that Liddell Hart was the creator of the
theory of mechanized and mobile war. The prolific
French military writer and senior officer, General
Lionel-Martin Chassin, thought that Liddell Hart
was the "greatest military thinker of the twentieth century whose ideas have revolutionized the
art of war."[32]   Michael Howard maintained that:
"Bernard Brodie and Sir Basil Liddell Hart in
works published in 1946, made prophecies which
twenty years later were to be commonplaces of
strategic thinking."[33]
Among the strategists there were only a few
who had access to power. Liddell Hart without any
doubt was foremost among them. He had indirect
contacts with those top political leaders who had
the authority to implement new ideas. Armstrong's
conclusion based on the interviews that he conducted with members of the leadership group, was
that:

It may be well to record the testimony
of several outsiders who are experienced
in inserting their views into the official machine. According to them, it is
not the brigadiers in the War Office or
the Assistant Secretaries in the Foreign
Office who should be the targets, but
the topmost political leaders. There
may be a hundred or so people in Whitehall who could be called strategists one
of them said, but only two or three of
them need to be convinced, if you get
the right ones, and these are the
Government's strategists, not the
government.[34]

The ability of men such as Fuller, Liddell
Hart, and to a lesser extent Slessor, Kingston-
McCloughry, Buzzard and others to be in contact
with the political leaders who were most influential among the strategists, resulted in a gradual
change in defense policy. In the following chap-
ters an attempt will be made to analyze the ideas
and to demonstrate their influence on the deployment of land forces overseas and especially in the
Middle East.

FOOTNOTES

CHAPTER II

1. Beloff, The Future of British Foreign Policy,
    p. 64.
2. Ibid., p. 69.
3. Stephen Kirby, "Britain's Defense Policy and
    N.A.T.O." in Michael Leifer, ed., Constraints
    and Adjustments in British Foreign Policy,
    (London, 1972) p. 71.
4. See Chapter 1.
5. Only a few studies are available on the
    subject. DeWitt C. Armstrong's unpublished
    Ph.D. dissertation ("The Changing Strategy of
    British Bases," Princeton University 1960) is
    valuable. Armstrong defined the strategist's
    role and measured his influence on defense
    policy formulation based on many interviews
    which he conducted with members of the
    leadership group in Britain. The study, The
    Military Intellectuals in Britain: 1918-1939
    by Robin Higham is also valuable because of
    its attempt to measure the influence of the
    military intellectuals on defense policy.
    Except for a few studies such as Jay Luvaas,
    The Education of An Army: British Military
    Thought, 1815-1940 (University of Chicago
    Press, 1964) and some articles in newspapers
    and periodicals, no other material is
    available for the postwar period. Therefore,
    in attempting to measure the influence of the
    strategists heavy reliance on these few
    sources is unavoidable.
6. Armstrong, loc. cit. p. 62.
7. Ibid p. 63.
8. Ibid, p. 73.
9. Ibid, p. 74.
10. Field Marshal B. L. Montgomery, Memoirs
    (London, 1958), p. 430.

11. The Royal United Service Institution was opened in 1857 with the intention of disseminating military knowledge and information about defense. Military officers, civil servants, commentators and sometimes leaders, attended its lectures. The RUSI can be regarded as a semi-official institution, because it was partly financed by the British Government. In an address given on May 18, 1857 the chairman of the Institution, Colonel James Lindsay said: "...after years of perserverance, we have at least succeeded in obtaining the countenance of the Government who, though unable to remit the charges we have to pay, have proposed to give us a sum with which to pay." (See "Address," JRUSI 1/1/1857, p. 2.)

12. J.F.C. Fuller, The Reformation of War (London, 1923) Chap. XI.

13. B. H. Liddell Hart, The British Way in Warfare (New York, 1933), pp. 93-114.

14. Armstrong, loc. cit. p. 332.

15. R. Higham, The Military Intellectuals in Britain: 1918-1939 (New Brunswick, 1966), p. 3.

16. Charles Owen, No More Heroes: The Royal Navy in the Twentieth Century: Anatomy of a Legend (London, 1945), p. 195.

17. Higham, The Military..., p. 30.

18. Ibid, p. 31.

19. Robin Higham, "The Dangerously Neglected - The British Military Intellectuals, 1918-1937" Military Affairs, 29/2 (Summer 1965), p. 16.

20. Armstrong, loc. cit. p. 355.

21. Francis Williams, Press, Parliament and People (London, 1946), p. 169.

22. Armstrong, loc. cit. p. 133.

23. See Chapter 4.

24. Cited in, Jay Luvaas, The Education of An Army: British Military Thought, 1815-1940. University of Chicago Press: 1964, p. 367.

25. Higham, The Military..., p. 49.

26. Ibid, p. 89.

27. Higham, The Dangerously..., p. 83.

28. Brian Bond, "Nuclear Age Theories of Sir Basil Liddell Hart," Military Review 50/8 (August, 1970), p. 10.

29. Cited in, James D. Atkinson; "Liddell Hart and the Warfare of the Future" Military Affairs, vol. 29 (1966) p. 161.

30. Ronald Lewin, "Sir Basil Liddell Hart: The Captain Who Taught Generals" International Affairs 47/1 (January 1971), pp. 79, 81-82, 84.

31. Sir Frederick Pile, "Liddell Hart and the British Army" in Michael Howard, ed., The Theory and Practice of War, London; 1965, p. 180. See also; Norman Gibbs, "British Strategic Doctrine, 1918-1939" in Howard, loc. cit., p. 187 and also Luvaas, p. 376.

32. Howard, "Biographical summary," p. 374. See also General L. M. Chassin, "Un grand penseur militaire britannique: B. H. Liddell Hart" in Revue de defense nationale (October, 1950) pp. 334-46.

33. Michael Howard, ed., "Studies in International Security," Problems in Modern Strategy (New York, 1970), p. 52.

34. Armstrong, loc. cit. p. 90.

CHAPTER III

THE QUEST FOR NEW SECURITY ARRANGEMENTS
AND ALTERNATIVE BASES

The ideas proposed by the strategists profoundly affected the deployment of forces overseas, and particularly in the Middle East. The
opinion of the majority of them was that, thanks
to technological and scientific changes, forces
could be reduced in size. There was a growing
conviction that deployment of forces in Europe and
overseas must be altered. On March 9, 1953 the
Secretary of State for War said:

> Eighty percent of our fighting units are
> overseas, and the Army is unduly
> stretched and strained in meeting our
> overseas commitments.[1]

Strategists of the postwar period emphasized
the importance of "strategic mobility," and "flexibility" of movement of forces. By strategic mobility they meant that forces could be stationed
in overseas territories close to potential trouble
spots, rather than in the metropolitan country.[2]
The strategists argued that it was useless to de-
ploy land forces overseas because they lacked "mobility" and "flexibility" needed in modern warfare. Liddell Hart was the first to advocate
withdrawal from permanent bases at distant areas
overseas. He observed:

> We are too much inclined to scatter our
> forces in non-operational packets for
> policing purposes. Soldiers are not
> suited to be policemen. In many areas
> we might do better to reduce the garri-

sons, and organize stronger police forces.[3]

Liddell Hart argued that highly mobile forces should be organized and that divisions of the newly formed "strategic reserve" could be supported by a series of regional centers, from which they could pick up heavy equipment on their arrival at a particular region. All these measures, he thought would help release a large number of men who could be utilized in British industry. In addition, contact between British forces and the indigenous population would be minimal.

The Churchill Government gradually began to rely on small forces. The idea of organizing a "strategic reserve" was popular throughout the fifties. It was officially adopted in 1957 as a basic element in the new defense system and as an integral part of Sandys' White Paper.[4] Strategists believed that a small, mobile, hard-hitting force could deal with any local trouble in the empire. While the strategic nuclear striking force was regarded as an instrument of a global nuclear war, the "strategic reserve" became a method to be used in case of a conventional attack by Soviet forces in overseas territories or in the case of local disturbances. Some even argued that local disturbances could be prevented without actual fighting and that even the awareness that forces could quickly arrive could be a deterrent.[5]

The army of the fifties had to be small in size due to the need for financial stringency. Therefore, the proposed strategic reserve had to be highly mobile and equipped with light arms. Such a force was also compatible with the policy of nuclear deterrence. Maneuverability and fire power were the essential elements of defense.

Liddell Hart was not the only strategist to advocate this idea. In 1946, S. L. Swain, a

Squadron Leader in the Royal Air Force, was awarded the Trench Gascoigne prize by the Royal United Service Institution, for an essay in which he emphasized the importance of "mobility" and "flexibility" in military operations. He argued that the ability to meet these characteristics could eliminate the need for static forces overseas.[6]

According to Swain's arguments, ships and aircraft could transport men, weapons and equipment with sufficient speed to meet any kind of emergency. Permanent forces stationed overseas on garrison duty were significantly less effective than a combined naval, air, and land force. A mobile unit could be a formidable striking force, and could improve the morale of the soldiers, since there would be no need for it to remain in overseas posts for long periods of time.

"Mobility" and "flexibility" could be achieved by using air and naval power in combat operations. The concept of "mobility," developed mainly by Liddell Hart and adopted by many other military and civilian officials, became an integral part of British defense planning. Postwar improvements in military technology made it possible to apply these concepts with greater ease. No longer did bases and static trench warfare dominate British strategic thinking.

As a result of these new concepts, the strategic reserve was developed and increased in size toward the late fifties. Forces which had been committed to garrison tasks were gradually decreased. In 1947, British forces evacuated Greece and Turkey. In 1948, the garrison of Palestine was withdrawn. The Agreement to evacuate the Suez Canal Zone in 1954 was an additional step in the same direction. The troops which were stationed in the United Kingdom as a strategic reserve became relatively free to concentrate on training.

Although defense of overseas territories remained a critical issue due to the need to protect them in the nuclear age, traditional garrisons in places such as Malaya, Hong Kong and Suez were regarded as too risky to maintain. Strategists questioned the value of the permanent bases in the era of the Cold War in view of the Soviet menace. The army of the Cold War era had to take care of the conventional aspect of a future war. According to the views of leading strategists, such an army had to consist of a very high proportion of lightly equipped mobile infantry, minimum supporting arms, some armoured car requirements, and a reduced proportion of administrative services.[7]

Apart from the heavier reliance on the nuclear deterrent, the defense plans of the Churchill Government remained as they were when Attlee was in power. According to those plans, the defense of Britain consisted of three major components: N.A.T.O. forces for global war in nuclear conditions, the "strategic reserve" for limited war and local colonial forces for the preservation of peace in overseas territories. No longer did traditional garrisons have any function for defense.

Criticism about traditional military thinking and the attitude toward bases had already been heard in the early postwar period. The role of British garrisons was explained and criticized[8] long before the lesson of Suez had been learned.

Writers had become fully aware of the fact that there were vital interests in the Middle East, of which oil was the most important, and agreed that they must be safeguarded. However, the traditional methods of protecting these interests were considered to be inadequate. The Middle East could not be defended by one division and a small air contingent based on the Suez

Canal. Even the fact that these forces could be reinforced by a further division with heavy air transport when needed could not be a solution to the problem, because, being untrained they would be incapable of deterring potential aggressors.[9] Trained reserves, which could be flown to any trouble spot throughout the Empire, were regarded as vital in the eyes of British defense planners.[10]

The argument was quite convincing, because the Middle East was an area of strategic interest relatively close to Britain, and it certainly did encourage thoughts about withdrawal of the garrisons from the area. The critics argued that forces in the wrong places could only defeat the purpose of defense.

The argument that the army should not fulfill police in addition to its duties as a fighting force, was frequently heard. Soldiers were a valuable commodity at that time, especially when British governments assumed that they might be needed in Europe in case of war. Soldiers, so the argument ran, were trained and equipped to fight European wars with full mobility and fire power and not to fulfill garrison tasks. The British also learned from the lesson they were taught in Palestine that "a British force that might have conquered three German divisions in 1945 was three years later helpless in the face of Jewish irregulars."[11] The men who served in the garrison force in Palestine during the Mandate period were not trained nor equipped to fight a local war. A mobile reserve could have been more effective in dealing with the Palestinian resistance.[12]

The general consensus in Britain at that time was that a war on a large scale might erupt at short notice and, therefore, forces in Britain, as well as in the imperial possessions, must constantly be on alert.[13] No longer could the British leaders rely on periods of preparations and on conventional weapons alone, and no longer could they disperse their forces in the traditional manner. The forces of the new era had to be stationed at home or somewhere in East Africa because a base in such a distant place was less vulnerable to Soviet attack.

The concepts of "mobility" and "flexibility" were widely discussed in the press. The Economist on April 8, 1950 stated: "the main strategic requirement in that era is mobility and striking power, rather than a show of overwhelming defensive force."[14] The Defense Minister, Harold Macmillan, said in his memoirs that one of the main objectives of Churchill's Government in 1954 was to reduce military commitments abroad and to build up a strategic force at home.[15]

This idea, originally propagated by Liddell Hart, found more and more supporters. John Slessor supported it enthusiastically.[16] By 1954, before the Agreement to evacuate the Suez Canal Zone was signed, the idea of using air transport for the proposed "strategic reserve" was dominant.[17] Thus, although the British forces at Suez had been viewed as a permanent garrison, and, according to the plans of the Chiefs of Staff, heavy arms depots with tanks and artillery units had to be established in order to reinforce the strategic reserve. However, it was decided that Suez was not to be maintained as a depot, due to its proximity to Egypt's big cities.

A British official gave an interview to The New York Times shortly before the Agreement on the evacuation of British forces from Egypt was reached. He was reported to have said:

The British Chiefs of Staff are evolving a long range defense plan that will enable Britain to airlift substantial numbers of troops from mobile reserves at home to trouble spots in the Mid-East, Southeast Asia, or the Far East within twenty-four hours.[18]

The White Paper on Defense of 1954 announced that:

It will be our aim gradually to reduce the total size of the Army, and to reconstitute the strategic reserve at home, the lack of which is at present, a serious, though unavoidable defect in our defense readiness.[19]

In 1954, a considerable part of the military elite was convinced that the strategic reserve would be the best solution for imperial defense problems.[20]

The "strategic reserve" in no way eliminated the need to maintain bases overseas. It was important to have small advanced bases with heavy equipment deployed around the Middle East. As early as 1947, Lieutenant Colonel H.R.R. Condor expressed his view that forces in the Mediterranean basin including Malta, Cyprus, and the Suez Canal Zone should be kept small, because of the danger that they might become isolated and completely defeated in case of war.[21] Eden said in his memoirs: "Smaller bases, redeployment and dispersal would serve our purpose better."[22] Smaller and cheaper bases were considered sufficient to protect Britain's Middle Eastern interests in a limited war.[23]

This departure from the outmoded reliance on a string of bases was received enthusiastically by Churchill's Government, and was considered a satisfactory alternative by most of those who favored withdrawal from bases.[24]

Advocates of the idea of "strategic mobility"

had convincing arguments regarding the need to
station forces close to the trouble spot rather
than in the metropolitan area. They argued that
response would be rapid, that troops would be
acclimatized to the area in which they were likely
to fight, and would become familiar with the region and its geographical characteristics. The
'strategic reserve' was to be moved to any spot in
the Empire by the Transport Command which was
beginning to take shape in 1954.[25]

In the original system of imperial bases,
India played an important part for many years.
The abandonment of India can be regarded as a
turning point in Britain's defense policy, although a complete reevaluation of Britain's role
east of Suez was made only after the Suez debacle.
There was a change in British policy even before
the evacuation of India. Leading generals,
diplomats, and advisors were called to London by
Attlee's Cabinet in October 1946, and "were informed more than consulted on the proposed shift
in imperial strategy: British forces would largely be evacuated from Arab lands."[26]

The Imperial General Staff consented to the
Foreign Office's demand to evacuate Egypt. Even
the military officials and the military professionals, who were usually being accused of narrow-
mindedness, supported withdrawal from Egypt, although the chiefs of the army wanted storage and
repair facilities, air bases, a labor force, and
fresh water supplies. They considered Palestine
as a suitable base and believed that Haifa with
its good harbor, pipeline, and refinery was appropriate for this purpose. Simultaneously they had
plans to develop Kenya as a base (details about
these plans will be discussed later). The Royal
Air Force believed that Cyprus could be a good
substitute. The army began to transfer stores and
equipment from Egypt to Palestine.

The move out of Egypt in the fall of 1946 was
accompanied by a parallel, almost covert move into
southern Palestine, where an extensive military
establishment was being constructed. The garrison
in Palestine was increased to 100,000 men. These
contradictory moves were made, due to the concil-
iatory approach which the Foreign Office was trying to foster towards Egypt. The attempt to reach
an agreement with Egypt was a result of calculated
steps to raise the prestige of the Arab League, to
extenuate the Egyptian opposition, and thus to
justify the Foreign Office in the eyes of the
Cabinet and the Parliament. The Foreign Office
was convinced that it would have been possible to
appease the Egyptian opposition by withdrawing the
troops from Cairo and the ships from Alexandria.
Thus, the British would be able to stay in the
Canal Zone for many years. The Foreign Office
tried to convince Field Marshal Montgomery to make
an impressive concession to Egypt. The service
chiefs were under pressure to release men from
service and therefore, consented.[27]

The belief that India would become the center
of a new regional defense grouping was abandoned
by the Chiefs of Staff. In addition, Palestine
lost its strategic importance in the years 1946-
1947 because it had turned into an arena in which
which the British were caught in a cross-fire of
Zionists and Arabs. The British were compelled to
continue the policy of limiting immigration of
Jews into Palestine in order not to antagonize the
Arabs. Also, they had to fight against Jewish
guerrilla organizations who were bent on forcing
the British to evacuate their forces from the
country. The British strategists regarded the
whole region from Malta to the Persian Gulf as one
entity and it was inevitable that some of them
would question the utility and practicability of a
British effort to play a major role in the defense

of this theater.[28]

Attlee felt that the traditional British policy in the Middle East could not continue without a major change. When the independence of India seemed imminent he became even more convinced that a change of policy must take place. Therefore, he raised the matter in September 1945, and again in February 1946. Hugh Dalton had written in his memoirs about Attlee's understanding of the change:

> Attlee is fresh-minded on defense. It was not good he thought, pretending any more that we could keep open the Mediterranean route in time of War. That meant, we could pull troops out of Egypt and the rest of the Middle East as well as Greece. Nor could we hope, he thought, to defend Turkey, Iraq or Persia against a steady pressure of the Russian land masses. And if India "goes her own way" before long, at the most, there will be still less sense in thinking of lines of Imperial communications through the Suez Canal. We should be prepared to work around the Cape to Australia and New Zealand.[29]

Lord Francis Alanbrooke also agreed that the loss of India would leave a great gap in the imperial defenses.[30]

Many historians of the British Empire and the Middle East believe that Britain did not leave the Middle East immediately after the independence of India due to British illusions about the Empire on which "the sun will never set" and as a result of a natural resistance to change.[31]

Elizabeth Monroe gave the same impression by saying that, by rights, the independence of India

should have reduced the British sense of responsibility in the Middle East, but habits die hard.
One can form the inaccurate impression that the
British had not done any serious thinking about
the loss of India and its implications.[32]   Although an overall reappraisal of British policy
did not occur, the strategic thinking did appre-
ciably change.   That immediate withdrawal did not
follow the independence of India does not prove a
failure on the part of the British Government to
understand that changes in the structure of the
Empire had taken place.   One pillar of the Empire
had fallen, and henceforth, the British Empire had
only one center, London.   Illusion about greatness
did not blind Attlee.   He questioned British presence in the Middle East.   This questioning proves
that commitments were not retained out of habit,
nor from illusions of grandeur.[33]   The retreat
from Palestine in 1948, the Suez in 1954, and east
of Suez in 1968 was a result of a gradual process
of change in defense policy.

   The independence of India changed the British
outlook about imperial defense, because there was
no source of military manpower left in the area.
Therefore, it was necessary to create a new
reservoir or to alter the pattern of deployment.
The British had to adjust themselves to the new
situation.   Other bases had to be found.   There
were frequent moves of soldiers from the Suez
Canal Zone to East Africa and from Cyprus to
Haifa, and these moves were accomplished in order
to protect the communications and to safeguard the
supplies of oil.[34]

   The loss of India caused a change in British
defense policy in the entire area east of Suez.
Once that link on the main chain of the traditional imperial system had broken, the whole system of
communication in the Indian Ocean and the Middle
East was adversely affected.   M. A. Fitzsimmons

explained that the independence of India was a turning point, because it signified a diminished willingness on the side of the British Government to use force.[35]

The loss of India was more devastating than the loss of the American colonies in 1783, because America had never meant as much, strategically or sentimentally, as India had.[36] The Middle East was affected by the independence of India because India had created Britain's concern for the Middle East and the Mediterranean, and had led to her increasing involvement in the area.[37]

The independence of India generated a feeling that there were not enough forces to defend the empire in the traditional manner. The separate armies of India and Pakistan could no longer be relied upon to defend the British interests in the area. The British did not feel that there had been an urgent necessity to fill the vacuum created by their withdrawal from India, because the mountainous nature of Northern India was such that a potential enemy could not easily penetrate.[38]

The loss of India was a crucial event in Britain's postwar overseas policy, although it did not force a total reappraisal of British defense policy east of Suez.[39] Thenceforward, there seems to have been no need to maintain British dominance in the Middle East at all costs. By losing India, Britain lost not only a reservoir of manpower, but also economic resources, communication, and military facilities, such as military installations, ports, and airfields. Britain's position in the area became much more vulnerable.

Although the basic defense network of the empire remained intact, some changes and adjustments had to be made. The British territories in the Indian Ocean became gradually independent, a fact which relieved Britain of her responsibili-

ties in the area. Britain was still committed to
the defense of Australia and New Zealand, but its
presence in India was no longer regarded as necessary for their protection. Even though the Government considered the possibility of signing a
defense agreement with India and Pakistan, no
formal treaty was negotiated. The Labor Government did not wish to be involved in an Indo-Paki-
stani conflict and it felt less obligated to
interfere in that part of the world.

Burma and Ceylon were granted independence in
the same year. Despite the fact that the Labour
Government had defense agreements with both, these
treaties committed Britain only to a limited degree. On October 17, 1947 a defense agreement was
signed with Burma. According to its terms Britain
had to send experts to guide the Burmese forces
but it had no automatic commitment to defend
Burma. The same can be said about Britain's
agreement with Ceylon signed on November 15, 1947.
These developments took place outside the United
Kingdom and they were external in nature. Nevertheless, only the strategists' understanding of
them and the substantial influence that they had
on Attlee's Government, made the latter aware of
the implications of these changes. The Government
was receptive to the strategists' ideas, and adjusted its policy accordingly. The above-
mentioned events in the British Empire, important
and substantial as they might have been would have
caused no change in British policy towards the
Middle East had it not been for the fact that
their significance was recognized by leading
strategists.

Liddell Hart, for example, was convinced that
with the loss of India, a basic tenet of British
traditional thinking about empire had drastically
changed. It must be borne in mind that Liddell
Hart's school of thought included numerous

strategists and other supporters, some of whom
held positions of substantial influence. An increasing number of civil and military officials
became convinced that stationing troops along the
eastern Mediterranean coast was a sheer waste of
resources.[40]   In addition; safeguarding the road
to India did not justify the maintenance of the
Suez Canal at all costs, for another reason because there was always a possibility that the
route to India would be blocked effectively at the
southern end of the Red Sea. The Labour Government understood that any tie with India would be
much looser than before. The independence of
India confirmed the feeling that Britain was losing its position as an imperial power, and once
the Government recognized this fact, it became
more receptive to withdrawal from Middle Eastern
commitments.

The British liquidation of imperial commitments cannot be properly understood without understanding the dilemma of Western defense, the North
Atlantic Treaty Organization, and the new presence
of the United States in the Middle East. Postwar
Britain had to fulfill both the traditional
demands of imperial security, sea communications,
and home defense, and also commitments which had
been created in the aftermath of the Second World
War. The commitments in Germany and Austria and
the need to secure European defense became the
first priority.[41]   The main aim was to build a
strong and prosperous Europe.

Defense efforts had been directed towards
Europe since 1948. On March 5, 1948, the assumption that the European powers would enjoy a period
of ten years peace with the Soviet Union had
changed. It was the siege of Berlin that changed
the British attitude towards the defense of Europe.[42]

The fear that the Soviet Union might attack western Europe increased the need to withdraw forces from overseas bases and to concentrate them in Europe. The Berlin Blockade had an immediate effect in the case of the evacuation from Palestine. From March 1948 when the siege of Berlin had begun, until the termination of the Palestine mandate in May 1948, the British forces were instructed by Attlee's Government to concentrate on smooth withdrawal without causing any casualties or loss of war material because there seemed to have been a need for them in Europe.[43]

Bevin, Field Marshal A. V. Alexander, and Field Marchal Montgomery advocated a firm British commitment to the defense of Europe. They believed that failure to do so would cause other western states to become too demoralized to make any serious efforts for their own defense.[44] Others, like Attlee and some Chiefs of Staff, Slessor in particular, still believed in the ability of air power to defend Europe. Consequently, both groups were led to believe that withdrawal from the eastern Mediterranean could by no means be detrimental to British interests. Although Attlee's Government was concerned about the Middle East, there was no doubt that Europe was given priority.[45]

N.A.T.O.'s experts argued that Britain's armed forces were not sufficiently large in order to cover all foreign commitments, and that the maintenance of forces overseas crippled the ability of the army to handle emergencies in Europe. Consequently, withdrawal from overseas commitments became urgent.

The increasing importance of Europe can be clearly seen also by reviewing the writings of civil and military officials. Lieutenant General H. G. Martin, the military correspondent of the Daily Telegraph, wrote in 1955:

As counters in the game for world domination, not even the oilfields of the Middle East can compete with the industries and industrial proletariats of Western Germany, France, the Benelux countries and the United Kingdom.[46]

In 1948, Attlee's Government approved the stationing of U.S. long-range aircraft on fields in the United Kingdom, an act which placed Britain in the front line in case of war. In the same years that the British began to abandon their commitments overseas, Britain not only allied itself closer to the United States, but also signed the Dunkirk Treaty, and the Brussels Pact (1948). Consequently, Britain's finest ground units were stationed in West Germany.[47] Attlee's Government did not fail to understand the need of choosing between alternatives.[48]

As Slessor noted, British strategy rested on the security of the United Kingdom (which made the continent of Europe the first area which must be protected in case of war). The retention of a hold on the Middle East and the maintenance of a British position in the Far East.[49]

It was a peculiar combination of domestic and external considerations that dictated withdrawal from the Middle East. Anti-Communism was the first priority of foreign policy, yet manpower badly needed for industry in Britain was not abundant. Therefore, a choice had to be made without adversely affecting Britain's security. As a result, overseas commitments were to be dropped. Germany loomed larger than any other area. "It is sheer lunacy," said Slessor, "to talk of withdrawing our occupation troops from Germany nothing can suit the Russians better."[50]

The pressure to increase the number of troops in Europe was mounting to such an extent that

British military authorities did not raise substantial objection to withdrawal from the Middle
East. The British military elite believed that
the Soviet Union was interested first and foremost
in occupying all Europe, and then the Middle
East.[51] They were convinced that concentration of
forces in Europe would keep the Soviets out of
Europe. It was a radical departure from principles and assumptions established in the past,
especially from the Ten Year Rule and it became
more evident with the creation of N.A.T.O. in
1949.[52]

     The traditional British maritime strategy
relied on the existence of major bases overseas.
In the nuclear age, defense of the British Isles
meant, not a maritime strategy, but a strong defense system in Europe. Consequently, major bases
overseas lost their priority. Airfields in key
bases were regarded as more important than huge
ground forces, as J.F.C. Fuller had already recommended in the early twenties.[53] This consideration was one of the major reasons for the British
willingness to relinquish their possessions in the
eastern Mediterranean. In the early fifties,
there was a widespread belief that air power could
handle emergencies more effectively, and with much
less casualties and expenses. This idea was
propagated by Hugh Trenchard, Viscount Templewood,
and Giulio Douhet.[54]

     In 1950, the correspondent of the Round Table
summarized the impact of defense policy in Europe
on the defense of the Middle East. He wrote:

     Few will dispute that Europe comes
     first, both from the selfish point of
     view of the immediate defense of
     Britain, and from the wider point of
     view, that a defeat in Europe would be
     decisive.... A wise Britain would feel

committed now to the provision of a
larger army and air force in Germany
with the prime object of showing the
French and the Germans that the West can
be successful against Russia.... The
defense of Iran and Iraq oilfields, of
Turkey and Greece of the same scale as
that forseen for the defense of Europe,
would involve a peace-time deployment of
force which is wholly inconceivable.[55]

Even the Korean War did not change the British belief that Europe was more vulnerable than
the remaining areas of the Empire. On August 26,
1950 Churchill said:

My eyes are not fixed upon Korea...the
supreme peril is in Europe. We must try
to close the gap on the European
front.[56]

The Korean War also, which erupted in June
1950, strengthened the Labour Government's conviction that western Europe should be defended
against any Soviet attempt to attack. Western
Europe seemed alarmingly exposed in June 1950.[57]
This policy of giving Europe the first priority
found expression in the White Papers on defense.
The logical outcome of this policy was to risk the
bases in the Middle East. On September 27, 1954
Eden said:

The United Kingdom will continue to
maintain on the mainland of Europe
including Germany, the effective
strength of the U.K. forces which are
now assigned to the Supreme Allied Commander, Europe-- four divisions, and
Tactical Air Force-- or whatever the

Supreme Allied Commander regards as equivalent fighting capacity.

The United Kingdom undertakes not to withdraw these forces against the wishes of the majority of the Brussels Treaty powers....[58]

The role of the Middle East had changed in the postwar era. Whereas previously it had been held as a safeguard for the passage to imperial possessions, now it became an essential area in containing possible Soviet encroachments in Europe and Africa, and in preventing the Soviet Union from capturing the oil fields. Suspicion of Soviet intentions constituted a major stimulant to concentrating forces in the Middle East.[59]

According to the estimates of N.A.T.O. experts, the adequate number of divisions needed for the defense of Europe was thirty of which six had to be British. Otherwise, they believed, there was no reality in Western defense.[60] The Middle East had to be defended by no more than two. The Middle East however, still retained its importance in the eyes of the chiefs of the services. They were convinced that the area would turn into a battle zone in case of war. Nevertheless, this consideration did not prevent the Churchill Government from abandoning the area. There was strong conviction in government circles that reinforcements could be sent there quickly from the Red Sea, and therefore, the forces could be reduced to one division and 160 aircraft.

Also, according to the military chiefs, the Middle East was an area of lesser strategic importance than western Europe. They believed that after dominating western Europe the Soviets would be capable of capturing the Middle East rapidly by sending a small force through the land bridge offered by Iran and Turkey.[61] Keeping all these considerations in mind, one can hardly doubt that the conviction that Europe had become the main theater of future war, was responsible for the relative neglect of the Middle East.[62]

Liddell Hart thought that British interests in the Middle East..."though important, are not so vital to her security as habit accustomed us to assume."[63] According to his view, an outbreak in Europe would be detrimental to British interests, because a war in Europe would mean a destruction of the entire continent.[64]

Although the British did not rely heavily on the help that could be obtained from the Commonwealth of Nations, some Britons thought that the Commonwealth could provide a viable chain of bases.

Because of the mood of disengagement and isolation in the United States, Britons began to believe that a Commonwealth defense agreement would be the best solution for British security problems. In 1946 and 1947, the idea of informal cooperation was accepted when the principle of allocating zones of responsibility with the Commonwealth was adopted by a number of Commonwealth members. A system of regional association was established and overall cooperation was obtained by the creation of a system of Commonwealth Liaison Officers.[65] Britain was hoping to create a viable regional arrangement, capable of protecting the Indian Ocean.[66]

There was a widespread belief that the Commonwealth would still maintain Britain's ascendency in every part of the empire. The Korean War had demonstrated that Commonwealth forces could be relied upon. The Commonwealth Division was a valuable fighting force.[67] General Van Fleet had described the fighting qualities of one of the Commonwealth units as: "The most outstanding example of unit bravery in modern warfare." It seemed as if the Commonwealth provided Britain a way to prolong its control in the Middle East, Africa and Asia.[68]

The feeling that the dominions should participate in the defense of overseas territories was shared by many.[69] It was one of the factors which contributed to the willingness of the British Government to evacuate its troops from overseas bases. Reliance on the dominions was considered essential for the defense of the Empire.[70] In an Address at Chatham House on June 27, 1950, Mr. Christopher Mayhew said that Britain had "...too many commitments which really belong to the Western cause as a whole. It is time responsibilities were clarified and shared...."[71]

In 1945 Attlee expressed his belief that since the Suez Canal was an international waterway, it could be entrusted by the Security Council to a regional defense association in the area if such an association could be created.[72] However, the Labour Government's feeling was that imperial interests were common to Britain and the Dominions, and as such, they required a joint defense.[73]

The emergence of the United States as a world power, and its increasing involvement in Middle East affairs, generated a feeling of security shared by most British leaders and military figures. This feeling stimulated a change in the traditional policy of maintaining bases. The military correspondent of The Economist commented, on April 1, 1950, that the coming of the United States into the Middle East as a full partner from the very beginning created a situation in which Britain no longer had to plan her strategic policy in isolation.[74] It was a turning point because responsibility for Middle East defense against the Soviet Union was shared by two powers.[75] Although Britain's commitments remained heavy, its military

and economic expenditures were decreased because
it no longer stood alone in the Middle East. Britain could increasingly hope for sympathy, interest, and aid from the United States. [76]

Churchill's Government had no illusions about
its ability to control the Middle East all
alone. [77]   The support that the United States was
ready to give the British Government, and American
willingness to see the Baghdad Pact of 1955 as an
important instrument in containing Communism, gave
the British an assurance that their interests
would not be jeopardized. [78]

Although in the beginning the American ini-
tiative in soliciting Arab cooperation for Western
defense caused suspicion in Whitehall, in the long
run it increased the feeling of confidence that it
was safe to evacuate British forces from the area.
Saudi Arabia, Lebanon and Jordan welcomed American
intervention in the Middle East, and towards the
mid fifties, American friendship with the Arabs
was becoming a reality. [79]

American and British interests in the Middle
East were identical. Both sought defense against
the Soviet Union, and free access to oil fields.
These interests were traditionally British. It
should be borne in mind, that throughout the nineteenth and twentieth centuries, British policy was
based upon maintaining the integrity of the Ottoman Empire as a buffer against Russian ambitions
in the Black Sea and the Mediterranean. The dis-
covery of oil reinforced this policy, but following the Second World War, another great power,
sharing the same interests, had emerged with
tremendous ability and vigor. The raison d'etre
of the British monopolistic policy in the area had
vanished. U.S. companies were already extracting
oil from the Middle East. The companies, Standard
Oil of New Jersey, and Socony Vacuum became part-
ners of the Turkish Petroleum Company as early as

1928.   The United States had a share of 23.75 percent of the Anglo-Persian Oil Company's shares. According to the Red Line Agreement of 1928, the Americans agreed not to seek separate concessions in the Asian territories of the Ottoman Empire. Although this agreement was violated in 1946, Attlee's Government was not alarmed.   The oil dispute with Persia in 1951 led to Anglo-American cooperation in the oil issue, because Western businessmen came to realize that they had more to gain than to lose by cooperating.   Besides, there was growing awareness in the esrly fifties, that if Britain wished to secure the defense of the Middle East, it must rely on Washington.[80]

Churchill's Government sought to prevent a controversy with the Americans.   Therefore, the best alternative was to be a partner under American leadership, since Britain no longer possessed adequate strength to maintain control of the Middle East alone.   Another important element to be taken into consideration in understanding Britain's reliance on the United States is the fact that the latter possessed the atomic bomb earlier than Britain.   Churchill thought that American nuclear power would be sufficient to deter Soviet aggression.[81]

The Truman Doctrine of March 12, 1947 which pledged American support for all free peoples who were resisting outside pressures, Communist or otherwise, demonstrated that both Britain and the United States were fighting for a common cause. Furthermore, British-American relations had steadily improved since the late forties, until the Suez crisis.

A change of attitude towards the main base in the Middle East--the Suez base--developed out of factors inherent in the base itself.   The need to change the strategic outlook on Suez had already been recognized by Liddell Hart in 1925.   He thought that the Suez Canal had lost part of its value in the face of technological developments. He was convinced that in a future war, Britain would be compelled to divert the line of communications around the Cape of Good Hope, due to the fact that the Suez Canal could be easily blocked by a potential aggressor. According to Liddell Hart; "the exaggerated importance still attached to it shows the fixity of conventional ideas."[82]

In 1935 when Ethiopia was invaded by Italy, the British fleet which was stationed at Malta, moved a considerable number of its vessels around the Cape. Reserve supplies were sent to such bases as existed on this route but these bases were not improved, nor expanded.

In 1937, Liddell Hart, after reexamining the problem of Middle East defense, submitted his research to the War Minister at the time. One of his conclusions was that, in the event of war, the British would be able to use the Suez Canal and the Mediterranean only to a meager extent, consequently, they would be forced to depend mainly on the route around the West Coast of Africa for their communications with Southeast Asia and Australia. Therefore, he recommended withdrawal from the Middle East and concentration on the development of the West Coast route.[83]

In a book written as early as 1946, W. L. Borden argued that the Mediterranean had ceased to be important for the West. His contention was that the Mediterranean lost its importance as a route to the Far East when German air power forced Britain to divert shipping around Africa. The lifeline of the empire was of no value whatsoever in the last years before the disaster in Hiroshima and Nagasaki, and therefore all the bases in the Mediterranean were completely worthless. As Borden noted:

> Gibraltar, Malta, the Dodecanese, Suez,
> Crete--all priceless assets in the era
> of preeminent sea power--scarely deserve
> to be plotted upon an aerial chart of
> the globe.[84]

In the immediate postwar years, most statesmen and military officials, though still adhering
to the old military traditions, realized that
Egypt was not an ideal base. Voices were frequently heard criticizing the value of the Suez
Canal Zone as a base. Undoubtedly, the Suez base
was still important, because of its proximity to
the oil resources and to other strategically important areas such as Cyrenaica, Abyssinia, Syria,
Greece, and Turkey. It was a useful naval base,
and it had facilities for ground and air forces,
however, it had some shortcomings, which became
apparent as the war progressed.[85]

The Churchill Government was uncertain as to
whether the base was an asset or a liability,
because no real support from Egypt could be
expected. Moreover, there was a strong conviction
that the Canal would be useless in a nuclear war.
Lieutenant Colonel A. D. Wilson wrote in January
1955,

> The Canal base was essential for the
> last war--it may well be essential for
> the next one, but let us not hang on
> these solely for reasons of prestige and
> pride.[86]

For the base to function in time of war there
was a need for a labor force, which had to be
imported, and these men had to be guarded. Also,
fresh food had to be imported, which meant that
shipping space would be lost. The options therefore, were whether to reoccupy Cairo and the en-

tire country, which would have been unthinkable, or to quit the base.

The availability of the Suez base was still considered important by the majority of the Conservatives and high ranking military officers. One has to bear in mind, however, that from December 1940 until September 1943, the campaign in the Middle East was supported by the Cape route. Abandoning the Suez meant losing some of the shipping from India, but the possibility of an atomic bomb destroying the Canal was considered very real and encouraged evacuation of the area. This was the main reason given by Churchill as a justification of his approval of the evacuation agreement with Egypt in 1954.[87]

Air Chief Marshal Sir C. F. Norris mentioned the important fact that during the war, passage throught the Mediterranean remained hazardous. Most troops and equipment had to circumnavigate the Cape to reach Egypt. Most aircraft flew through the central African route.[88] The Canal Zone was never secure in any direction, and the war had demonstrated that it could be threatened by an enemy. Liddell Hart argued that during the war the British were compelled to abandon the Mediterranean as a main traffic route.[89] He concluded that the army had to find another base if possible. He and other critics argued that installations which took many years to build and which required substantial amounts of money had to be placed in secure areas. Furthermore, they thought that base installations could not be moved quickly in wartime.

As long as the Mediterranean remained open the Suez base was valuable. Once the Mediterranean was blocked, shipping had to be carried by the Cape route. Furthermore the base never did secure the access to the oil fields. For instance the use of the Haifa pipeline could have been denied to the British had the Raschid Ali rebellion in Iraq been successful. Even troubles in Palestine could have prevented the British from using this line. Controlling Egypt by no means guaranteed that the British could secure the way to the Persian Gulf. The Red Sea was vulnerable to air and submarine attacks, especially from Italian-held territory.

The flow of oil depended not on the control of Egypt by British forces, but on Arab cooperation. Besides, Egypt was never an ideal base because it had only a small industrial sector.

The economic pressure to reevaluate Britain's defense needs was a constant. There were, moreover, other strategic arguments which found expression in the press. The correspondent of The Economist expressed the view that the heart of the British defense system which used to be located in Suez, was now to be found in the Persian Gulf, and therefore, a British force with sufficient striking power should be stationed in the northwest corner of the Indian Ocean.[90] The strategists assumed that Egyptian forces were inefficient, and that Egypt could easily become a target for an air attack or rocket bombardment. Therefore they regarded the base as vulnerable even in case of a conventional war. They even thought that passing through the Suez Canal might be risky.

The new importance attached to the Northern Tier states--Turkey, Iran, Iraq, and Pakistan--in the mid-fifties was partially responsible for the belief that the Suez base was unnecessary. The defense of Iraq became more important than ever, because it had oilfields and refineries, and it was also adjacent to the oil regions of the Persian Gulf. The main concern of the British was to contain any Soviet advance towards the Persian Gulf--the main source of oil. The strategists believed that Iraq suited this purpose better than

Suez, because reinforcements could arrive there faster than to the Suez base because the Suez base was situated too far to the south.[91]   Maintaining 50,000 troops in order to provide security for 30,000 who maintained the base was thought ludicrous.

The chiefs of the services brushed away the argument that called for reducing the size of the garrison force to a brigade or a division and pulling back to a small area on the Bitter Lakes. They argued that more troops were needed to hold the line of communication for a hundred miles along the Canal from Port Said to Suez.[92]   By 1954, the chiefs of the services came to the conclusion that maintaining a base at the Suez Canal Zone was no longer reasonable.   In addition, some of them thought that since the Anglo-Egyptian Treaty would come to an end by 1956, there was no sense in occupying Suez any longer.[93]

In the early fifties, Turkey, Greece and Yugoslavia were regarded by the strategists as a single unit which could contribute substantially to Western defense if Yugoslavia could become a part of a Western alliance.   They hoped that these countries would constitute a strong bastion against the Soviet Union and its satellite countries.   This region could become a springboard for an attack against southern Russia.   Furthermore, N.A.T.O. maintained naval bases in the north along the coast of the eastern Mediterranean.   The area was mountainous and extremely hard to penetrate. It could be an excellent barrier against airborne or land attack by Soviet forces.   Egypt could be protected more easily if British forces were stationed in the Northern Tier.   Moreover, forward bases in the eastern Mediterranean littoral, and on the northern shores of that sea did not have to depend on the Suez Canal Zone.

In the traditional thinking about defense, the Suez Canal had been described as the lifeline of the Empire, as an essential base for the defense of the Middle East and the Far East, and as a supreme necessity in the event of war. Yet, the British were victorious in two world wars despite their inability to use the Canal. Since Churchill assumed that Britain would be unable to use the Canal in a future nuclear war, he must have counted to some extent on the Cape route. The probable inability to use the Canal, compelled the Churchill Government to develop air power, in order to transport troops and equipment to any area at any time without the need to rely on the Suez Canal base.

The British took pains to prevent the possibility that the Soviet Union would dominate the Abadan refinery and the Persian Gulf region. Air bases were developed in Iraq in striking distance of southern Russia. The assumption was that a small force could delay any Russian advance in the Persian mountains. The army did not plan to hold points beyond the line from the Taurus mountains in Turkey to Akaba on the Red Sea.[94] The result of this planning was that the importance of the Suez base was decreased even more.

In February 1952, Greece and Turkey joined N.A.T.O. and thus brought with them a reinforcement of some thirty divisions to the defense of Europe and the Middle East. Turkey was considered essential to the defense of southeast Europe and the Middle East. It controlled the exits from the Black Sea on which Russia's only warm water ports lay. By the terms of the Montreux Convention of 1937, Turkey was entitled to refortify the zone of the Straits. As a belligerent nation, it could block the Straits to foreign warships whenever a danger seemed imminent. Turkey was a base from which an attack on the oil fields of the Caucasus and the industrial area of the Ukraine, could be launched.

The incorporation of Turkey in N.A.T.O. was regarded as a major contribution to the defense of Europe. Therefore, the Churchill Government saw even less reason to defend the Suez Canal Zone. The reliance on Turkey rather than on Greece or Persia, gave the British good grounds to believe that the Northern Tier would be protected in case of Soviet aggression. Turkey was heavily support- ed by the United States. It was granted nearly one billion dollars in American aid, and N.A.T.O. airfields were built on Turkish soil.[95]

Some strategists believed that Turkey's mem- bership in N.A.T.O. constituted a guarantee for a superior defense system. Sir Anthony Head, the Secretary of State for War, said: "the likelihood of our being able to take part in a more forward strategy on Turkey's right flank in the defense of the Middle East is much increased."[96] Other strategists believed that Turkish forces were the best in the Middle East and could not be easily defeated if they were to fight in defense of their country.[97] Therefore, the Northern Tier seemed secure.

There was a tendency to rely on the Army of Pakistan to hold the southern approaches to the Gulf of Oman. In addition, there was some degree of confidence that the Jordanian Arab Legion and the Israeli Army would fight against Soviet invad- ing armies if needed despite the fact that Israel could not be incorporated into an alliance with Britain and the Arabs.[98] According to the opinion of N.A.T.O's experts, the immediate threat to the security of the Middle East was a Soviet airborne operation, capable of seizing Mosul, Baghdad, and Basra. However, they believed that there was no danger that Soviet land forces would follow very quickly, since the land routes from Georgia (the place from which an attack was most likely to start) to Iraq were very long and difficult to pass.

The idea of insuring the security of the Middle East by regional defense systems had found many adherents since the end of the Second World War.[99]   In March 1947 the correspondent of the Round Table wrote:

> The interests of the British Empire and the Arab League are in this respect (defense) completely complementary: neither can be safe without a regional system of security worked out in partnership.[100]

By the early fifties, the British military planners became convinced that the defense of the Middle East could be secured by treaties with the friendly powers in the area. The Iraqi air bases would serve the air force on its flights to the East from Cyprus. These bases were regarded sufficient to enable the R.A.F. to strike at any Soviet force that might attempt to penetrate Iran and other areas in the Middle East.

The area of northwestern Iran was protected by natural barriers, such as mountains. Air power and British forces in the area could readily be used against the Soviets. There were three divisions and four air squadrons in Iraq. They could be assisted by forces in Cyprus, Libya, Jordan and Iraq.

Evacuation of British forces from the Suez Canal Zone did not seem detrimental in the early fifties. Even die-hard imperialists had begun to realize that the independence of India had removed the justification of the defense of the Canal. Furthermore, efforts to secure the Northern Tier-- the region where a conflict with the Soviet Union

was most likely to erupt--were quite successful.
Despite the failure of the Baghdad Pact which was
signed in 1955 and included Britain, Iraq, Pakistan and Turkey, the Northern Tier seemed secure
because Turkey and Iran--the two large states
blocking the Soviet entrance to the Mediterrane-
an--had joined N.A.T.O. Belief in the Middle East
Defense Organization was quite strong prior to the
Iraqi revolution.[101]

The belief in a viable defense organization
revolving around the Norther Tier was widespread.
It stemmed from the assumption of the leading
strategists in Britain, that new bases in the area
would force the Soviets, should they decide to
attack, to concentrate a large number of their
forces in order to break through the southern
flank.[102] The belief developed that defense could
be organized only through regional groupings of
allies, especially after N.A.T.O. became a reality
and enhanced the position of those who advocated
an immediate withdrawal from the Suez Zone. Thus,
new ideas and suggestions concerning defense were
brought to the attention of the British leaders,
and it was their business to consider new security
arrangements since they were interested to prevent
a financial crisis.

In April 1955 the British joined the Turkey-
Iraq Pact which came to be known in 1959 as the
Central Treaty Organization [CENTO]. This Pact
replaced the Anglo-Iraqi Treaty due to expire in
1957. The Pact provided for joint training in
peacetime, British assistance to Iraq, and the
availability of airfields to Britain. It was
considered a great asset for Britain which "far
more than compensates us for the partial loss of
the Canal Zone."[103]

Iraq had been a useful staging post on the
air route to the Far East and Australia. It also
controlled the possible approaches of Communist

invaders through Persia.   Iraq was becoming important also due to political changes in Sudan.
There was no assurance that the British would
enjoy free access to facilities on the southern
air route through Khartoum in the future.   The
alliance with Iraq guaranteed Britiain's ability
to use the air routes in the area, and thus eliminated the need to maintain bases in Egypt and India.

Although Iraq did not have a strong army, the
alliance serving as a buffer could allow time for
British and N.A.T.O. forces to send reinforcements
to the area.   The facilities of Habbaniya air base
could also be expanded if necessary.   Jordan had a
well-equipped airfield at Amman.   There were military workshops at Zarqa, and other supply centers.
Air reinforcements and armored divisions could be
deployed rapidly from Cyprus and Libya, and even
from the United Kingdom.   It was hoped that the
expansion of the Baghdad Pact would give Britain
some other important facilities, such as ports and
railroads.

According to the treaty of friendship and
mutual support between the United Kingdom and
Jordan, the R.A.F. was allowed to station units in
Amman and Mafraq, and by 1955 Britain maintained a
fighter squadron there.   The British were allowed
to move troops through Jordan into any territory
they deemed necessary.   Also they could station
additional units in Jordan for joint training with
the Jordanian forces.   The fact that Jordan was
financially supported by Britain in a very
substantial way, helped to create a feeling of
confidence that Jordanian good will would serve
British interests if needed.

There were some strategists who advocated
stationing forces in the Northern Tier, but most
disagreed.[104]   The latter argued that there was no
need to invest money in areas which could be de-

fended by other means; that there were not enough forces available for this purpose; and that the local populations in the area would raise objection to rule by force. Therefore, it seemed desirable to withdraw British troops from independent countries in the Middle East and to concentrate them on British territory.[105]

Successive British governments had tried to conclude treaties and alliances with Middle Eastern countries, thus hoping to gain the cooperation of the Arabs in order to avoid local conflicts. Also the British wished to encourage Arab unification as a basis of friendship against Communist penetration. Britain regarded treaties with Arab countries as a guarantee of her right to re-enter these countries in case of a threat to peace. After the British decided to abandon their base in the Suez Canal Zone they considered establishing a base in Kenya. Attlee had attempted to persuade the Chiefs of Staff and the Defense Commitee, that Britain should retreat to a line from Lagos to Kenya after World War Two.[106] Attlee believed that such a base would better suit Britain's security needs. He believed that geographical obstacles could protect Africa against the Soviet menace. Dalton welcomed this scheme for financial reasons.[107] However, the Chiefs of Staff thought that Kenya was too remote and until January, 1947 they insisted that the Middle East be held. The resistance of the military had lessened even prior to the announcement on the withdrawal from Palestine. Those strategists who believed that the loss of India required adjustments in imperial defense planning favoured this idea.

In September, 1947, 300 Royal Engineers arrived in Kenya in order to build a depot for military installations. Work was begun to improve the communications between Nairobi and Mombasa.[108]

Substantial work was done in Kenya and in McKinnon Road, and it seemed that the area would be developed into an important base.[109]   As the 1957 White Paper noted, "For this task, [defense of the Persian Gulf], land, air, and sea forces have to be maintained in that area, and in East Africa."[110]   The reason for the above mentioned decision was that Defense Minister Duncan Sandys thought that the strategic emphasis had shifted south of the Suez Canal to the Arabian Peninsula.[111]   He thought that this was the case because he felt that the oil, located mostly in the Persian Gulf, was of prime importance to the British economy.

Fitzsimons argued that the British concession in Suez in 1954 was made because bases in Gaza and Kenya were being considered.[112]   As long as the British could find an alternative to the bases in the eastern Mediterranean in places such as Kenya, Malta and Cyprus, from which they could control the lines of communication, there was no need to be overly concerned about the bases in Palestine or Suez.[113]   Even the military chiefs were willing to accept other alternatives.

The idea of developing the Simonstown base in South Africa was also considered by the British Government as a good alternative to the naval base in Alexandria.   The base was to be used in wartime in return for arms which Britain agreed to sell to the Union of South Africa.   This idea remained in the minds of the British leaders until the 1960s when it was rejected by the Labour Government because of South Africa's long distance from the Middle East.[114]   In addition, there were other alternative bases in the Middle East itself, such as in Jordan, Cyrenaica, Palestine, and Sudan. Some strategists believed that friendship with members of the Arab League could provide a guarantee to the defense of the Middle East.[115]   These plans were seriously considered throughout the entire period. Ultimately, Bevin's attitude was to evacuate all bases when and if possible,[116] an attitude Churchill shared.

Another factor which undoubtedly contributed to Britain's readiness to withdraw from the area was the rapprochement with Libya. In July 1953 Britain signed a treaty of friendship and alliance with Libya, the terms of which committed Churchill's Government to assist Libya financially. In return, Britain could use the military facilities and installations of Cyrenaica and Tripolitania for a brigade group of British troops and R.A.F. The fact that Libya provided a new base for British forces was considered as a clear addition to the security of the Canal route.[117]

Prior to the Suez fiasco, there was a widespread feeling among strategists that Britain possessed sufficient power in the eastern Mediterranean to enforce its will. There was also an assumption that its power could be applied so quickly in wartime, that the Canal would be back in British hands before any other power could intervene.[118]

During the war, the R.A.F. had operated many airfields in the eastern Mediterranean and the Middle East. In the postwar era, some of these airfields were improved and turned into permanent airfields. There were air bases in Tripoli, Sudan, Somaliland, Egypt, Jordan, Iraq, the Persian Gulf, Cyprus and Malta. Until the Suez crisis, the R.A.F. could use several air routes despite restrictions on flights which were imposed by the states of the area at one time or another. The British could use the airfields of Amman and Mafraq in Jordan. They also had large bases in Habbaniyah and Shaibah in Iraq. The British navy was able to use the ports of the north African coast. Therefore, one can easily understand why

British defense in the area was by no means totally dependent on the Suez base. Moreover, the
United States had already occupied bases in the
area. There was a large air base at Dhahran in
the Persian Gulf and it was superbly equipped for
bomber and fighter units. In addition, the air
base on Cyprus was in the process of improvement,
and it served both the American Air Force and the
R.A.F. Some believed that if the Kashmir dispute
were settled, Pakistan might cooperate in the defense of the Persian Gulf area.

The Churchill Government did not lose hope
that friendships with both Israel and the Arab
nations would continue. Although no formal agreement with the Israeli Government existed, there
was hope that British forces would be allowed to
use Haifa when necessary, because of Israel's
anti-Communist convictions. Besides, Israel's
developed heavy industry could be used to repair
British equipment. Hopes for renewal of treaties
with Iraq and Jordan did not die, because the
countries of the Middle East continued to deal
with London despite the fact that they resented
Britain's pro-Zionist policy in Palestine, and its
refusal to evacuate their lands. The Arabs still
overrated Britain's strength. Therefore, the
British believed that the good will of the Arabs
could be secured by offering them economic and
technical aid.[119] Also, the British thought, that
since they were a big consumer of oil, the Arabs
would refrain from breaking relations with them.
Slessor believed that since the Arabs were dependent on Britain for their markets, they would remain friendly to the West.[120]

In addition to all the bases previously
mentioned, Cyprus was also considered as an alternative to Suez. The idea of developing Cyprus as
a base and as an airfield prevailed in 1952-1954.
Among those who argued on these lines were the

Minister of Defense, and the Secretary of State
for War. Their influence was so crucial that
Churchill complained of their turning all the soldiers against him.[121]   Cyprus became a possibility
because it could meet the requirements of the
R.A.F. That Cyprus did not have a convenient
harbor did not seem to bother the British in the
early fifties due to the excessive reliance on air
power at that time. The island could be an air
base as well as a training ground. Besides, Cyprus was less turbulent than Egypt. The army
chiefs did not object strongly to using Cyprus as
an alternative base. As H. G. Martin predicted,
"After their bleak experience in the Canal Zone,
our troops would be glad to find a place where
they could live and train in peace."[122]   Cyprus
was considered a valuable air base in the context
of the defense of both the Middle and the Near
East. Its importance increased after the Suez
operation. In 1956 Eden emphatically said: "No
Cyprus, no certain facilities to protect our supply of oil. No oil, unemployment and hunger in
Britain. It is as simple as that."[123]
Undoubtedly, consideration of building a base in
Cyprus influenced Britain's willingness to withdraw from Suez in 1954.

The idea of a strategic reserve seemed to fit
well into the new arrangements proposed by the
strategists. The strategic reserve could be located in Cyprus, Benghazi and Tripoli, all of
which were accessible to the sea and had no hostile population. Their bases could be staging
posts for operations in Iraq if such operations
should be necessary. They could be used for ammunition storage, for maintaining equipment and as
repair facilities. Also, a certain degree of dis-
persion against atomic bombs could be achieved in
this way.

There were other plans which had been discussed throughout the period, and these ideas came
from influential strategists. As has been said,
Liddell Hart believed that the eastern Mediterranean should have been abandoned and that developing the route westward would have been more bene-
ficial.[124]   Members of the Keep Left group within
the Labor Party, especially Ian Mikardo and R.H.S.
Crossman, thought along the same lines.[125]   Liddell Hart argued that excessive attention was
given to the eastern Mediterranean and the Suez
Canal; that the burden of the Near East was not a
necessity; and that the consequent loss of the Far
East could have been avoided if withdrawal had
been carried out long ago.

The idea of shifting military bases to West
Africa was frequently discussed in Whitehall, and
was eventually accepted.[126]   Liddell Hart thought
that west Africa would be a good substitute,
because of its long distance from the Soviet Union. According to his plans, the posts of Mombassa and Dar-es-Salaam, as well as the main ports
of Gambia, Nigeria and the Gold Coast should be
fully developed military installations. Kenya and
Tanganyika should be linked by rail and road
northward to the Sudan, and southward to Rhodesia
and the Cape. The air route across central Africa
which was one of the great innovations of the war
should be maintained. By developing facilities in
African airports at Kano, Fort Larmy and El
Fashar, Liddell Hart suggested that the British
cooperate with the French in a joint development
of the North African airfields. He also thought
that a railway should be built across Africa link-
ing East African bases with the Atlantic coast.

Major B.H.D. Barnes agreed that East Africa
would be a alternative to bases in the Middle and
Near East. In support of *his* argument he said
that East Africa was at the heart of Allied terri-

tory, protected by desert, mountains, and swamps; that communications, manufacturing, and repair facilities were not expensive to develop; and that the area possessed important minerals. East Africa had other advantages such as a supply of manpower, and land available for training grounds. for the forces. It was located close to the whole area from Tripolitania to Persia. Barnes thought that East Africa was the best alternative to locating bases in the Middle East. He argued that Somaliland was too small and had no facilities for any task force. Sudan's political future was uncertain, and the Egyptians were unlikely to accept British presence in the area. Moreover, Sudan had only one harbor, Port Sudan, which needed major improvements and was vulnerable to air and rocket attack.

There was one disadvantage to East Africa-- its long distance from the Middle East. This disadvantage, according to Barnes, could be outweighed by other advantages such as lack of political objection to British presence there; the availability of training areas and installations; and an adequate supply of water.[127]

Lieutenant Colonel H.R.R. Condor, like Liddell Hart and others, thought that Africa was valuable because of its untapped natural resources, and because it was protected from the north by the Mediterranean and the deserts of the Middle East. He thought that the area between Kenya and Southern Rhodesia could be developed, and that the proposed strategic reserve could be stationed there.[128]

One of the reasons for the declining importance of the Suez base was the growing number of bases which were being developed elsewhere to provide facilities for the R.A.F. These bases required no more than a small force for their

protection.   Such a force could be stationed in
any area, and not necessarily in the Canal Zone.

Great importance was attached to air bases in
Jordan and Iraq because of their proximity to the
Soviet border;   consequently, extensive improvement of these bases took place.   According to the
estimates of British and N.A.T.O. experts, the air
force could contain a Soviet attack until sufficient forces arrived.   Therefore, there was less
need to station forces in Suez.   Besides, the
growing needs of the R.A.F. necessitated more airfields.   The elite of the R.A.F. held the opinion
that air attack would be decisive in the next
war.[129]

The defense treaties which were signed with
the Arab states were designed mainly to guarantee
the R.A.F. landing rights in the Middle East.   The
Air Ministry required a reliable staging post between Cyprus and Aden, or Bahrein.   Global considerations dominated the British thinking about
bases in the Middle East.   The coming of the Cold
War and the financial stringency forced the British to reevaluate the nature of their defense
system, and particularly the deployment of forces
in the Empire.   Also some of the strategists believed, that holding on to the Middle East might
provoke the Soviet Union since "they are apprehensive of our aims there...."[130]

Presence of troops in Middle Eastern bases
was risky because it could stimulate the Soviets
to intervene on behalf of the indigenous populations.   On the other hand, disengagement from
these areas could be more conducive to Soviet cooperation.   As early as 1946 Attlee believed that
British withdrawal from areas in which clashes
with Soviets were likely to occur might remove the
grounds for friction between East and West.[131]
Also, there was an opinion that the forces stationed overseas, adequate as they might have

seemed, would fail to deter a major power from attacking. Slessor insisted that overseas forces "were never adequate to meet the major threat of attack by a major power."[132]

The British strategists were aware of Britain's financial difficulties, and constantly thought of ways to reduce Britain's commitments overseas. Liddell Hart mentioned the possibility of recruiting native forces for local defense. He even talked about the creation of a British Foreign Legion from the reservoir of trained soldier refugees from Europe.[133] The argument that African troops could replace the British was occasionally mentioned in the press. On April 1, 1950, the correspondent of The Economist wrote that in view of the growing commitments, the British Government must consider recruiting colonial forces to maintain law and order in overseas territories.[134]

Following the independence of India, some officials argued that a great colonial army in Africa should replace the Indian Army. R. A. Butler had said the same thing as early as 1946.[135] The war had proven that African forces could quickly be expanded, and the notion that Africans made second-class soldiers seems to have been forgotten, especially by those members of the Labor Party who constantly demanded withdrawal. R.H.S. Crossman and H. R. Mackeson advocated this policy.[136] Hugh Trenchard suggested the opening of a big training school at which Africans could be trained in mechanical work. These suggestions were accepted by the Labour Government. According to an agreement with the government of Nepal, Gurkha soldiers were recruited to serve in the British Army.[137] The idea of recruiting forces to replace the Indian forces was prevalent in the years 1946-1952. In March 1951 back benchers asked the Government to investigate the possibility of raising larger forces in the colonies and their motion was passed by a majority of 182.

Many Labor politicians, and even some conservatives questioned the need for conscription.[138] Objection to military service was traditional in Britain. There was constant pressure to reduce the period of service not only due to economic difficulties that a longer period of service entailed, but also as a result of pacifist tendencies. The National Service Bill of March 1947 proposed a period of 18 months service, but opposition within the Labout Party compelled the Government to reduce the period to 12 months. With such a length of service, it became harder to retain British bases overseas with the same number of troops. It was with extreme reluctance that the War Office accepted the 12 month period and then on condition that the period be extended if overseas commitments had not been liquidated.

Many Britons, including Liddell Hart, argued that raising forces by conscription was a wasteful method, due to the need to train new recruits by highly trained men. Also, they believed that it did not make sense to employ short service troops for short tours of duty in distant places, where travel and acclimatization substantially shortened the time available for their active service in the area. This argument strengthened Hart's conviction that there was a need to create an air-lifted strategic reserve. The belief that the next war would be sharp and decisive, and that "neither time, nor strategy employed will admit the use of large armies" contributed to the anti-conscription mood.[139] This position countered the argument of the Minister of Defense, A.V. Alexander, who held the opinion that conscription would help to fulfill British commitments abroad and keep overseas garrisons up to strength.

In 1948 Anthony Head stated in the House of
Commons that the period of full-time training
should be reduced from one year to six months, and
that instead of training or seeking to train the
National Serviceman to take his part in the regular forces, no more should be attempted than to
give him a basic military training. Such a proposal, he argued, would reduce the strain of the
National Service scheme on the national economy
and its interference with individual lives.[140]
This idea was contradictory to the traditional
pattern of deployment of forces which entailed
heavy strain upon the soldiers and the budget.
However, military experts had begun to doubt the
possibility of building effective front line and
reserve forces by means of conscription and favored an elite volunteer army with emphasis upon
armor. This thought was influential and was
shared by military intellectuals and politicians
alike. Sir Eric Speed, the Permanent Secretary of
the War Office for instance, doubted the value of
conscription.[141] Public opinion was overwhelm-
ingly against conscription, and its abolition
required substantial reduction of overseas commitments.[142]

The belief that a base in a hostile land
would not be useful in wartime, was common to many
strategists. Troops could be harmful, because
they might raise the objection of the local population and this could lead to resistance instead
of cooperation.[143] The army desired the cooperation of the indigenous population. British needs
could be obtained only if the Egyptians were ready
to cooperate. They could not be expected to cooperate as long as British forces were occupying
their land. It was clear that a base in a hostile
land would be useless. This condition was one of
the main reasons for the British retreat from
Palestine in 1948.[144]

The same consideration compelled the British to withdraw from the Suez Canal Zone. This base became useless because it depended heavily on Egyptian labor which was no longer cooperative.[145] These factors were the main external reasons which influenced the British readiness to withdraw from the Eastern Mediterranean. Successive British governments had to take into consideration the need to protect the area in case of war. This problem, caused by the emergence of Arab nationalism, affected Britain's policy in a very substantial way, as Liddell Hart had observed.[146]

Major General L. O. Lyne wrote in 1953, "We can retain our present position only at the expense of continued hostility and deteriorating relations with Egypt."[147] The desire to have allies in the Middle East who would be willing to cooperate was a factor which contributed to the decision to evacuate Suez. The forces of nationalism were never so powerful as to be the sole cause of withdrawal. The army was strong enough and willing to deal with local disturbances of any kind.[148]

It was stated in a paper of the Imperial Chiefs of Staff, that the maintenance of a military base in hostile territory was impossible in the long run.[149] Churchill's Government could not pursue its defense policy in the area with complete disregard to the political consequences. The exclusive pursuit of the strategic aims diminished the prospect of success politically.[150] There was a need to secure the good will of the Arabs. The British Government did not wish to create an atmosphere of hatred.

Arab attempts to gain independence could not be ignored for humanitarian reasons. Pressures of Laborites and pacifists on the Government to withdraw increased considerably. One of the critics wrote:

> We thought too much of treaties and
> bases. The Middle East was a place
> where people lived, not merely a place
> to which troops could be sent. Treaties
> were not required: <u>ad hoc</u> arrangements
> between General Staffs were much bet-
> ter...the British could have any facil-
> ities they wanted anywhere; but they
> must treat the Arabs as friends, and
> gain their trust and confidence, and not
> seem to care more for bases than for
> Arab goodwill.[151]

In summary, as has been said, Britain sought the
goodwill of the Arabs mainly because of the need
to have the strategic advantage of landing in
Middle East airfields, of using the local installations, and, above all, access to Middle East
oil. Keeping large garrisons overseas involved
not only problems of dealing with local nationalism. It raised objection at home. British
soldiers and military personnel were separated
from their families. This aspect also helped lead
to reduction in the number of troops overseas and
the creation of a central reserve force.[152]
Churchill realized that there was a need to
attract men to join the Army as Regulars. According to <u>Army Estimates 1953-4</u>, there were 325,500
British troops in the United Kingdom, and 123,000
British troops overseas. The European garrison
was about 100,000 men or the equivalent of four
divisions.[153] (This was not only a larger
proportionate commitment than was shouldered by
the army of any other country, but also a larger
proportion than any peacetime army had ever sent
overseas.[154] He also understood that as long as
Britain maintained the same pattern of deployment,
a soldier in a field-force unit had to serve three
years in Germany and then be sent abroad again for

a further three years after his initial training for three years outside Europe. During all this time, the soldier could not be posted in the United Kingdom except for a brief course of instruction. Overseas posts did not have accommodations for families. Therefore, military service was not attractive to married men. It involved separation of soldiers from their families because they often had to serve in a different regiment. Moreover, there were no schools to which they could send their children. Churchill concluded, as had others, that was essential to maintain the morale of the men in service, and that could be done only by withdrawing the troops and by posting them in the United Kingdom where they could be expected to serve in the proposed strategic reserve.

The fact that the British Government did not formulate a general policy with regard to the Middle East and the whole area east of Suez until 1957 has been emphasized by many historians. This omission led to some degree of pragmatism and flexibility which characterized Britain's willingness to abandon the Middle East. The British Chiefs of Staff were constantly working on a long-term defense program[155] despite the fact that the military was more conservative in its views about deployment of overseas forces. Montgomery mentioned in his memoirs that in January 1947, Attlee was threatened with the resignation of all three service Chiefs of Staff if he had persisted in challenging the necessity of holding on to the Middle East. Eventually, however, even these military officials became convinced that retaining the Middle East could be harmful.

Defense policy was under constant review. Some strategists argued that evacuation of the Suez Canal Zone would not be detrimental to Britain's interests because the Canal Convention of 1888, which guaranteed that the Suez Canal would be kept open to free navigation of all nations, was an adequate guarantee that Britain could still maintain its influence in the Middle East.

The Suez fiasco of 1956 was a culmination of all these tendencies toward withdrawal. Some historians argued that the Suez Affair was a radical turning point in British defense thinking, and thought that it was responsible for the complete reassessment which place in 1957. Armstrong, for instance argued that the Suez crisis was a great shock which awoke the British to a new understanding about deployment.[156] The Suez debacle can be regarded as a coup de grace to the traditional thinking which was under constant attack since the Second World War, because successive British governments recognized earlier that changes had occurred. The invasion of Suez was a natural attempt on the part of Eden's Government to regain a lost prestige, and not to lose in a fight against local nationalism. Moreover, the need to safeguard the flow of oil was stronger than ever, becasue the output of oil from the area increased. It would be inaccurate to argue that until 1957 no change in British strategy toward the Middle East had taken place. The Suez experience accelerated the process of re-evaluation of the bases. Sandys' White Paper of 1957 is an expression of tendencies that were in existence long before 1957.

The examination of Sandy's White Paper proves that most of its points were not novelties. The main point of this document was that Britain was indefensible against nuclear attack, a fact which was recognized long before 1957. The idea that Britain must strive to prevent a war rather than to prepare for one, belonged to the immediate postwar years.[157]

Abandoning the eastern Mediterranean was advocated by critics who argued that if Britain would be forced to withdraw, it would seem as if the empire was crumbling. The critics argued that maintaining forces overseas might increase the prospects of war and that there was no way to secure the safety of any force in a hostile land. Liddell Hart described the imperial commitments as an overinflated balloon which was susceptible to puncture.[158] Maintaining the Suez base meant that Britain would have to commit the entire strategic reserve to defend the area.

The tendency to reduce military commitments in the Middle East was also a result of Britain's commitments in other areas. According to Macmillan, there was no question about the necessity of holding on to Hong Kong.[159] The Anglo-Persian oil dispute of 1951, the Egyptian coup d'etat, the rebellion in Kenya, and the Malayan conflict, all required additional troops. Also, there was an urgent need to send troops to British Guiana in August 1953. The Far Eastern Conflict was a source of anxiety for the British Government because Churchill was concerned about American relations with the Chinese Nationalists. Moreover, he was anxious not to abandon Australia and New Zealand after the Singapore disaster of 1942. The signing of the S.E.A.T.O. Pact increased rather than reduced Britain's military obligations. In summary, withdrawal from the Suez Canal Zone meant that more forces could be available to the Far East.

Some strategists were convinced that the next war would be total.[160] Total war meant a nuclear war and since Britain had the ability to create nuclear weapons in a short time, the entire deployment pattern in the eastern Mediterranean could easily be allowed to alter. There was also a school of thought, the most prominent spokesman of which was John Slessor, who held the view that even if a conflict erupted, it could be localized. Such a view would assure the British that they could localize conflict in the Middle East and would not endanger the British Isles, and that the abandonment of the area did not mean ex- posing Britain itself to enemy attack. The next war they thought, might be: "a localized testing out of how much we or they mean business."[161]

Towards the end of the fifties there was no doubt that bases were much less valuable than they used to be. Armstrong wrote at that time: "...strategic bases are no longer thought to be valuable. That is, the few people--mainly politi- cal leaders, civil servants, military officers, and commentators--have discounted their former valuation of deployment."[162]

The number of troops at the end of the war was far larger than the normal requirements and the strategists felt that it could be de- creased.[163] The Ten Year Rule was a stimulant to withdrawal even when danger from the Soviet Union seemed imminent. Churchill expressed his opinion in the House of Commons that war between the Sovi- et Union and the West was neither imminent, nor inevitable, and this was the view of the great majority of informed observers in 1950.[164] The chiefs of the military believed that until 1955 nothing would happen. It was the "magic date," as Slessor called it. The assumption was that if war started before 1955, it might continue until the Soviet Union used the atomic bomb which could defeat the United Kingdom. If it started after this date, it might start immediately with the atomic bomb. In both cases overseas bases would be useless.

British strategists hoped that the outbreak of a future war might be prevented by the help of the programs for the recovery of Europe. Slessor thought that since the Soviet Union believed that the capitalist system would collapse anyway, they would not start a war.[165] Therefore, no danger was imminent either in Europe, or in the Middle East.

Developments outside the United Kingdom could take place without substantially affecting British defense policy. However, the fact that the strategists who often were prolific, eloquent and persuasive writers, understood the significance of these developments, led the British policy-makers gradually to absorb their ideas about defense and to change their policy in defense matters. One may thus argue that defense policy was determined, in large measure, by domestic factors. External factors are stimuli to domestic pressures which often lead to a change in policy.   External factors may not cause a change in policy or attitude, unless they are kproperly understood by people who have access to policy-makers as indeed many of the strategists had.

FOOTNOTES

CHAPTER III

1. H.C. Debates, Vol. 512 Col. 846 (9 March, 1953).
2. See Neville Brown, Strategic Mobility (New York, 1967).
3. Liddell Hart, Defense..., p. 210.
4. "Defense: Outline of Future Policy," Command 124 (April, 1957).
5. H. A. Deweerd, "Britain's Changing Military Policy," Foreign Affairs 34/1 (Oct. 1, 1955) p. 106. See also Brigadier C. N. Barclay "The Problem of the Arab World," Brassey's Annual (1959) p. 145 and also Philip Darby, British Defense Policy East of Suez: 1947-1968 (London, 1973), p. 84.
6. S. L. Swain, "How can the lessons learnt from the development of the Services in organization and technique since 1939 be applied to the solution of Imperial Defense problem?" JRUSI, Vol. 92 (May 1947) p. 175.
7. Brigadier K. R. Brazier Creague, "The Local Defense of Overseas Territories," Brassey's Annual (1956) p. 223.
8. The Round Table is a Conservative quarterly which first appeared on November 15, 1910 with the aim to provide a regular, unbiased account of the developments in Britain's overseas possessions. Articles contained in this quarterly were usually written in the Dominions and the colonies.
9. "Manning the Defenses." Round Table 41/161 (December 1950) p. 50.
10. Ibid., p. 46.
11. Ibid.
12. Ibid.
13. B.H.D. Barnes, "Future Strategic Importance of the Middle East to the British Common-

wealth of Nations," JRUSI 57/1 (October, 1945) p. 177.

14. Bartlett, British Defense Policy, p. 120.

15. Harold Macmillan, Memoirs III, Tides of Fortune: 1945- 1955 (London 1969), p. 573.

16. John Slessor, "Air Power and World Strategy Today," Foreign Affairs Vol. 33 (Oct., 1954), p. 51.

17. Armstrong, loc. cit. p. 223.

18. "British to Expand Military Aircraft," The New York Times (Feb. 9, 1954), pp. 2-3.

19. "Statement on Defense" 1954, Cmd 9075.

20. Major General R. H. Bower, "Air Support for the Army," Brassey's Annual (1954), p. 183.

21. Lieutenant Colonel H.R.R. Condor, "Future Developments in Imperial Defense," JRUSI (1947), p. 381.

22. Eden, The Memoirs III: Full Circle (London, 1960), p. 260.

23. Bower, loc. cit..

24. Edward Skloot, "About East of Suez," Orbis, Vol. 10 (1966/7), p. 949.

25. Monroe, Britain's Moment, p. 176.

26. Howard M. Sacher, Europe Leaves the Middle East: 1936-1954 (New York, 1972), p. 407.

27. Kimche, Seven Fallen Pillars, pp. 67-68.

28. Sacher, Europe, p. 15.

29. Dalton, Memoirs, pp. 101, 105.

30. "Commonwealth Defense: Lord Alanbrooke's Proposal," London Times (Nov. 7, 1946) 2:2.

31. Darby, British Defense Policy, pp. 21-22.

32. Monroe, Britain's Moment, p. 159.

33. Rosecrance, Defense, p. 44.

34. Thornton, The Imperial Idea, p. 334.

35. M. A. Fitzsimons, Empire By Treaty: Britain and the Middle East in the 20th Century (Notre Dame, 1964), p. 53.

36. Correlli Barnett, Britain and Her Army: 1509-1970 (New York, 1970), p. 480.

37. Ibid.
38. John Slessor, The Great Deterrent (New York, 1957), p. 81.
39. Darby, British Defense Policy, p. 10.
40. Liddell Hart, Defense..., p. 249.
41. John Baylis (and others), Contemporary Strategy: Theories and Politics (London, 1975), p. 269.
42. The Forrestal Diaries (Entry for February 25, 1947) Walter Millis, ed., (London, 1952), p. 242. (New York, 1951), p. 245.
43. Monroe, Britain's Moment, p. 169.
44. Ibid. p. 254.
45. Darby, British Defense Policy, p. 45. See also Kirby, "Britain's Defense," in M. Yiefer, ed., Constraints and Adjustments (London, 1972), p. 70.
46. Lieutenant General H. G. Martin, "The Eastern Mediterranean and the Middle East," Brassey's Annual (1955), p. 96.
47. DeWeerd, "Military Policy," Foreign Affairs 34, p. 105.
48. Ibid., p. 113.
49. Slessor, The Great Deterrent, p. 78.
50. Ibid., p. 92.
51. Ibid.
52. Denis Healey, "Britain and N.A.T.O." in Klaus Knorr, ed., N.A.T.O. and American Security (Princeton, 1959), p. 214.
53. See Fuller's comments about air power in CHAPTER 2.
54. See Viscount Templewood, Empire of the Air: The Advent of the Air Age, 1922-1929 (London, 1957), Chapter 7. See also CHAPTER 4 in this study.
55. "Manning the Defenses," Round Table 41/161 (Dec. 1950), p. 46.
56. Observer (August 27, 1950).
57. Bartlett, British Defense Policy, p. 57.

58. Cited in Major General J. W. Moulton, "The Role of British Forces in the Strategy of Flexible Response," Brassey's Annual (1965) p. 24. (Moulton did not indicate on what occasion this speech was delivered).

59. Rosecrance, Defense, p. 21.

60. "The Strategic Emphasis," The Economist 158/5562 (April 1, 1950) p. 693; see also "Balanced Forces," The Economist 158/5563 (April 8, 1950) p. 756.

61. Rosecrance, Defense, p. 83.

62. Bartlett, British Defense Policy, p. 120.

63. Liddell Hart, Defense..., p. 85.

64. Ibid., p. 143.

65. Baylis, Theories and Politics, p. 267.

66. "The United Kingdom Strategic Interests," R.I.I.A. (London, 1950), p. 54.

67. Anthony Verrier: An Army for the Sixties: A Study in National Policy, Contract and Obligation (London, 1966), pp. 109-110.

68. Cited in David Rees, Korea: The Limited War (London, 1964), p. 250; see also Andrew J. Pierre, Nuclear Politics: The British Experience with Independent Strategic Force 1939-1970 (London, 1972), p. 68.

69. Lieutenant General Sir Francis Tuker," Pacts, Bases and Commonwealth," The Twentieth Century. Vol. 161 (February, 1957), p. 115.

70. Major General Sir Ian Jacob, "Principles of British Military Thought," Foreign Affairs 29/2 (January, 1951), p. 228.

71. Christopher Mayhew, "British Foreign Policy Since 1945," International Affairs 26/4 (London, October 1950), p. 485.

72. "The Empire and the Middle East," Round Table Vol. 36 (1945) p. 32.

73. Darby, British Defense Policy, p. 27.

74. Air Commodore W. Carter, "The Middle East in Modern Strategy," Brassey's Annual (1961) p. 119.

75. Monroe, Britain's Moment, p. 159.

76. "South of the Soviets," The Economist 160/5625 (June 16, 1951), p. 1414.

77. "Middle Eastern Alternatives," The Economist 169/5752 (Nov. 21, 1953), p. 561.

78. Rosecrance, Defense, p. 161.

79. John C. Campbell, Defense of the Middle East (New York, 1958), p. 208.

80. The Economist (Nov. 21, 1953) p. 5621.

81. "Tory Reform for Defense," The Economist 166/5714 (Feb. 28, 1954), p. 549.

82. Liddell Hart, Defense..., p. 243.

83. Ibid., p. 245.

84. William L. Borden, There Will be No Time: The Revolution in Strategy (New York, 1946), p. 162.

85. Barnes, "Strategic Importance," Army Quarterly 57, p. 64.

86. Lieutenant Colonel A. D. Wilson, "The Relevance of Air Mobility to the Middle East," Army Quarterly 69/2 (January 1955), p. 169.

87. See CHAPTER 5.

88. Air Chief Marshal Sir C. F. Norris, "Marshal of the Royal Air Force Lord Tedder" in Michael Carver, ed., The War Lords: Military Commanders in the Twentieth Century (Boston, 1976), p. 489.

89. Liddell Hart, Defense..., p. 246.

90. "The Strategic Emphasis," The Economist 158/5562 (April, 1950), p. 693.

91. "Agreement on Suez," The Economist 172/5788 (July 31, 1954), p. 343.

92. "Britain, Egypt, and the Canal Zone Since July 1952," The World Today: Chatham House Review 10/5 (May, 1954) p. 195.

93. "The Anglo Egyptian Treaty," The Economist 161/5649 (Dec. 1, 1951) pp. 1314-5.

94. Monroe, Britain's Moment, p. 160.

95. Ibid., p. 176.

96. Cited in Fitzsimons, p. 115.

97. Wilson, "Relevance of Air Mobility," Army Quarterly 69/2, p. 170.

98. Ibid.

99. Round Table 41, loc. cit.

100. "The Empire and Middle East," Round Table Vol. 37 (March, 1947) p. 107.

101. Martin, "Eastern Mediterranean," Brassey's Annual 1955, p. 109.

102. Campbell, Defense, p. 159.

103. Martin, loc. cit., p. 103.

104. Barnes, "Strategic Importance," Army Quarterly 57, pp. 170-171.

105. Ibid.

106. Dalton, Memoirs, p. 105. See also, the influential memorandum of Liddell Hart, Defense..., pp. 249-255.

107. See CHAPTER I.

108. "Military Stores from India and Egypt: Huge Depot in East Africa," London Times (Sept. 13, 1947), 3:7.

109. "Kenya Stores Depot," London Times (Sept. 16, 1947) 3:3.

110. "Defence: Outline of Future Policy" 1957, Cmd. 124.

111. "Mr. Sandys Back from Tour: Early Decision on Mid-East Base," London Times (June 24, 1957) 6:3.

112. Fitzsimons, p. 95.

113. Captain A. O. Shipley, "Imperial Defense and the Rise of Nationalism in Colonial Territories," Journal of the Royal Artillery Vol. 84 (1957), p. 242.

114. Swain, "Imperial Defense Problem," JRUSI 92, p. 180.

115. Kimche, Seven Fallen Pillars, p. 61.
116. Sacher, Europe Leaves, p. 410.
117. Armstrong, loc. cit. p. 194.
118. Ibid., p. 196.
119. Monroe, Britain's Moment, p. 160.
120. Slessor, The Great Deterrent, p. 85.
121. Bartlett, British Defense Policy, p. 86.
122. Martin, "Eastern Mediterranean," loc. cit., p. 107.
123. Bartlett, British Defense Policy, p. 90.
124. Liddell Hart, Defense..., p. 246.
125. See CHAPTER I.
126. Liddell Hart, pp. 248-249.
127. Barnes, "Strategic Importance," Army Quarterly 57, p. 172.
128. Condor, Imperial Defense, p. 382.
129. Slessor, The Great Deterrent, p. 84.
130. Liddell Hart, Defense..., p. 251.
131. Rosecrance, Defense, p. 59.
132. Cited in Armed Forces in New States (London, 1972), p.v.
133. Liddell Hart, Defense..., p. 215.
134. "The British Colonial Army," The Economist 160/5616 (April 14, 1951) pp. 844-5.
135. H.C. Debates Vol. 420 co. 55 (4 March, 1950).
136. H.C. Debates Vol. 434 col. 1622 (13 March 1947); see also H.C. Debates Vol. 435 col. 673 (20 March 1947).
137. H.C. Debates Vol. 445 col. 34-5 (1 Dec., 1947) Also "Future of Gurkhas: Tripartite Agreement," London Times (Dec. 2, 1947) 3:2.
138. Darby, British Defense Policy, pp. 104-5.
139. Liddell Hart, Defense..., p. 218.
140. W. T. Wells, M.P., "Defense and Imperial Conference," Fortnightly Review Vol. 170 (1948), p. 93.
141. Bartlett, British Defence Policy, p. 26.
142. Rosecrance, Defense, p. 197.

143. Tuker, loc. cit.
144. Francis Williams, Socialist Britain: Its Background Its Present and an Estimate of Its Future (New York, 1949), p. 182; see also Richard H. S. Crossman, "The Role Britain Hopes to Play" Commentary Vol. 5 (June 1948), p. 496.
145. Rosecrance, Defense, p. 201.
146. Liddell Hart, Defense..., p. 250.
147. Major General L. O. Lyne, "Middle East--A Strategic Survey," Brassey's Annual (1953) p. 112.
148. Monroe, Britain's Moment, p. 157.
149. R. M. McClintock, The Meaning of Limited War (Boston, 1967), pp. 94-95.
150. "Darkness in Egypt," The Economist 162/5658 (Feb. 2, 1952) p. 258-9.
151. Lord Strang, Home and Abroad (London, 1956), p. 261.
152. Wilson, "Relevance of Air Mobility," Army Quarterly 69/2, p. 161.
153. "Memorandum of the Secretary of State for War Relating to the Army Estimates: 1953-54" Cmd. 8770.
154. "An Army Extended," The Economist 170/5766 (Feb. 27, 1954) p. 660.
155. Slessor, The Great Deterrent, p. 77.
156. Armstrong, loc. cit., p. 189.
157. John Slessor, "British Defense Policy," Foreign Affairs Vol. 35 (July, 1957) pp. 551-63.
158. Liddell Hart, Defense..., p. 245.
159. Macmillan, Tides..., p. 573.
160. Lord A. V. Tedder, "A Defense Warning to Britain," Sunday Express (October 19, 1947).
161. Slessor, "British Defense Policy," Foreign Affairs 35/4, p. 94.

162. DeWitt C. Armstrong, "The British Revalue Their Strategic Bases," JRUSI Vol. 104 (1959), p. 423.
163. Rosecrance, Defense, p. 60.
164. "Forward in Europe," The Economist 158/5562 (April 1, 1950), p. 691.
165. Slessor, "British Defense Policy" loc. cit., p. 93.

CHAPTER IV

AIR POWER AND THE STRATEGIC DEPLOYMENT

The postwar years witnessed a change in the internal structure of the British armed forces. This change was so radical that it was bound to have a great impact on British defense policy, particularly in imperial matters. The emergence of air power as a dominant element in the armed forces, and the parallel decline of naval power dealt a major blow to the traditional concepts of imperial defense. Overseas bases lost their priority. Air enthusiasts increased in number and aggressiveness and constituted an internal pressure group whose voice the Government coult not ignore.

Those strategists, especially those who had constantly written about the impact of air power on Britian's defense, became increasingly convinced that air power was the most important element of defense. The Government, torn between the need to promote the welfare of its citizens and to defend the Empire, was compelled to acquiesce to demands made by those who came to be known as specialists in defense matters. Air power had emerged supreme in the years that preceded the abandonment of the Suez Canal Zone. It seemed able to offer the flexibility needed in global war, limited war, and local disturbances in the colonial possessions.

The development of highly sophisticated aircraft profoundly affected the deployment of ground forces and garrisons throughout the Empire. Aircraft had continuously improved since the First World War. Consequently, a change of attitude towards imperial defense became inevitable although a few clung to the old principles of war.[1]

As a result of the postwar revolution in technology, ground forces and garrisons ceased to

be the major component of defense.   Other methods
such as radar and electronics, a system of ground
observers, an efficient air force supported by a
modern aircraft industry and airfields throughout
the empire became more accepted among military observers and increasingly used.   In addition to the
innovations in the use of air power and naval forces, the emergence of the nuclear weapons, eliminated the need to station large garrisons overseas, especially in areas adjacent to the United
Kingdom.   Air strategists did not recommend
immediate evacuation of all troops from every spot
in the Empire; however, they argued, that the
number of troops deployed overseas could be reduced substantially.[2]   Most military observers and
scientists realized that technological innovations
were bound to cause a change in thinking about
defense.

Various newspapers and magazines carried
articles that reflected the opinion of the military elite, the Chiefs of Staff, and ministers
involved in defense matters.   Most of those who
wrote articles in the periodicals had held high
positions in the army, or in the Government at one
time or another.   Most writers believed that the
unprecedented growth of air power made it mandatory to make adjustments in the defense system.
Lieutenant General Sir Francis Tuker, for instance, believed that nuclear rockets would inevitably change strategic thinking because of their[3]
power of devastation, speed, and accuracy of aim.
Slessor thought that since conditions in the
international and technological fields changed
dramatically it became necessary to review
Britain's defense needs more frequently.[4]

In the wake of the scientific innovations
came the conviction that the Suez base had become
obsolete and that it was necessary to shift the
lines of communication further south.   Sea and air

power, they argued, could safeguard the defense of the empire if they were supported by a system of bases spreading outward from Africa.[5]

The development of new weapons supplied with the most sophisticated electronic devices gave the British military experts confidence that imperial possessions could be defended without maintaining large garrisons. Attlee's Government decided to construct a long-range bomber force capable of delivering atomic weapons and bombing targets inside the Soviet Union. It is noteworthy that despite the relative neglect of the Royal Navy, greater importance was attached to aircraft carriers in the immediate postwar years.[6] It was only later that British air strategists questioned the usefulness of carriers and began to stress their vulnerability. The R.A.F. strove to get a larger share of the defense budget by minimizing the importance of the Navy in warfare. Thus, concepts such as mobility, flexibility and speed were given priority. Reliance on these concepts was inevitable since the Government was compelled to find the cheapest way to secure Britain's interests. New elements such as electronic communications, navigational aids and refuelling techniques had to be reckoned with.

As has been said, the effect and decisiveness of air power was already recognized by many strategists before World War I, but it was not until after World War II that it affected traditional defense policies. The influence was cumulative and gradual. The technological innovations of the postwar period affected air power more than any other branch of the defense system. Air power had become decisive. In order to understand the impact of air power on British defense thinking it is necessary to trace its development, and to examine the theories about air power and their impact.

The main proponent of air power was Giulio
Douhet, an Italian strategist who saw warfare as
an affair of super bombers imposing terms of surrender on a tenaceous enemy in a very short time.
Douhet's theory, which was discarded by most
strategists as sheer nonsense in the post-World
War I era, became an article of faith for many
strategists later on.

According to Douhet, an enemy could be
defeated solely by air attack, a factor which
eliminated altogether the need to station ground
forces or garrisons in overseas territories, for
these were immobile and therefore vulnerable.
Douhet argued that because air power had become
the most important element of warfare, land forces
should be small in size because there would be no
need to hold the enemy in check; air attack would
be decisive, and therefore most of the nation's
efforts should be concentrated on the development
of air power; that air power should be used to hit
enemy targets behind the front, and not in support
of ground forces. Command of the air was the decisive element in war; therefore, in order to
guarantee a full command, the enemy's air power
must be destroyed on the ground. Furthermore, he
recommended that enemy aircraft should be destroyed first, then the factories which produce them.
Attack should be preemptive and the bomber must be
able to protect itself against enemy aircraft.
Aircraft should be used to break the morale of the
civilian population and not simply against enemy
aircraft in the air.

This idea of the exclusivity and the special
mission of the R.A.F. was derived directly from
Douhet, because, for Douhet, air power was self
sufficient and therefore, independent of any other
branch of the armed forces. Douhet[7] virtually
ignored other forms of military power.

These arguments became influential despite

the fact that the experience of World War II had proved that the bomber was indecisive, that the morale of the population was not shattered by the bombing as Douhet had predicted it would be, and that bombers were never enough to win the war. Billy Mitchell's theory of air power drew upon similar ideas. Although both men were over optimistic about air power in some aspects of their theories, the British strategists never-theless, followed them by attaching excessive importance to air power and undervaluing land forces and garrisons overseas.

Douhet gave the land forces a purely defen-sive function. He thought that with proper devel-opment in the use of air power, the battle would be swift; hence, minimal military action would be needed to delay the enemy's infantry forces and to keep them from advancing until the air force could arrive and destroy them. Douhet overestimated the ability of air power.

Douhet also thought that an air fleet capable of dropping hundreds of tons of bombs would be easy to construct. Also, he thought that an air force would be cheaper to maintain than ground forces. He was convinced and he convinced others, that aircraft and bombs required limited re-sources. Douhet also argued that a powerful air force could be organized within a short time with-out attracting the attention of the enemy.

Douhet, like Liddell Hart, Lord Trenchard, Slessor, and others, was extremely influential; however, part of Douhet's theory proved overly optimistic or even erroneous. Nevertheless, the trend of air power development and the formulation of general strategy followed his theory.[8]

Marshal Petain and Bernard Brodie thought that Douhet's philosophy of air power was highly innovative, convincing and logical.[9] Douhet's contribution was extremely valuable because he

turned upside-down the old military axiom derived
from Jomini, that methods change, but principles
do not.   Douhet was influential because he developed a well integrated philosophy with exceptional
internal consistency and built it up in a logical
way.
                                                10
      Those who believed in Douhet's theory
thought that most of the nation's resources should
be allocated to the development of air power and
that land and naval forces should be confined to
defensive purposes and therefore must be limited
in size.   Garrisons, they thought, were nonessen-
tial in the era of air superiority.   Emphasis was
placed on strategic bombing; consequently, the
emergence of strategic nuclear weapons made Douhet's theory appear more valid than ever.
      Military officials held the view that once
air superiority was achieved, it would be possible
to use airborne forces both in an offensive role
and as a mobile reserve.   Airborne forces were
considered by the strategists as the best type of
mobile reserve for use in any theater.   The following statement sheds light on the influence of
Douhet's theory about air superiority.

> It could be said that, as it is agreed
> both by the Army and the Royal Air Force
> that 'Air Superiority' is the prime re-
> quirement from which success in war in
> an atomic age must flow, all resources
> should be concentrated on achieving it
> at the earliest possible moment and
> maintaining it throughout the con-
> flict.[11]

These views were held by some influential strategists and by the elite of the R.A.F. who were in a
position to convince the government to adjust
their concepts about defense.   The most well known

of these air strategists were Hugh Trenchard, Lord
C.F.A. Portal, Leigh-Mallory "Mary" Conningham,
John Slessor, C.F. Harris and Sir Robert Saundby.
They were not only theoriticians of air power.
Their influence on the Government was far greater
than theoreticians like Douhet and Spaight, because they held high positions in the R.A.F. in
addition to their writing about air power. Their
influence from the fact that their writings "Never
seemed to possess the artificiality, or purely
theoretical flavor of the doctrines of Douhet and
Mitchell, and their disciples."[12] The most brilliant and influential of these men was Lord Trenchard.

Armstrong claimed that Trenchard was the most
highly respected airman.[13] Trenchard rarely said
anything in public and was represented by his ju-
nior officers, his disciples, Charles MacKay and
John Slessor. He was also helped by Sir Maurice
Hankey, the Secretary of the Committee of Imperial
Defense and of the Cabinet. His power was formidable because he could lay down the basis on which
discussion would take place and no one could challenge him because he was considered "the only commander of an independent air force."[14] Trenchard
was among those strategists who retained their
influence in the postwar era. He was known as the
father of the Royal Air Force.

In order to understand the influence of the
elite of the R.A.F. and the supporters of air
power on the Government, one has to bear in mind
that these men held high positions in the Government and its ministries and not only in the army.
Lord Templewood, for example, was both Air Minister and Foreign Minister. Lord Portal and Lord
Trenchard were the two most famous retired Chiefs
of the Air Staff and their arguments in the House
of Lords made a deep impression.

Lord Templewood thought that air power was

the solution to the dilemma of defense. In one of the debates in the House of Lords, he said:

> I am convinced that for the years immediately before us, a dominant Allied Air Force can hold up and disorganize a Russian advance.... It needs also a determined effort to convince the countries of Western Europe and particularly France (who for years past has ignored the teachings of air strategy), that air force is the most effective defense against Russian military aggression. Most of all, it needs the closest possible cooperation with the United States Air Force.... By these means...we can most effectively prevent war....

Lord Trenchard agreed completely with these words. He was convinced that Russian forces could defeat any garrison, anywhere, and that the only way to stop them was by air power. Liddell Hart also agreed that air power would be important in a future war, but he never did rely on it as the sole means of defense. He wrote: "I agree with its basic thesis-so long as this is not carried too far."[15]

Trenchard attributed great importance to the ability of the bomber to determine the outcome of future wars. Trenchard's influence caused the postwar Air Staff to pressure the Labour Government under Attlee to provide them with funds for a force of 180 land-based V bombers. Their argument was that since the manned bomber had been useful in the Second World War, the modern bomber would be even more important in the next war.[16] Although the Bomber Command had not won the war single-handed as Trenchard believed, and despite the fact that strategic bombing in the Second

World War was generally ineffective as has been pointed out above, the R.A.F. continued to pressure the Government to invest money in expanding the Bomber Command. Trenchard thought that the bomber which was capable of flying at high altitude could very easily evade almost any type of aircraft. Largely due to Trenchard's popularity, the British Government failed to heed the actual lessons of the war regarding the effectiveness of strategic bombing, the belief in the ability of air power to handle any situation was shared by many. Sir John Kennedy, Director of Military Operations for Field Marshal Alanbrooke wrote in his diary in the middle of the war:

> In my view, the only well-founded ground of criticism of making our central war direction now lies in the use we are making of our Air Force.... If we had diverted, say, 20 percent of our long-range bomber aircraft to the Middle East, it is doubtful whether Rommel could ever have started his offensive and more doubtful whether he could have sustained it at its recent tempo.[17]

The belief in the ability of air power to win wars and to preserve the integrity of the empire was an important factor in British defense planning because it affected the attitude toward bases. Believers in the ability of air power to solve all the problems of imperial defense never did attach importance to bases. Trenchard himself thought that in the era of air superiority there was no need to station garrisons overseas.

Because of the support it was receiving, the R.A.F. achieved an independent status for itself. Nevertheless the Air Force gained independent status only after the First World War.

Trenchard's theories on the decisiveness of air power were responsible for the overconfidence of prewar British foreign policy. Churchill however, late in 1941, said that he was misled by the Air Staff in regard to the effectiveness of air power:

> The Air Staff would make a mistake to put their claim too high. Before the war we were greatly misled by the pictures they painted of the destruction that would be wrought by air raids.[18]

Nevertheless, Trenchard's ideas were accepted without any attempt to alter them. The R.A.F. became so important that money had to be cut from other services. The influence of the R.A.F. could not have been stopped, because air strategists had viable arguments about the independent function of aircraft. The Air Staff did not change Trenchard's philosophy when radar and other revolutionary developments occurred.[19]

Frederick Sykes and P.R.C. Groves, who belonged to the air power school, developed the theory of the deterrent which was further developed by John Slessor. The latter was an important figure especially when he became a member of the Chiefs of Staff Committee. He was in a position to submit recommendations to the Government. According to Armstrong, Slessor was one of the most highly esteemed strategists in the innermost circle for many years.[20] Slessor developed the theory of strategic nuclear bombing and his ideas were embraced by the Churchill Government in Britain. He did not see any purpose in stationing forces in the various areas of the empire. He thought that in order to gain strategic freedom of action, Britain should liquidate the "outlying commitments" of ground forces.[21] The confidence that liquidation of all ground commitments would not be detrimental to British interests stemmed from the belief in the superiority of air power.

Obviously, not all the leading strategists were air power enthusiasts. Air Force advocates became disappointed after the experience of the Second World War, but they remained convinced that air power was the most important weapon of the future, and the emergence of the atomic weapons only strengthened their belief in air power. Michael Howard commented that "In spite of their disappointment in the Second World War (caused by the fact that strategic bombing was not as effective as they thought), the advocates of air power seemed at the beginning of the 1950's to have emerged supreme."[22]

Sir Frederick Sykes thought that the airplane would be a good substitute for manpower in overseas territories, and that it would relieve the British from the expensive commitments there, and in Europe. He wrote in his memoirs, that the aircraft "may prove the greatest service to such a nation as ours with a tempermental dislike to military service." In a memorandum to the Cabinet in 1918 he wrote:

> In the next war, the existence of the British Empire will depend primarily upon its Air Force. The giant aeroplane of today will inevitable develop in striking power to something analogous to an aerial dreadnought.[23]

The British leaders had great respect for the officers of the R.A.F.. The R.A.F. was extremely popular between 1945-1955. Movies about air warfare such as: One of Our Aircraft is Missing were produced in abundance in these years in Britain and the air force was also landed greatly

in the United States.   This was the era of the
swashbuckling General Le May of the Strategic Air
Command (S.A.C.).   Books about the subject were
also numberous, and increased the popularity of
the R.A.F.   One political leader believed that
R.A.F. officers were most flexible and least
dogmatic in their strategic thinking.   Also, he
thought that they were more talented than the
officers of the navy and the army.[24]

The elite of the R.A.F. was so influential in
the fifties that ministers were directly affected
by them.   Senior officers were often complaining
that Mr. Duncan Sandys, the Minister of Defense,
was..."In the pocket of the airmen."   It was not a
mere coincidence that he was nominated a Minister
of Defense despite the navy's bitter objection.
He was a candidate of the Air Marshals, and this[25]
gave him substantial leverage in the Government.

It has been recognized that in every operation and in every condition of warfare, the result
of the next war would be "dependent upon the degree to which air power, properly handled, could
be brought to bear upon it by one side or other."[26]

There was a firm belief among Britons that
air power was decisive in the Second World War.
The ability of air power to determine the outcome
of war was proved not by saturation bombing in
Germany, but in the Mediterranean campaign in
World War II.   In the words of Air Chief Marshal
Sir C. F. Norris: "It introduced in rather brutal
terms, the new factors of 'air superiority' and
its effect on the operation on land and sea forces.... One of the outstanding characteristics of
air power proved to be its flexibility."[27]

Quite a few air enthusiasts made extravagant
claims about the ability of the air power to win a
war by itself.   They thought that air power could
protect shipping by bombing U-boat bases, by

destroying industrial centers and military installations, and, most of all, by destroying the
morale of civilians. Although these men did not
constitute a majority of the strategists, the idea
that air power might become decisive in a future
war gained wide acceptance. The principle of 'air
superiority' and the supremacy of the offensive in
aerial war became an article of faith in the
R.A.F. [28] In a lecture at Cambridge University in
1947 Lord Tedder said:

> I am utterly convinced that the out-
> standing and vital lesson of this last
> war is that air power is the dominant
> factor in the modern world, and that
> though the methods of exercising it will
> change, it will remain the dominant
> factor as long as power determines the
> fate of nations.... It can be the
> guardian of peace until that happy day
> when nations realize that wars don't
> pay. [29]

Major Alexander de Seversky, a distinguished
aircraft designer and strategist said, "the air
ocean is one and indivisible, and must be controlled by a single homogeneous force." [30] Like
other air enthusiasts, de Seversky tended to regard bases overseas as unnecessary commitments.
He thought that air power could be a cheaper and
better substitute. Seversky was not the only one
who came to this conclusion. He wrote in his book
Victory Through Air Power:

> It is sheer waste to maintain advanced
> bases instead of hurling the full aerial
> potential   directly   against   the
> adversary. The entire logic of aerial
> warfare makes it certain that ultimate-

ly, war in the skies will be conducted from the home ground with everything in between turned into a no-man's-land.[31]

In a lecture on air power published in the Air University Quarterly Review de Seversky said that the West must build a most powerful air force. He thought that since aircraft had sufficient range, there was no need for refueling and therefore, no need for bases. He said, "In the future, we shall strike the enemy across any distance from our home bases." In the era of global war and modern air power, there seemed to have been no value to land bases because the cost of maintaining, protecting, and supplying such bases became ludicrously out of proportion to the benefit they offered.[32]

The ideas about air power held by such prominent men were bound to have tremendous influence on defense planning. Edward Mead Earle, one of the leading writers about strategic matters, wrote:

> No instrumentality in the long history of warfare has exerted so revolutionary an influence upon strategy and politics as the military airplane and its related airborne weapons including the atomic bomb.[33]

In summary, bases became increasingly vulnerable since enemy aircraft could destroy them quickly. Prior to the emergence of air power, strategy was based on the assumption that troops stationed in overseas territories should be able to defend the empire, or at least to hold off an attack until reinforcements arrived. The possibility that local garrisons might suddenly be threatened with an attack, created a feeling that

overseas territories could no longer be defended
with land forces.[34]   Of course, as has been said,
when financial restrictions became a necessity,
the British Government was compelled to develop
the R.A.F.. Air defense became most important.

Even in 1938, the bulk of the British military elite had favored the termination of imperial
commitments. Only the infantry remained concerned
about the defense of imperial commitments such as
Egypt and India, while the Royal Navy was concerned with Japan and the need for a capital ship
fleet. The R.A.F. was occupied chiefly with developments in Europe.[35]

Also, the majority of the strategists were
convinced that only with the help of air power
were other forces capable of operating in an
offensive role. Montgomery said "The first and
basic principle is that you must win the air battle before you embark on the land and sea battle."[36] The great advantage of air power over
stationary bases was that air power was highly
flexible. It could be switched to army or navy
support, or to strategic air offensive, according
to the priority of the moment. Aircraft had the
advantage of speed and elevation, and possessed
the ability to destroy stationary targets on the
ground while remaining comparatively invulnerable.

The recommendations of the strategists regarding the need to give priority to the air
force, were accepted by Churchill's Government and
duly implemented.[37] The army was the first to be
affected by this intruder, because by the mid-
fifties even ordinary Britons thought that it was
possible to rely heavily on air power. Accordingly, overseas garrisons were reduced. Ultimately,
air power was looked upon as an indispensable
force and rendered other kinds of forces relatively unimportant. According to Air Marshal Sir
Robert Saundby, air power could be used to trans-

port forces and supplies to the scene of action, to establish air superiority, to provide direct support in battle, and to interdict the battle zone.[38]

With the development and spread of nuclear weapons, the victory of the R.A.F. was sealed. Like many other strategists, Saundby thought that air power could be used, not only in global war, but also in a limited war. They argued that a fighter could carry small atomic bombs.

Colyer argued that the war had ended in victory for Britain largely because the Allies recognized the significance of air power earlier than their enemies. The fact that they possessed overwhelming air power enabled them to impose their will on Germany. Emphasizing the fact that technology and science were the most important element in defense planning he continued:

> Go to the scientists and technicians, for all they can possibly give in the way of speed, mobility, and economy, and then develop the whole time with an eye on the other two members of the team in cooperation not in competition.[39]

Slessor said about the same point:

> I believe that in this critical sphere of air power, the scientific, technological, and industrial superiority of the western powers remains of cardinal importance and value.[40]

The development and construction of aircraft in large quantities was made possible only after the war. In 1947, the air force as a result was able to build a series of long-range bomber aircraft. They started to build the <u>Vulcan</u>, the

Valiant, and the Victor medium bomber, and also the Canberra light bomber. These bombers were scheduled to be completed in the early fifties. Many other aircraft such as the Meteor, Venom, and Vampire were ordered. There were plans to pur- chase a four-engined jet bomber, advanced fighters and jet night fighters. In addition, there were plans to purchase the Sabre fighter and the Nep- tune reconaissance plane from the United States. The purchase of fighters required L54.78 million. The jet fighter strength of the Fighter-Command was doubled.[41]

Advances in technology and industry, however, resulted in a significant decrease in the army's budget. Production for the army was cut back again in 1950. Whereas the estimated expenditures for the air force and the navy rose by 50 million pounds and 40 million pounds respectively between 1948 and 1950, those of the army fell by 6 mil- lion pounds.[42] This trend became more discernible with the progress of the nuclear program. In the early fifties, a few years before the agreement on Suez was reached, the British Air Force possessed more aircraft than all the European allies com- bined. In 1951 more than 1,000 planes were being produced

Attlee's Government had ordered a large num- ber of aircraft without providing funds to pay for them. Arthur Henderson pointed out on March 2, 1955 that the 1951 air plan had aimed at strengthening the Air Force by building and purchasing between 3,000 and 4,000 planes. Slessor pressured the Government to expand the R.A.F. by equipping it with every kind of air- craft, but he put a strong emphasis on the V- bomber and called it "the natural successor of the battle-fleets of Nelson and Jellicoe."[43]

The belief that the Pax Britannica depended on the bomber force and not on traditional garrisons along the lifeline of the empire was commonplace among the military Chiefs. Slessor thought that "The bomber holds out to us the greatest, perhaps the only, hope of that. It is the great deterrent."[44]

The bomber was built to meet the requirements of the new age. Flexibility, mobility, and the ability to maneuver were the main foundations of British defense policy in these years, and these aims could not be achieved by land forces, nor by permanent garrisons. Warfare in the new era required the ability to switch instantly from one kind of operation to another, which only could be accomplished with bombers. The bomber could be used to attack enemy air forces, to support the army, or to lay mines in enemy waters.

Air power had proved useful in the past in preserving peace within the Empire. The confidence with which Britain had abandoned its commitments in the Middle East stemmed not only from a theoretical belief that air power could eliminate the need for permanent garrisons, but also from a long experience in the use of air power in controlling various areas in the Middle East. The British had used the air force in order to free Colonel Jacob's mission in Yemen. The R.A.F. also had been used in the Sudan against the Garjaks. There were other air operations in the area which proved to be successful and inexpensive. After one of the air attacks, Churchill said that the R.A.F. achieved more on this expedition than the Army was able to do before, and at a much lower cost.[45]

The British in 1920 used the air force to maintain control in Somaliland a task which it concluded successfully. It then crushed a rebellion in Iraq, which the 60,000 troops stationed there had failed to do. As a result, it was decided at the Cairo Conference in 1921 to transfer

the responsibility of preserving order in the area
to the Air Ministry. The R.A.F. in Iraq defended
the area with the assistance of a small force of
local Assyrian irregular troops. This experiment
was a success. Rebellions were crushed immediately.

This method was gradually applied to the
entire Middle East where tribes were scattered
about the deserts. The topography of the region
made it more feasible to use the air force rather
than ground troops. That is, other areas under
British rule were tropical, mountainous or urban,
but the bulk of the Middle East was flat and open,
without much vegetation. Enemies could be easily
found and hit from the air.[46] The British, were
impressed by the successes of air control, and the
policy was carried over to the postwar period
until 1959 in the Middle East.

The revolutionary method of dealing with
colonial rebellion in open areas by bombing and
strafing represented one of the most remarkable
achievements of the twenties and the thirties and,
although it failed in Palestine in 1937-8 (because
most of its areas were urban or heavily populat-
ed), the bombing role of the R.A.F. dominated British thinking. The new method continued to be
employed in the Arabian Peninsula and the Persian
Gulf. Targets in the Middle East were easy to
identify; therefore, it was possible to use it
constantly until 1958-9.[47]

All the R.A.F. required was safe bases from
which to operate and the whole country could be
brought under surveillance within a very short
time. This was the reason for Britain's insistence upon keeping the airfields of the Middle
East until forced to evacuate them. Signing
treaties with the states in the area for use of
airfields was the best guarantee of local control
when a crisis erupted. Thus in the fifties Bri-

tain retained the privilege of using the airfields
in Jordan, Iraq, and Egypt. In addition there was
a constant search for alternative airfields in the
Middle East throughout the entire postwar era.

Air enthusiasts even argued that air blockade
could be as effective in highly organized society
as it was against tribes, because civilized people
were more sensitive than nomads to any disturbance
in their way of life. This argument was widely
accepted but some strategists questioned the effectiveness of air power in civil disturbances on
moral grounds.

In addition to its many functions air power
had the advantage of frightening enemies. Therefore, it was assumed that the employment of the
R.A.F. in this capacity was more economical than
sending a large body of troops to distant territories. The speed of the aircraft made it possible
to create an impressive show of force in a very
short time with relatively little effort. The
enthusiasts believed that aircraft could deter
political enemies by its noise alone.

Air Commodore C.F.A. Portal thought that the
use of air power on a regular basis could be extremely helpful in administering overseas territories. Referring to the experience of policing
Aden in the mid-thirties, he said that this area
could be administered more effectively and more
economically by using air power. In his words:

> There is nothing in the Aden protector-
> ate that justifies the expense, in money
> and life, entailed by military expedi-
> tions or occupation if the required
> standard of law and order can be main-
> tained in any other way.... If, then, we
> rule out military occupation, the puni-
> tive military expedition, and wholesale
> bribery as methods of maintaining law

and order, there remains only the system which uses the Air Force as the primary police instrument, and thus has been used successfully in Aden since 1928. [48]

Portal had a firm belief that control of overseas territories could be maintained without occupation.   He argued that the 'Air Control' method could be more effective because of its ability to drive the tribesman away, whereas the Army's punitive expedition had no such frightening effect. [49]

Officers of the R.A.F. constantly encouraged the Government to entrust to them the defense of the Empire.   This pressure had been ceaselessly exerted since the end of the First World War.   It was not a mere coincidence that the Baldwin-Chamberlain program of 1935-9 aimed at the creation of an Air Force which would render the stationing of large forces in the imperial possessions unnecessary.   The emphasis on air power as a substitute to garrisons appeared before the war, and continued in the postwar period.   The concept of 'Air Control' caused a radical change in British thinking about imperial defense.   Slessor wrote about the impact of this change:

> I think the really interesting development in those years [between the wars], was the emergence of a quite new concept of the use of force in which not only was the aeroplane used as the primary arm, but the whole method of enforcing our will upon the enemy underwent a radical change. This concept came to be known as Air Control. [50]

Air Vice Marshal W. Carter, a highly esteemed commander in the R.A.F., also thought that the

'Air Control' method provided a large part of the
answer to the problem of maintaining overseas territories.   Although 'Air Control' was not very
helpful in India, its effectiveness in the Middle
East was an accomplishment which the elite of the
R.A.F. was proud to point out.   The R.A.F. aircraft operating with their own armored car units,
were able to discourage tribal attempts to organize and revolt.   The R.A.F. increased its efficiency and, thanks to significant improvements
such as flying boats and land-planes, it was
possible to control the route to India and
Singapore.

If the Second World War had taught the British how important it was to have a powerful Air
Force, then the emergence of nuclear weapons was a
further proof of such a need and, at that point,
the British Government could no longer ignore the
voices of the strategists continuously warning it
not to ignore air power.   The confidence that aircraft were capable of hitting any target on the
ground with remarkable accuracy was strong not
only among airmen, but also among other services.
Troops in overseas territories had been calling
the R.A.F. fighters to hit targets which often
were located no more that 25 yards from their own
positions.[51]   Therefore, the R.A.F. gained tower-
ing prestige in the eyes of the Government and the
public.

The overwhelming opinion among the military
elite was that had it not been for the 'Air
Superiority' achieved by the R.A.F. in World War
II, the British Army would have been pushed into
the sea.   Indeed, 'Air Superiority' was decisive
in the Second World War.   This element made the
British more concerned about the availability of
as many airfields as possible throughout their
imperial possessions.   This lesson was learned in
the Second World War as Major General R.F.K.

Goldsmith had stated:

> The acquisition of suitably located
> airfields or their denial to the other
> can truly be said to have had a
> tyrannical effect on Allied Strategy in
> the Mediterranean from the invasion of
> North Africa onward.[52]

Undoubtedly, one of the great capabilities of
air power was to transport troops and equipment by
air. Air Transport had a far-reaching effect on
British military thinking about imperial defense.
The strategic reserve depended heavily on air
transport--a concept which directly influenced
Britain's willingness to abandon its commitments
overseas. In 1931 and 1932 British troops were
transferred from Egypt to Cyprus and Iraq by eight
Vickers Victorias. It had been the quickest way
of moving forces at that time. This operation
according to Wilson "pointed the way to the future."[53] Strategists of the postwar years estimated that British soldiers could arrive in less
than thirty-six hours atany spot of the Empire.

The idea of creating an air lifted strategic
reserve originated in those early days. Portal
was only one of those innovative strategists who
thought that there was an opportunity to form
special battalions that could be flown to any spot
of the empire. The ability of the aircraft to
carry bombs and supplies was valuable in police
operations carried out in India and throughout the
Middle East. The aircraft of the prewar period
could carry as many as 650 18-pound shells in
addition to 24 machine guns and thousands of
rounds of ammunition.[54] The value of the aircraft
for transportation had been proven in India especially, where there were no communication facilities and air fields or when weather or enemy

action temporarily prevented the normal traffic on the ground.

After the Second World War, some strategists concluded that an entire army unit with its heavy equipment and vehicles could be carried to a trouble spot in case of need.[55] This opinion was held by Liddell Hart himself. Since the early fifties, the military Chiefs of Staff were working on a plan for military operations in the Middle East. They believed that brigades from the strategic reserve could be flown from the United Kingdom to any area, and these could be supported by armored brigades stationed permanently in the Middle East. Their assumption was that if each airborne brigade would join one of the permanent brigades stationed in the area, the permanent garrison could be kept to a minimum. They regarded the garrison as an untrained an immobile force incapable of serving any valuable purpose at all other than simple routine duties. The achievements of air transport and air trooping were impressive enough to encourage the British Government to change its attitude toward defense problems. Slessor wrote in 1948:

> Who, ten years ago, would ever have believed that within ten years whole brigades and their transport, 9,000 fighting men and 1,200 mules, with all supporting weapons and equipment, would be landed by air in an enemy's rear in the jungles of Burma?"[56]

Furthermore, because Britain could not afford to maintain large garrisons overseas, airborne divisions could be used for imperial defense.

The ability of the aircraft to cover long distances at a very high speed, the ability to carry troops, and the relative independence of the

aircraft from ground facilities were advantages
which the British strategists did not fail to see.
For airborne operations such as the dropping of
paratroops or supplies, the aircraft did not even
require a landing ground at its point of destina-
tion. Only a few landing areas were required for
the delivery of supplies. A transported force
could perform various tasks such as participating
in airborne assault and reinforcing ground forces.
At last, a solution to the problem of transportation of heavy equipment was found. It was inevitable that these changes and improvements would
affect the deployment of forces in overseas territories.

   With the improvements in transporting troops
and equipment by air, the main foundations of the
strategic reserve had been laid, although suitable
aircraft had to be maintained for lifting the
troops at a few hours notice. Churchill's Government adopted this policy and took measures to
improve the troop carrying capacity of the R.A.F..
[57]
   The development of troop deployment by air on
a substantial scale took place in the early
fifties. The Viking, York, Bristol, and Wayfarer
were the main aircraft used. During 1951 and 1952
troops were carried to the Middle East in these
aircraft. The R.A.F. Transport Command carried
troops to and from the Middle East with Yorks,
Hastings, and Valettas. In 1952 the Government
decided that moving troops by air was the best
method for rapid deployment of forces overseas.
It was stated that "It is in our strategic interests to increase and encourage air trooping...even
if this means the withdrawal from service of some
of the older troop ships before the end of their
useful life. As a result of this decision, the
following years witnessed the rapid increase in
the movement of troops by air to all overseas
stations.[58] By the mid-fifties, this became the

normal means of travel for troops and personnel to overseas territories. Once the advantages of 'Air Trooping' were recognized, British forces did not have to stay in permanent garrisons overseas. The British Government could thus hope to make enormous financial savings by diminishing the number of bases or even evacuating them altogether.

Toward 1954 when the question of withdrawal from the Suez Canal Zone was debated, the carrying capacity of the transport aircraft was quite impressive. While the Bristol Britannia could carry about 100 soldiers with light equipment, the Blackburn Beverley, an aircraft designed for tactical roles, could carry about 170 fully armed men or two armored cars with their crews. Whereas previously it took two weeks to transfer troops to the Middle East in ships, aircraft could travel the same distance in ten hours. It had been estimated that if troops were moved by air, the aircraft would pay for its initial purchase within a period of six years and the number of men in transit would substantially be reduced by as many as 8,000 a day. The policy in these years was efficient enough to make it possible to withdraw British forces stationed in the Canal Zone and to use them as part of the strategic reserve.

The air force of the mid-fifties could be used in a variety of functions which virtually eliminated the need for ground forces and garrisons which were never adequate for Britain's security needs in overseas territories. Air power could be used as a means of communication and also for reconnaissance purposes. The importance of aircraft increased with the advent of nuclear weapons. Arthur Henderson once said:

It is sometimes suggested that it is a
waste of money continuing to build new
types of man-carrying aircraft when the

scientists have brought push-button
equipment within our view. The answer
to that suggestion is two-fold. Press-
button warfare as the major factor is
not yet a practical reality. Even if
and when the technical problems which it
involves have been solved, there will
still remain many air force functions
which can only be carried out by manned
aircraft.

While research and development are
being pushed on unmanned weapons, it is
clear that concurrently with that, we
must continue research and development
towards the production of the aircraft
.... It would be unwise to go into expensive large-scale production of types
which would soon be out of date.[59]

In summary, Slessor and others believed that
even in the era of total war the aircraft would
remain the principal agent of war, and the ability
to exert pressure on the enemy by using air power
would remain the dominant factor for a long
time.[60]

The most radical thinking about defense matters came from the Services, and especially from
Slessor, from scientists associated with defense
such as Henry Tizard, Patrick Blackett, A. V.
Hill, A. P. Rowe and F. A. Lindemann and from
influential ministers such as Duncan Sandys and
Harold Macmillan.[61]

It has been mentioned earlier that some of
the strategists such as the Chiefs of Staff, the
senior military officers, and the military intellectuals exerted great influence on the Government. The fact that these men held important
positions in the services and in the Government
placed them in a position to persuade the Govern-

ment to implement their new ideas about defense.

The most prominent strategists of the period--those who enjoyed direct or almost direct access to the Government--were Sandys and Macmillan who were the Ministers of Defense, and Slessor who was the Chief of the Air Staff. Sandys was the architect of the 1957 White Paper on Defense which was adopted as the official policy of the British Government in defense matters. These men were influenced by the military intellectuals who wrote extensively about defense matters, and also by the scientists who came into prominence with the innovations in the air force and later with the advent of nuclear weapons.

The military had to rely on the advice of the scientists as to the applicability of the sophisticated weapons to a military situation. The combined pressure from these groups on Churchill's Government led to a gradual but persistent change in defense policy. Believers in the dominant role of air power constituted an efficient pressure group. Sometimes they overstated the case for air power. Some of them sincerely believed in the ability of aircraft to provide a solution for imperial defense others simply felt that they had to justify the existence of the newly born R.A.F. as an independent service, and therefore advocated the use of air power in any kind of warfare. The result was the same, their arguments created an atmosphere receptive to change. Furthermore, such arguments came at the precise time when the Government was searching for ways to reduce the economic burdens which imperial defense entailed.

FOOTNOTES

CHAPTER IV

1. Slessor, The Great..., p. 104.
2. Condor, "Future Development..." JRUSI 92/567, p. 380.
3. Armstrong, "The British Revalue...," JRUSI 104 p. 160.
4. John Slessor, "A New Look at Strategy for the West," Orbis vol. 2 (Fall 1958) pp. 320-6.
5. Condor, loc. cit. p. 381.
6. Armstrong, loc. cit. p. 430.
7. Bernard Brodie, "Technological Change, Strategic Doctrine and Political Outcomes," Klaus Knorr, ed., Historical Dimensions of National Security Problems (New York, 1976), p. 296.
8. Edward Warner, "Douhet, Mitchell, and Seversky's Theories of Air Warfare" in E. M. Earle, ed., Makers of Modern Strategy, (Princeton, 1973), p. 492-494.
9. Bernard Brodie, "Some Notes on the Evaluation of Air Doctrine," World Politics 7/3 (April, 1955), p. 351.
10. There was, and there still is a controversy among strategists and historians as to the influence of Douhet on British thinking about air power. Bernard Brodie believed that Douhet was responsible for the growth of both British and American air theories. (See: Bernard Brodie, Strategy for the Missile Age (Princeton, 1959), 71ff.) J. M. Spaight thought that Douhet had some influence in Britain (See: J. M. Spaight, Air Power in the Next War (London, 1938); Air Marshal Sir Robert Saundby believed that Douhet was the prophet of air power (See: Air Marshal Sir Robert Saundby, "Prophet of Air Power," The Aeroplane, 4 May, 1956, pp. 342-343.) Edward

Warner and Eugene Emme were also convinced
that Douhet contributed to British theories
about air power. (See: Warner, loc. cit.
pp. 495-6.)

Liddell Hart saw the British air power
theory as the R.A.F.'s doctrine (See:
Liddell Hart, The Revolution in Warfare (New
Haven, 1947), p. 10) Slessor argued the same
thing (See: Slessor, The Central Blue, p.
39). Noble Frankland and Robin Higham
thought also that Douhet had no influence in
forming British air power theory (See:
Higham, The Military..., pp. 258-9).

There seems to be no consensus about
this point. Yet, it is possible in my
opinion to assume that Douhet had some
influence. The writings of the British air
strategists, especially Slessor's, show
a striking resemblance to Douhet's theory.

11. Major General R. H. Bower, "Air Support for
    the Army," Brassey's Annual (1954) p. 184-
    186.

12. Eugene M. Emme, "Technical Change and Western
    Military Thought: 1914-1945," Military
    Affairs vol. 24 (Spring, 1960) p. 13.

13. Higham, The Military..., p. 139; see also
    Armstrong, loc. cit. p. 179. Armstrong's
    contention was based upon interviews
    conducted with officers and retired personnel
    of the R.A.F. and other services.

14. Liddell Hart, Defense..., p. 122.

15. Cited in Liddell Hart, Defense..., pp. 122-4
    (date of debate is not indicated).

16. H. R. Allen, The Legacy of Lord
    Trenchard (London, 1972), p. 186.

17. Major General John Kennedy, The Business of
    War (London, 1957), p. 247.

18. Winston Churchill, The Second World War, vol.
    III, pp. 451-2.

19. Allen, op. cit. p. 68,70,74.
20. L. W. Emme, "The Market for Strategic Ideas in Britain in the Sandys era," American Political Science Review 56/1 (1962) p. 25; see also Armstrong, loc. cit. p. 175; see also Robin Higham, Guide..., p. 571.
21. John Slessor, Strategy for the West (London, 1954), p. 72.
22. Michael Howard, "Bombing and the Bomb," Encounter vol. 18 (January, 1962) p. 22.
23. Higham, The Military..., pp. 125, 150-9.
24. Armstrong, loc. cit. p. 116-117.
25. "Defender of Defence," The Economist 172/5972 (Aug. 28, 1954) p. 639.
26. Air Marshal Douglas Colyer, "Air Warfare," Fortnightly Review vol. 170 (1948), p. 168.
27. Norris, p. 498. WORK NOT CITED.
28. John Slessor, "Air Power and the Future of War," in JRUSI vol. 159 (August 1954) p. 346.
29. Lord A. V. Tedder, Air Power in War (Westport, Conn, 1975), pp. 123-4.
30. Donald Cox, "A Dynamic Philosophy of Air Power," Military Affairs 21/3 (Fall, 1957), p. 134.
31. Cited in Earle, op. cit. p. 501.
32. Major Alexander de Seversky, "A Lecture on Air Power," in Air University Quarterly Review vol. 1 (Fall, 1947) p. 32.
33. Edward Mead Earle, "The Influence of Air Power Upon History," in Yale Review 35/4 (Summer, 1946) p. 579.
34. Basil Collier, The Defence of the United Kingdom (London, 1957), p. 27.
35. Norman Gibbs, "British Strategic Doctrine: 1918-1939" in Howard Michael, ed., The Theory and Practice of War, p. 204-210.
36. Swain, JRUSI 92, p. 171.
37. Slessor, The Great..., p. 104.
38. Herbert S. Dinerstein, "The Impact of Air

Power   On   The   International   Scene: 1933-1940," Military Affairs 19/2 (Summer, 1955), p. 67; see also Air Marshal Robert Saundby, "Air Power in Limited War" in JRUSI vol. 103 (1958) p. 387.

39. Colyer, "Air Warfare," Fortnightly Review 170, p. 171.

40. Slessor, The Great..., p. 105.

41. "Defence Orders and Aircraft Employment," The Economist 158/5560 (March 18, 1950) p. 612.

42. Keith Feiling, The Life of Neville Chamberlain(London, 1946), pp. 258-314.

43. Bartlett, The Long Retreat, p. 49.

44. Slessor, The Great..., p. 124.

45. Liddell Hart, The British Way in Warfare(New York, 1933), p. 141.

46. Slessor, The Great..., p. 58.

47. Darby, British Defense Policy, p. 90.

48. W. P. Snyder, The Politics of British Defense Policy 1945-1962(Columbus, 1964),p. 52; see also Captain B. S. Cartmel, "Maintenance of the Royal Air Force Overseas," in JRUSI vol. 92 (1947), pp. 100-105;see also Wing Commander J. A. Chamier, "The Use of Air Force for Replacing Military Garrisons," JRUSI vol. 66 (1921), p. 209.

49. Air Commodore C.F.A. Portal, "Air Force Cooperation in Policing the Empire," Ibid. vol. 82 (1937) p. 346350.

50. Slessor, The Great..., p. 55.

51. Air Vice Marshal W. Carter, "Air Power Confronted," in Brassey's Annual (1965), p. 170, 175-176.

52. Major General R.F.K. Goldsmith, "The Development of Air Power in Joint Operations," Army Quarterly 95/1 (Oct., 1967), p. 59.

53. Wilson, "The Relevance of Air Mobility," Army Quarterly 69/2, p. 162.

54. Portal, "Cooperation," JRUSI, p. 345-346

55. Wilson, loc. cit. p. 36.

56. John Slessor, "Some Reflections on Airborne Forces," in Army Quarterly 56/2 (July, 1948), p. 161-166.

57. Vice Air Marshal A. C. Collier "Air Transport" in JRUSI, vol. 90 (1945), p. 145-147.

58. Cited in Lieutenant Colonel T. S. Craig, "Trooping Today," in The Army Quarterly 76/2 (July, 1958), p. 215.

59. Wells, "Defense," Fortnightly Review 170, p. 92.

60. Slessor, The Great..., p. 78.

61. Bartlett, op. cit. p. 131.

CHAPTER V

SUEZ AND THE HYDROGEN BOMB

The progress of technology profoundly affected the nature of warfare and decreased the value
attached to local garrisons and navies. Even before the acquisition of the hydrogen bomb by Britain in 1954 the Government deemed it necessary to
adjust its defense policy. This was particularly
true of Middle Eastern defense policy. By that
time, military observers had already noted the
uselessness of maintaining garrisons in the area.
H.R.R. Condor had written in 1947 that if the
Mediterranean became unsafe for transporting
troops and no aid could be expected from India,
then...

> any garrison located in the Middle East
> at the start of war, might be defeated
> in detail before other Imperial forces
> could be concentrated to its aid, and
> that the continued use of the area as a
> source of oil fuel, as a communication
> center, and as a base might be denied to
> us.[1]

Steady improvements in transportation, navigation, and speed had substantially decreased the
limitations of distance. Airborne forces could be
flown to any spot in the Empire, and especially to
the Middle East, in which there were bases closer
to the United Kingdom than other bases such as
those at Singapore or Hong Kong. The increased
range of aircraft, the capability of delivering
many soldiers with their equipment, the improved
methods of refuelling in the air, the nuclear sea
power and the nuclear missiles made it easier to
defend overseas territories by means other than
local garrisons. Modern technology had altered the

entire basis of military planning.[2] The British
came to believe that their security depended on
the nuclear deterrent. With the development of
the atomic bomb, the bomber became the main agent
of war.[3]

The importance of technical efficiency in a
future war had been emphasized by the leading
strategists. Some of them had argued that since
there was a danger that war techniques and war
materials might become outmoded and obsolete, efforts should be made to concentrate on nuclear
weapons, and on the improvements of war tactics,
rather than on ground forces and garrisons. Liddell Hart emphasized the uselessness of the battle
fleet and naval bases because these were bound to
become obsolete within a short period of time.[4]

The growth of nuclear weapons with their
impact on the nature of war had profoundly affected British thinking about overseas bases.[5] The
devastating power of the atomic bomb made total
war a possibility. Attlee's Government therefore
assumed that an enemy would refuse to take the
risk of war, and therefore, there would be no need
to protect overseas territories. This conviction
had led Attlee to adopt the Ten Year Rule which
spelled out that no major war was likely to erupt
in the forseeable future. The sudden collapse of
Japan in 1945 left no doubt in anyone's mind that
the atomic bomb was a turning point in the history
of warfare. Military observers called upon the
Labour Government to take into consideration the
devastating effect that a nuclear war might cause.
Liddell Hart wrote:

> It is well to remember that 'Port
> Arthur' in 1904 was followed by 'Pearl
> Harbour' in 1941 and we should not
> overlook the possibilities of a third
> trick in the series.

Liddell Hart also maintained that nuclear power had rendered a large conscript army obsolete and senseless.[6]

When the hydrogen bomb became available in 1954, military officers and commentators wrote extensively about the need to disband the overseas bases in the wake of the emergence of the hydrogen bomb. At the Royal United Service Institution in 1950, Admiral C. C. Hughes Hallet said that the atomic weapons made it mandatory to disperse overseas bases. The full power of the hydrogen bomb became known in the summer of 1954. It was claimed that it had the destructive power of five hundred Hiroshimas.[7] The atomic bombs used at Hiroshima and Nagasaki had explosive power of 20 kilotons--or and equivalent of 20,000 tons of T.N.T. The hydrogen bomb exploded on November 7, 1952 had explosive power of five megatons, or five million tons of T.N.T..

Churchill's Government considered the effect of the atomic bomb very seriously. John Slessor said at that time:

> Now it is useless to minimize the very serious consequences of the appallingly vulnerable nature of the United Kingdom to attack by weapons of mass destruction, whether airborne, or directed by other means.[8]

Ground defenses were regarded as vulnerable elements. Michael Howard, a distinguished professor of war studies at the University of London, explained also pointed out that the power of atomic weapons had brought about the decline in the effectiveness of ground forces and the navy. He said:

Increasingly during and since the Second

World War, the struggle for mastery has been transferred from the battlefields of the land, sea, and air, to the laboratories and factory work benches.[9]

Land forces remained important only for the defense of Europe. N.A.T.O. generals regarded the presence of British troops in Europe as essential, even in a thermonuclear war, in order to hold back the Soviet ground forces. Troops were still needed for conventional military operations in which nuclear weapons could not be used. Also, ground forces were needed for the strategic reserve scheme, and in order to help Britain maintain its influence in N.A.T.O.. Garrisons in overseas bases could not fulfill a significant function in a future war and therefore could be drastically diminished.

There was no need for excessive explanation on the part of military officers, scientists, or politicians, to convince the Labour Government that the atomic revolution had changed the nature of war. Although British leaders were painstakingly emphasizing the peaceful uses of atomic energy, they had grasped the political and military implications of nuclear applications at an early stage.[10]

The emergence of nuclear weaponry occurred when Britain was weak and impoverished. The domestic weakness of Britain found its expression in an army crippled by the ordeal of the Second World War. There were growing demands to abolish conscription. The army was ill-equipped and lacked the most modern weapons produced at the time in the United States and the Soviet Union. This army, demoralized, disorganized and scattered all over the imperial possessions, could not even fulfill garrison duties in those days when nationalist movements in Asia and Africa were becoming violent.   Only a qualitative change could have saved the British Army in a future war.   It is only against this background that the departure from reliance on overseas bases can be properly assessed.   The emergence of nuclear weaponry created a new surge of confidence that a quick and decisive solution to Britain's defense problems had been found.   Military analysts believed that a nuclear war would be total and most destructive. The strategists believed that the Russians realized this, and, as a result, atomic weapons were capable of deterring the Soviet Union in a very effective way.[11]   Traditional military concepts had radically changed.   The deployment of land forces in overseas territories had to be adjusted to the needs of a modern era in warfare.   Furthermore the nuclear deterrent was less costly than huge arsenals of conventional weapons.

The overwhelming majority of the strategists believed that in the next war the major powers would be totally involved, until one side would win decisively.   General Andre Beaufre, one of the leading scholars in French defense matters, explained the pessimism which had overcome many governments.

> The result of the advent of the nuclear
> bomb has been a vague feeling that the
> burden of national defense has its roots
> in obsolete traditions.   Unable to un-
> derstand the new rules, in any case too
> contradictory, too conjectural, and too
> fluid to carry conviction, we have been
> driven to take refuge at one time in the
> great illusion of disarmament, and at
> another in the abdication of our respon-
> sibilities.[12]

The advent of nuclear weapons created the

feeling that there could be no defense against a
nuclear threat. The result of this assumption was
that overseas territories would be the first to be
affected. Furthermore, garrisons were considered
to be useless in case of an atomic attack and
therefore, useless to maintain. Besides, from a
budgetary point of view it was impossible to invest money both in the nuclear deterrent and in
conventional weapons at the same time.[13]

Nuclear weapons were bound to affect the entire defense planning in which overseas forces had
an important part. The impact of nuclear weaponry
on defense policy was far greater than the threat
to empire from forces of local nationalism had
been. Attlee had been told that the future
development of the atomic bomb would not be very
expensive, a consideration of utmost importance at
that period of economic difficulties, and hence
demanded a review of defense policy.

With the emergence of the nuclear weapons
some old strategic policies lost importance.[14]
The nuclear era raised the element of 'massive retaliation' into prominence. In the era of 'massive retaliation' only vital interests could be
defended. Obviously, the most vital interests
were those pertaining to the security of the United Kingdom, and the adjacent European continent,
and not the Middle East.[15]

One of the traditional doctrines spelled out
the need to maintain large forces in key bases
along the route to India and the Far East. The
vulnerability of bases in an atomic war was known
to the Labour Government, but, it was not until
1954 that the Conservative Government took this
fact into consideration. The American nuclear
tests provided the incentive for the revaluation
of the Suez Canal Zone.

Overseas territories remained important, but
theories on the method of defending them had

changed. Bases, especially those in the Middle
East, were still regarded as indispensable for the
defense of Europe, but Harold Macmillan argued
that colonial possessions must be protected by
nuclear weapons, and not by land forces or garrisons because they were essential for the defense
of Europe.[16]

Slessor suggested that it would be most
prudent for the British Government to avoid clumsy
lines of communication, now that the deterrent was
available, and that missiles represented an increase in the power of the deterrent. The Labour
Government was prepared to accept the change
created by the advent of the new weapons as indicated in the White Paper on Defense of 1946.

The decision to produce an atomic bomb was
made in the early postwar years. It was almost
certain that nuclear weapons would be produced
because the momentum created by the great scientific effort was great enough to assure this outcome.[17]

During the war, scientists already recommended that the Government establish a nuclear research center, and a plutonium facility of 100.000
kilowatts. The Government approved both during
1945. As early as April 1945 the Coalition Government had accepted the basic designs of a low-
separation gaseous diffusion plant for the production of U-235.[18]

It had been clear to Attlee and Bevin that
the atomic bomb could be used in the future.
There was no doubt that Britain would become a nuclear power. The decision to build production
reactors at Windscale was made in March 1946. In
October, initial steps were taken in creating the
low separation diffusion in the R.A.F.'s plant at
Capenhurst. By mid-1947 the R.A.F. had begun to
plan on the availability of the nuclear weapons.
By the end of 1947, the British were beginning to

complete the plutonium process in the chemical separation plant at Windscale. The plutonium fabrication plant was completed at Aldermaston between April 1950 and March 1951. By early 1952, military quantities of plutonium were beginning to be produced, and Britain's first atomic test was held on October 3, 1952 in the Monte Bello Island near Australia.

Investment in the bomb appeared less expensive than maintaining forces in many areas of the Empire. Attlee thought that the project would be much less expensive and less complicated than was proven later, because in those days, no one thought about problems of delivery of the bomb, about ballistic missiles, or warning systems. Bombs, they believed, could be easily delivered by a bomber, and being inexpensive, could serve as an excellent substitute for land forces and garrisons. The atomic potency was a great leveler, and a means of retaining Britain's position as a world power.[19]

Churchill's Government, which assumed power in 1951, invested most of its resources in the nuclear deterrent. As a result, conventional weapons were neglected even though successive White Papers did not disregard the need to improve conventional weapons, the nation's resources were invested mainly in nuclear weaponry.[20] British strategic thinking in the early postwar era was summarized in the Global Strategy Paper of 1952.[21] Nuclear deterrence was accepted as the basis for defense.

Manpower had to be cut in favor of new weapons. Conventional capability was to be reduced as a sacrifice to the nuclear deterrent. As a result, land forces and garrisons along the traditional lifeline of the Empire assumed a secondary importance at best.[22]

The decision to concentrate on the develop-

ment of the nuclear weaponry came from the Chiefs
of Staff Committee, and resulted in heavy reliance
on the deterrent.   The White Papers mentioned the
nuclear deterrence as the main foundation of defense in the period up to 1956.   The papers prove
the acceptance of the nuclear deterrent by the
Government.   Excessive reliance on the nuclear
weapons stemmed from two major reasons.   First,
the desire to be an independent power, free from
the domination of the United States, and to maintain Britain's prestige in Europe.   Secondly, the
realization that it was wiser to invest money in
the development of nuclear weapons, than to accu-
mulate a large arsenal of conventional weapons
which might turn obsolete in a future war.

The emphasis on the deterrent stemmed from
the belief that the need of the new era was not to
fight and win a war, but rather to prevent it.
The concept of deterrence was developed as a result of this kind of thinking.   Developed by Slessor and supported by Liddell Hart and other influential strategists, it made a deep impression on
the Labour Government at that time.   In one of his
speeches at Chatham House, Slessor said that the
aim of Western defense policy was not to fight a
war even if victory were its definite outcome, but
rather to prevent it, because a war might result
in destruction of Europe and Britain.   According
to this line of thinking any element in the defense system which might provoke war, had to be
eliminated.   Overseas bases were provocative as
well as vulnerable.   Besides, the atomic threat
made the British leaders more concerned with the
defense of Europe.   Liddell Hart and many other
strategists argued that what Britain needed was
not forces scattered overseas, but troops in the
Island to defend the home front.   The British
Government, influenced by the strategists and
their interpretations regarding the impact of the

atomic weaponry, refrained from committing forces
to actual fighting, and concentrated on the deterrent.

Arms control, disarmament and peace-keeping
became the dominant elements in British strategic
thinking. The development of the hydrogen bomb in
the years 1952-4 rendered a long war and a large
concentration of troops impracticable. Macmillan
saw the nuclear deterrent as the real answer to
the Soviet threat before he became Minister of
Defense. His experience in this Ministry
reinforced his belief.[23]

The possibility of using the nuclear weapons
was not a remote one. It was quite openly contem-
plated at the time. Besides, this concept was
economically acceptable and was prevalent up to
the time of the Suez debacle.[24] Nuclear deterrence had to be guaranteed, but it also maintained
that conventional arms also should be developed to
fight a global war should the use of nuclear weapons prove unsuccessful. They were proved to be
inappropriate for some purposes in the Suez Affair. Eden's Government, as a result, decided to
develop conventional weapons. The invasion of
Egypt in 1956 illustrated the limitations of the
nuclear weapons. The belief that nuclear weapons
would be used in case of war was held by most decision makers of the period until the Suez episode.[25]

Awareness that the hydrogen bomb was highly
destructive did not deter the Churchill Government
from thinking seriously about using it. The use
of nuclear weapons seemed certain at least until
the Soviet Union had developed the hydrogen
bomb.[26] But even then, the possibility of using
atomic bombs remained open. Nevertheless, military analysts believed that only atomic weapons
were capable of preventing the Soviet Union from
dominating the Middle East. Jules Menken, a well

known strategist, was convinced that had the Soviets decided to take control of Middle Eastern oil fields, the forces stationed in the area as garrisons would have failed to stop them.[27]   Macmillan, as noted above, believed that nuclear war was the only possible form that war could take in the future. He did not believe that conventional weapons could be relied upon because in a conventional war Britain would be crushed whether in the Middle East or on the Island.[28]

In order to understand the importance which the Churchill Government had placed on the deterrent, and the resulting abandonment of the Suez base, the influence of the scientists on the Government has to be assessed properly, because in a large measure they were responsible for the drastic revision in British strategic thinking after the advent of nuclear weapons. Scientists had not been highly influential until the Second World War. They had some influence in the prewar period and even before. When Britain was forced to compete with Germany, Japan and the United States in the industrial field, the government was compelled to encourage industrialists to conduct scientific research, and for that purpose, the Department of Scientific and Industrial Research had been established in 1916 with Sir Henry Tizard serving as its permanent secretary. Scientists became increasingly employed in industry, especially in the chemical, electrical, and aircraft industries. The National Research Development Corporation was founded after the First World War for the purpose of allocating money to new inventions. The Ministry of Defense became a large employer of scientists. The Chief Scientific Adviser to the Ministry of Defense became the most influential of all scientists. The war pushed many scientists into the government and thus they became a vital element of the defense system.

Such officials in the United Kingdom had greater power and more influence in determining policy than their counterparts in the United States.

C. P. Snow, the writer, once made the observation:

> In England they [the scientists] are right at the heart of the establishment, and in a good many ways, are more steadily and continuously important that their political bosses.[29]

The Air Ministry, under the influence of the scientific adviser H. E. Wimperis and the government's scientist A. P. Rowe, set up a Committee for the Scientific Study of Air Defense. The Committee was established in order to apply scientific and technical knowledge to the improvement of air defense. Tizard became the chairman of the Committee which included eminent scientists like A. V. Hill and P.M.S. Blackett. The Committee received substantial amounts of money from the Government without difficulty--as Snow said: "Within a short time, the Tizard Committee was asking for millions of pounds and getting it without a blink of an eye."

Tizard could easily convince the senior officers of the necessity of certain weapons and they were ready to be convinced as soon as he started to talk.[30] The Tizard Committee was extremely effective. It stood behind Churchill, the anti-government spokesman, in 1934 when he had challenged the Government's underestimation of the size of Hitler's air force. Tizard himself became influential thanks to his major contribution to the defense of Britain. He was responsible for the development and installation of the radar system that proved indispensable in the Battle of Britain in 1940.[31]

In the summer of 1940, Tizard persuaded the Coalition Government to send to the United States a mission of which he was the chairman. The mission was to include the famous black box containing blueprints and reports of nearly all important new British war devices, including the magnetron. By 1941 he was widely recognized by Whitehall and the armed forces. His ability to bring scientific knowledge into the Allied war effort was recognized by the British and the American governments.[32]

Another influential scientist who exerted considerable influence on the British war Government and especially on Churchill was F. A. Lindemann. The latter had more influence on Churchill by virtue of his friendship with him. Being rich, determined, and brilliant, Lindemann managed to develop wide contacts with government officials. He became an intimate friend of Lord Birkenhead and through him, met Churchill. Lindemann became Lord Cherwell, and a member of the Cabinet in the Second World War. He was the only scientist in the Cabinet whose proposals were accepted by all.

While Tizard was highly influential because he had political and administrative leaders behind him all the time, Lindemann was an extremely powerful scientist thanks to his friendship with Churchill. No scientist has ever achieved anywhere near Lindemann's influence. Government's officials often complained about the magnitude of Lindemann's influence. However, protected by Churchill, Lindemann had no reason to fear. He continued to exert significant influence within government circles. Snow quoted someone as having said: "The Prime Minister and the Professor have decided, and who are we to say then 'nay'?"[33]

Blackett was not only a scientist, but also a well-known commentator on international affairs and on the political consequences of the atomic bomb. He wrote extensively about the impact of the bomb on the bases and on the Suez base in particular. He became a most influential political spokesman among top scientists, and was well known for his strong left wing views and suspicions of America. Furthermore, he played an important part in atomic research, became deeply concerned with the relations between government and scientists, and helped to set up the Advisory Council for Scientific Policy.

Blackett had argued that the scientists could persuade the Government to apply their suggestions when they were organized as a group. Writing about the Government's decision to attack the center of civilian population in Germany, made in the spring of 1942, and proven ineffective, he said:

> If we had only been more persuasive and had forced people to believe our simple arithmetic, if we had fought officialdom more cleverly and lobbied ministers more vigorously, might we not have changed this decision?"[34]

Scientists became increasingly in demand with the emergence of the atomic weapons. As a result, they became a privileged class. The lull of the atomic era and the uncertainty regarding the role of the fighting forces had tremendously increased the influence of the scientists. The confusion in defense planning provided them with the opportunity to be involved in the political implications of the atomic weapons. They became an extremely effective pressure group and wrote articles and memoranda concerning the impact of nuclear weapons on Britain's position in the world, and on the value of overseas bases in light of these weapons. In this respect, their influence on the government was as great as other strategists. It was not a mere coincidence that Churchill became convinced that the Suez base was vulnerable in case of an atomic war and expressed his willingness to withdraw in the summer of 1954. Who could possibly convince Churchill, the staunch believer in empire, that abandonment of the Suez Canal Zone was not harmful, and even necessary if not scientists like Lindemann and Blackett? These scientists were recognized by Churchill as experts in matters relating to the impact of atomic weapons on imperial defense, perhaps even more than Liddell Hart, Slessor, Kingston-McCloughry or Saundby.

Reliance on the scientists was heavy in the mid-fifties. It is worthwhile to note that Defense Minister Duncan Sandys, the architect of the revolutionary White Paper on Defense from 1957, relied heavily on his scientific advisors.[35]

The vulnerability of the Suez Canal Zone was agreed upon by most military observers and strategists even before the advent of the hydrogen bomb. It was vulnerable because of its proximity to the Soviet Union. Strategists of the fifties concluded that nuclear weapons would be used only against very important targets, and only under conditions or ranges in which they had a very good chance of hitting the target area. The accuracy of rockets was such that an error of only ten miles at 500 miles range could be expected.[36] Therefore, the best way to defend bases overseas, it was thought, would be to place them at such a distance that they would become less vulnerable. Strategists believed that if chances of a direct hit were small, the enemy would not risk one of its few atomic bombs to hit the target. Withdrawal to East Africa was strongly recommended. One of the strategists had suggested that, instead of relying on the Suez base, Britain should use the Cape route

as the main artery to the Middle East, and develop
the transcontinental route between the West and
East coasts of Africa.[37]

In summary, the hydrogen bomb offered an
opportunity for Churchill's Government to relinquish the heavy financial and military commitment
of Suez. The domestic pressures had been inten-
sifying since the end of the Second World War
which had left Britain impoverished, tired and
lacking the desire to dominate other cultures. A
solution had to be found and the Government was
compelled to yield to these pressures. How could
anyone imagine that Churchill, the most imperial-
minded leader, would give up this important artery
without being influenced by domestic constraints?
Churchill was the one who pressured Attlee's Government into evacuating Palestine in 1947. The
same factors led him to abandon the Suez Canal
Zone in 1954. As the head of a Conservative Government, Churchill could not decide to abandon the
Suez Canal base and thus alienate most of his
Conservative supporters.[38]

But the momentum of social reform started by
the Labour Party could not be stopped and the
interests of the working people could not be
disregarded in the name of imperialism. Any
government had to consider these facts if it
wished to stay in power. Many politicians were
convinced that the hydrogen bomb provided an
excuse to cut military manpower and to divert
money to more popular causes.[39] That is, they
thought that the Suez Canal Zone could be evacuated with many less repercussions because of its
vulnerability than the elimination of the programs
for social welfare and health insurance. Withdrawal was a necessity, and an excuse had to be
found. Fortunately the pretext was valid and
convincing enough for a challenge of any kind.
The hydrogen bomb provided the means to escape

from the ordeal of having to divide the nation's resources between two essential goals.   However, it is obvious today that excessive emphasis was placed on the effects of the hydrogen bomb.   Some strategists today even talk in terms of surviving a hydrogen bomb attack.

Churchill's belief that the Suez Canal Zone had become obsolete stemmed from the excessive reliance of the Government on the nuclear deterrent.   Thinking in terms of global war, he was bound to conclude that conventional commitments were of secondary importance.   This line of thinking had begun to influence the Government since 1952.[40]

The withdrawal from the Suez Canal Zone in 1954 reflected the triumph of the thermonuclear strategy over geographic interests.   Reliance on the nuclear deterrent had led to reduction of the size of overseas garrisons.   The Suez base was the first to be affected by this policy.   The decision to sign an agreement with Egypt was also a triumph for the domestic pressures in Britain.   Most historians tend to attribute this change of policy to military reasons alone.   There is a negative correlation between the demands of a society for welfare and reduction of taxes on the one hand, and an aggressive defense policy on the other.[41] Apart from the very serious strategic concerns, the disrupted economy, the poor morale of the English people, the war fatigue, the objection to conscription inherent in the British society, the apathy and the lack of desire for military adventures and for ruling subject peoples all contributed to the willingness to withdraw.   In addition, the Government was pressed to give up the Zone because Egyptian nationalists were pressing for independence and the departure of foreign soldiers from their soil.

Military historians, trying to trace the

origins of the new defense policy inaugurated in
1957, had come to the conclusion that the emergence of nuclear weapons was the main reason for
this change. Darby, commenting about the White
Paper of 1957, noted that recent advances in technology and science, encouraged the Government to
escape from the traditional dependence on large
armies. The framers of the White Paper on Defense
of 1957 assumed that the nuclear weapons and the
airlift capability would enable Britain to decrease substantially the manpower in overseas
territories.[42]

The possession of the hydrogen bomb by the
Soviets had made it impossible for the West to
deter the Soviets by a threat. Show of force in
the bases could be provocative and might trigger a
global war. Also, the possibility of using small
atomic bombs was out of the question because no
one could possibly predict where the Soviets would
stop in case of a piecemeal atomic war. Thus,
bases overseas were increasingly regarded as vulnerable. The vulnerability of the permanent bases
provided the Royal Navy with an important new role
to play in the nuclear age by means of the
aircraft carrier.

The financial inability of Britain to maintain the commitments overseas had accelerated the
process of developing the hydrogen bomb. The
success achieved by the completion of the bomb
influenced, in turn, the willingness to abandon
the draining commitments. The report of the
Eniwetok test explosions of the hydrogen bomb by
the United States, which, in 1954, came to the
hands of Churchill, had completed the process of
policy change which started in the early fifties.

The report stated unequivocally that the
value of bases such as the Suez Canal Zone must be
reassessed in light of the explosions. This
analysis had a great psychological effect on the

conservative leadership. It seems that the alarm created by the alleged vulnerability of the United Kingdom and overseas territories in the nuclear age led to the reassessment of the Government's strategy for all overseas bases. Churchill's speech about the vulnerability of the Suez base was delivered in August 1954, and barely two months later, the agreement to evacuate the base was signed. It seems that the turning point for the decision to evacuate Suez came in July 1954.[43]

The fact that the Suez Canal Zone had become less important than in the prewar years was known to the British leadership. One of the lessons of the war was that the area was inessential. Also, it was ineffective in protecting oil supplies, because these were located too far. Nevertheless, there was a need for cogent arguments to convince the die hard imperialists that it was no longer necessary to maintain Suez. In an atmosphere of global conflict, heavy emphasis on nuclear deterrence and the emergence of two super powers, bases overseas could not count for much in the eyes of British leadership.

Traditional British thinking about the Middle East and the Suez Canal Zone was a product of a non-nuclear era. The fact that the war of the future was seen as global, quick and mobile, a war in which weapons would be sophisticated and long range, dwarfed the Middle East and diminished the importance of the Suez Canal Zone.

The new concepts were not only a result of rational motives and cool considerations, but also a product of irrational thinking which stemmed from pessimism caused by the emergence of nuclear weapons. The British leaders were thinking in terms of a devastating war which might leave the United Kingdom and the entire European continent in complete ruin. This belief had generated a pacifist school of thought which contended that since there was no protection against the nuclear threat, no matter how well prepared the British Army was, there was no reason to conscript young men into the Service, and post them in overseas territories. Besides, it did not make any sense to spend money for fruitless defense.[44]

It is difficult to say whether the act of withdrawal from the Suez base was an act of irresponsibility. It is likely however, that that feeling, coupled with the fear of the disastrous effect of the bomb, was influential in the change of policy towards the Middle East, which resulted in the abandonment of the base.

Defense policy is determined by numerous causes, domestic as well as external, rational as well as irrational. The excessive reliance of Britain on the nuclear deterrent stemmed from a fear of the consequences of an atomic attack upon bases of the home islands. As a result, the Government became convinced that overseas bases were not only non-essential, they were also dangerous to maintain. The vulnerability of the bases to nuclear attack was officially recognized in the Sandys White Paper on Defense of 1957, which integrated all these ideas into a clear and coherent policy on defense matters.[45]

FOOTNOTES

CHAPTER V

1. Condor, "Future Development..." in JRUSI 92/567, p. 376.
2. Armstrong, "The British Re-Value...," JRUSI 104/616, p. 215.
3. Air Vice Marshal W. M. Yool, "The Royal Air Force: Fifty Years of Service, "The Army Quarterly vol. 96 (April, 1968), p. 42.
4. B. H. Liddell Hart, Memoirs: 1895-1938(New York, 1965), p. 332.
5. Armstrong, "The British Re-Value...," p. 423.
6. Liddell Hart, Revolution in Warfare(London, 1946), p. 98.
7. Liddell Hart, loc. cit., pp. 103-4. Admiral C. C. Hughes Hallet, "Naval Logistics in a Future War," JRUSI vol. 95 (May, 1950), pp. 234-235 and also, Bartlett, The Long Retreat(New York, 1972), p. 111.
8. Slessor, The Great Deterrent, p. 79.
9. Michael Howard, "Bombing and the Bomb," Encounter vol. 18 (Jan-June, 1962), pp. 13, 24.
10. H. A. DeWeerd, "Britain's Changing Military Policy," Foreign Affairs vol. 34. (October, 1955) p. 112.
11. Slessor, The Great Deterrent, p. 105.
12. Andre Beaufre, Deterrence and Strategy(New York, 1966), p. 11.
13. Liddell Hart, Defense..., p. 376.
14. C. Attlee, Twilight of Empire(New York, 1962), p. 98-100.
15. T. E. McKitterick, "What Are British Interests?" Political Quarterly 31/1 (Jan.-March 1960) p. 8, 14.
16. Harold Macmillan, Tides of Fortune: 1945-1955(New York, 1969), p. 572.
17. "Statement Relating to Defence," 1946, Cmd

6743.

18.   Alfred Goldberg, "The Atomic Origins of the British Nuclear Deterrent," International Affairs (July, 1964), p. 426; see also Margaret Gowing, Britain and Atomic Energy: 1939-1945 (London, 1964), pp. 334-6.

19.   Leonard Owne, "Nuclear Engineering in the United Kingdom-The First Ten Years," Journal of British Nuclear Energy Society 2/1 (January 1963), p. 23.

20.   Rosecrance, Defence, p. 37 and 42;Baylis, Theories and Politics, p. 276.

21.   "Statement on Defense," 1952 Cmd. 8475.

22.   Bartlett, The Long Retreat, p. 95; see also "Statement on Defence" 1953 Cmd. 8768; see also Darby, British Defense Policy, p. 70.

23.   Liddell Hart, Defense..., pp. 97, 134, 140, 193.See also Bartlett, The Long Retreat, p. 96.

24.   Brian Bond, "Nuclear-age Theories of S. B. Liddell Hart," Military Review 50/8 (August, 1970), p. 15.

25.   Roger Carey, "The British Nuclear Force: Deterrent or Economy Measure," Military Affairs vol. 36 (December, 1972) p. 134.

26.   Campbell, Defense of the Middle East (New York), p. 160.

27.   Jules Menken, "Problems of Middle Eastern Strategy" in Brassey's Annual 1956) p. 139.

28.   Macmillan, Tides of Fortune (London, 1969), p. 567.

29.   C. P. Snow, Science and Government (Cambridge, 1961), p. 21.

30.   Ibid., pp. 28 and 29.

31.   P.M.S. Blackett, Studies of War: Nuclear and Conventional (New York, 1962), p. 122.

32.   C.P.M. Blackett, "Tizard and the Science of War," Nature 185/4714 (March 5, 1960) pp. 647-53.

33. Snow, Science and Government, p. 65.
34. Blackett, Studies of War..., p. 126.
35. William J. Crowe, Jr., The Policy Roots of the Modern Royal Navy 1946-1963. Unpublished Dissertation(Princeton, 1965), pp. 188-9.
36. "Atomic Energy, Its International Implications" in Royal Institute of International Affairs, p. 50.
37. See CHAPTER III.
    Barnes, "Future Strategic Importance of the Middle East...," Army Quarterly 57/1 (Oct., 1948) p. 175-177.
38. Eden, Full Circle(London, 1960), p. 368.
39. Hartley, A State of England(London, 1963), p. 127; see also Cyril Falls, "A Window on the World: Obscurities of Defense," Illustrated London News (August 11, 1956) p. 218.
40. Denis Healey, "Britain and N.A.T.O." Klauss Knorr, ed., NATO and the American Security(Princeton, 1959), p. 217; see also Rosecrance, Defence, pp. 201-203
41. Norman Polmar, Aircraft Carrier(New York, 1969), p. 575; see also Michael Howard, "Britain's Strategic Problem East of Suez," International Affairs 42/2 (April, 1946) p. 181.
42. Darby, British Defense Policy, pp. 119-120.
43. Terence Robertson, Crisis: The Inside Story of the Suez Conspiracy(New York, 1965), p. 3; see also Air Chief Marshal Sir Philip Joubert. "The Hydrogen Bomb--The Impact on Military Strategy," The Listener (June 3, 1954) p. 954; and A.J.C. Groom, British Thinking About Nuclear Weapons(London, 1974), pp. 96-7.
44. Rosecrance, Defense, p. 161; see also "Defense: Outline of Future Policy" 1957: Cmd. 124. "Report on Defense: Britain's Contribution to Peace and Security" 1958:

Cmd. 363.

45. Air Vice Marshal E. J. Kingston-McCloughry,
     "The Future of the Armed Forces--The effect
     of the new weapons" Brassey's Annual (1956)
     pp. 41-2.

CHAPTER VI

THE ROYAL NAVY AND THE MOBILE BASE POLICY

Bases and colonies had been essential to Britain in order to maintain its sea power throughout the centuries. By controlling strategic bases, such as Gibralter, Cyprus, or Suez, Britain was in a position to exert a large measure of power and influence in the Mediterranean which, according to Alfred T. Mahan, ..."played a greater part in the history of the world, both in commercial and military point of view, than any other sheet of water of the same size."[1]

By establishing bases in the Mediterranean, Britain gained control over foreign lands bordering the Mediterranean basin. Commercially, the bases served as an outlet for British trade and as a support for the naval forces safeguarding sea communications. Bases were considered essential for naval supremacy. In his classic book about naval power which appeared in 1890 Mahan had written that a navy without bases is like "land birds unable to fly far from their shores."[2] A base without a fleet or air force operating from it, would be equally meaningless.[3]

Naval bases which Britain annexed during four centuries such as Bermuda (1609), Jamaica (1655), Halifax (1713), Cape Town (1805), Ceylon (1805), Singapore (1805), Malta (1814), the Falkland Islands (1832), Aden (1839), Hong Kong (1841), and Suez (1882), made it possible for the British to operate the most formidable navy in the world and the Royal Navy made Britain the most powerful nation in the world.[4] It was only at the end of the nineteenth century that British ascendancy came to an end with the emergence of the American, Japanese and German navies.

According to Mahan, the basis of power lies in major trade, large mechanical industries and an extensive colonial system in which bases can be located. Between 1860 and 1890 Britain lost its ability to out compete such powers as Germany and the United States in industry and trade and, after the First World War, Britain gradually began to lose its naval supremacy as well.

The development of submarines and aircraft further threatened the supremacy and effectiveness of the Royal Navy, for the submarine and the airplane rendered such tactics as a surface blockade a less terrible weapon than it had previously been.[5] Mahan, who had insisted in 1900 that "water remains and must always remain the great medium of transportation"[6] and that fortified bases with garrisons constituted the necessary foundation of power at sea, was unable to predict that maritime transportation could be threatened, not by superior naval forces but by the airplane. Indeed air power did deal a major blow to naval bases and as a result, to shipping. Once a naval power had lost control over its all-important bases, it was no longer in a position to protect sea communications. In the case of Great Britain, after its navy had lost supremacy over the sea lanes and its bases became vulnerable, its exports also began to decline. The decline in trade, in turn, reduced the importance of a strong navy and the bases which supported it. The reduction in the power of the navy, of course, also affected Britain's ability to defend her Empire.

The decline of the Royal Navy after World War II resulted, in part, from a decision by the British to concentrate on the defense of Europe.[7] The Admiralty lost some of its importance, as a

result, because European defense required a
commitment of land and air forces. The Royal Navy
was given less attention and a reduced budget.
Furthermore, the armed services were placed under
the Ministry of Defense at a time when the
aircraft carrier, airborne divisions and the
development of amphibious techniques made
cooperation between the services more essential
than ever.

Since the commercial and industrial strength
of Britain was the main foundation of its naval
supremacy the increasing importance attached to
bases maintained that supremacy. The economic
depression that England experienced after World
War II made a strong navy less essential because
the decline decreased the need for colonies and
bases as trade diminished. Finally, the economic
crisis was accompanied by the Government's efforts
on behalf of social reform. The cost of social
reform, however, demanded heavy expenditures and
the result was that the budget for the navy was
reduced.[8]

Britain showed the classic symptoms of a
declining empire according to Carlo Cipolla's
analysis:

> When needs outstrip productivity,
> capability, a number of tensions are
> bound to appear in society. Inflation,
> excessive taxation, difficulties in the
> balance of payments are just a small
> sample of the whole series of possible
> tensions. The public sector presses
> heavily over and against the private
> sector in order to squeeze out the
> largest possible share of resources.
> Consumption competes with investment and
> vice versa. Within the private sector,
> the conflict group tries to avoid as

much as possible the necessary economic
sacrifices. As the struggle grows in
bitterness cooperation among people and
social groups fades away, a sense of
alienation from the commonwealth
develops, and with it, group and class
selfishness.[9]

These factors had a clear influence on
defense policy. Since the economy was in decline,
it became harder to encourage technological
innovations. For the most part, British society
did not protest the weakening of the naval forces,
or even the collapse of the Empire. They were
weary of suffering the privations of war and
wanted to improve the quality of their own lives.
Also, as Mahan already sensed in 1890: "Popular
governments are not generally favourable to
military expenditure, however necessary, and there
are signs that England tends to drop behind."[10]
Ultimately, inflation, a rise in the cost of
new weapons, the objection to high taxes, domestic
pressures for improved social services and health
care, all combined to make it impossible for
postwar Britain to conduct an aggressive foreign
policy. One of the most important means for
imposing imperial policy was a strong navy, with
supporting bases overseas. As the influence of
Great Britain waned in foreign affairs, the
importance of a strong navy also declined. Then,
in the postwar years, military planners began to
think that the navy's function of protecting sea
lanes and convoys could be carried out more
effectively by shore-based aircraft. Others
thought that, since the next war would be short,
the outcome would be decided before shipping could
be interrupted.
The navy responded by trying to assume a new
role in the policy of deterrence. This was done

by adopting the aircraft carrier as a major ship and by emphasizing that carriers were much less vulnerable to atomic attack than even small land bases. Even when the Navy had succeeded in stressing the need for the aircraft carrier, its victory was achieved at the expense of overseas bases. During World War II, the Admiralty had developed new methods for the transfer of fuel, supplies, equipment, food, ammunition, spare parts, and people at sea, under any condition of sea and weather. Traditionally, the Royal Navy was 'short legged' because bases were available in many locations. That is to say, vessels used to operate within a short radius. With the growing radius of action for individual ships, the development of mobile logistic fleet support, and later, nuclear power for ship propulsion, the need for naval bases, for refuelling, repairs, supplies, recreation and shelter had drastically diminished.[11] Although the navy had been heavily dependent upon shore bases located throughout the world, it began to rely on support ships to increase the range of the fleet. Also, it began to build nuclear-powered ships, which further reduced the need for land bases. By 1954, when withdrawal from the Suez Canal became an issue, the innovations were highly developed. Despite all the innovations, the navy continued to face opposition to its expenditures.

The Royal Navy had been an instrument of power around which a legend had been built over the years. It was regarded as a police force <u>par excellence</u>, as a gigantic apparatus in charge of securing peace that was essential for the smooth operation of international trade. The Royal Navy was not regarded as an instrument of 'gun-boat diplomacy,' although it had been used for that purpose numerous times. The Navy's function was regarded as altruistic in nature. The remoteness of the Navy from the British Isles and its traditional function of suppressing piracy at sea reinforced the myth of the Navy as a powerful and dispassionate instrument of world order.

The Royal Navy had been given credit for numerous events which had taken place in the nineteenth century. It implemented the British Abolition of Slavery Act of 1807. It intervened to help peoples fight for their freedom in places such as Portugal (1820) and the South American colonies of Spain and Portugal (1818-1825). It destroyed the Fleet of the Egyptian leader Muhammad Ali at Navarino Bay in 1827 and thereby secured the independence of Greece. Even the unification of Italy was attributed to the intervention of the Royal Navy. In short, the Royal Navy was regarded as the chief contributor to the Pax Britannica.[12]

Many experts had argued that the battleship was already obsolete in 1916, by the time of the Battle of Jutland; others held that the battleship was doomed after May 21, 1941 when the largest battleship of the British fleet, <u>H.M.S. Hood</u>, was sunk by the German battleship <u>Bismark</u>. In fact, the Pacific War had proved that the battleship had become obsolete. In the great battles of 1942, on the Coral Sea (May) and around Midway Island (June), carrier-borne aircraft were the main weapons. Surface ships did not come within firing range at all. Japanese and American vessels were sunk from the air. Yet, in spite of these realities which led many a battleship to the scrapyard after the war, the mythology lived on.[13]

It was widely believed that the Empire, trade, the Navy and the bases were all components of the British system and not one could exist independently.

The jealousy and animosity which existed between the services made the Navy's adjustment to

the new situation even more difficult. The R.A.F.
was a new service with widespread support and the
ability to manipulate politicians. Thus, it
managed to get the largest share of the defense
budget. John Slessor attacked the Royal Navy
while stressing the ability of air power to handle
any kind of emergency. In a speech at the U.S.
National War College in April 1948, Slessor even
indicated the vulnerability of the carrier:

> In my view, the battleship and the heavy
> fleet carrier are irrelevant in these
> days...I believe the fleet action to be
> as dead as the Dodo. I do not believe
> there will be opposed landings on an
> enemy shore in the future war. I think
> the carrier or heavy ship that floats
> about within easy range of future
> shore-based aircraft, will be blown out
> of the water.[14]

Field Marshal Montgomery also thought that it
was unwise to spend money on aircraft carriers.
The result was the White Paper on Defense of 1954,
which placed increasing emphasis on nuclear
deterrence at the expense of the navy.[15] In
addition, many felt the navy had become obsolete
because it was vulnerable to enemy nuclear
weapons. As H. G. Thursfield, the chief editor of
Brassey's Annual wrote in 1949:

> Guided missiles, it is said,
> perhaps carrying atomic explosives are
> now being developed to fly for hundreds
> if not thousands of miles; bombers are
> being built that can fly faster than
> sound, and carry a bomb load across an
> ocean and return without refuelling.
> Such weapons were unheard of, even

> unthought   of   when   Mahan   wrote;
> therefore runs the argument, there can
> be no validity in his arguments and
> conclusions.[16]

The atomic bomb and the hydrogen bomb which
followed it appeared to have rendered land and sea
bases obsolete.

The fleets of Germany, Italy and Japan had
been entirely defeated.   The Soviet navy did not
seem powerful at the time because the Soviet Union
was regarded as a land power and the United
States, the only great naval power, was Britain's
ally.   Therefore, the British let their navy
deteriorate.   Also since the British economy was
strained, only the most essential weapons could be
maintained.   The Churchill Government continued
Labour's policy of relying on the nuclear
deterrent and air power.[17]

Sharp cutbacks in the Navy's budget resulted
in a severe shortage of skilled personnel.   By
1955, the Royal Navy was in urgent need of
carriers, ships with guided weapons, escorts to
support the carriers, a shore-based air force,
submarines and minesweepers. The Suez Affair had
demonstrated the need for these vessels.

At the time, the role of the Royal Navy was
not clear.   It was obvious that Churchill's
Government was not willing to spend money on a
service whose role was inadequately defined. The
Royal Navy ceased to be the dominant factor in
defense and there was less need for naval bases.
Air bases were still needed, however.   Britain
managed to secure the right of using airfields
located in Arab countries by treaties signed for
this purpose. Objection to British flights in the
Middle East came only in 1956 when the Suez
operation was carried out.

The Royal Navy lost most of its functions

after the Second World War.   There was no longer
any need to guard the flow of oil from the Middle
East since Britain could not use this oil without
agreements or treaties with Arab states.   The
appearance of nationalist regimes after the Second
World War also prevented Britain from maintaining
bases there.   Nor could Iran's nationalization of
the oil industry in 1951 be stopped by British
naval action.   The nationalization of the Iranian
oil industry was an expression of revolutionary
nationalism which could no longer be dealt with by
naval force.   The impotence of the navy   further
diminished its importance in the eyes of defense
planners. [18]

The Royal Navy was in decline not only
because of its diminished role in imperial
defense, it also lost its position as an
instrument of foreign policy because of a decline
in the old elan of Empire.   As Charles Owen
observed:

> Leadership...no longer expresses the
> same self assurance of an elite 'born'
> to command.   It is more tentative, less
> physical...the confident public school
> twang was virtually no more....Officers
> looked plumper, less heroic, not so much
> men of muscle as bank managers on a
> spree. [19]

The Navy's morale was affected because it was
gradually deprived of its highly respected role of
policing the Empire and safeguarding the lines of
communications.   As a result, the Navy had lost
its importance in the eyes of the British public
which served to demoralize the personnel even more
than did the diminished role in defense.   In
addition, many people, including students,
intellectuals and the educated middle class had

developed a resentment against the old upper classes. Since most of the officers of the old navy had derived from the privileged class, the navy had also thereby suffered.

Most of the officers of the R.A.F. were given extensive indoctrination regarding the superiority of aircraft. While the Royal Navy was losing its popularity in the years 1945-1955, the R.A.F. was gaining even higher prestige. Most naval officers were educated in the Royal Naval Colleges at Osborne and Dartmouth. Only a few attended public school and hardly any had attended a university.[20]
It seems that in the public mind at least, officers of the Royal Navy were regarded as more conservative in attitude and outlook than the officers of the R.A.F., although opinions on this point varied.

The impression that the Royal Navy was more conservative than the R.A.F. stemmed partly from the fact that the Royal Navy had often trained and provided personnel for certain positions, especially in intelligence. Moreover, the elite of the R.A.F. were younger men and could look into the future and point to the usefulness of air power in a future war. Naval officers also became victims of the negative connotation which conservatism implied in the public mind, i.e., dogmatism, resistance to change and inflexibility. It was unfortunate and even unfair to some degree that the Navy's conservatism had been criticized. In reality, the officers of the Royal Navy were not narrow-minded. Some even argued that they were the most adaptable of the three services because they managed to gain employment in civil industry with surprising ease. However, with the advancement in technology there was an increasing number of trained people among middle class civilians; consequently, naval officers and seamen lost their previous competitive edge.

Aside from the fact that the Government had decided to rely on nuclear deterrance as the basis for defense for economic and social reasons, the vulnerability of ships was amply demonstrated when the United States detonated atomic bombs at Bikini Atoll, which destroyed or damaged ships a mile away from the site of the explosion. This revelation did not, however, change the Government's attitude that conventional forces would continue to play a great part in defense immediately. The British Admiralty was convinced that vessels could be widely dispersed to protect most of them from an atomic blast. However, the hydrogen bomb made the strategists unsure that the Royal Navy could be useful in war. Ships could not survive a thermonuclear explosion and they could no longer be relied upon to supply overseas bases. Since bases could not be supplied, they could not contribute to a war. It seemed that there was no sense in maintaining them. And if bases were no longer relied upon, the most important function of the navy--defense of sea lanes--became meaningless.[21]

Then, in 1954, The Defense Statement of 1954 introduced the idea of "broken backed" warfare. The Royal Navy was given the important assignment of achieving victory in case atomic weapons failed to inflict total destruction on the enemy. Despite the fact that the navy was now required to defeat enemy forces at sea, to promote the undisturbed movement of supplies and troops and to support the air and land forces, it still was not considered as essential as it had been in the past.

The Navy League tried to gain support for the navy from the public and the government. Its members worked to remind everyone that the security of their country had depended on the navy and that the livelihood of the British people was

assured because the navy protected the uninterrupted flow of shipping. The League said that the
Soviets were building a fleet that could interdict
British shipping, assuming that the next war might
not be nuclear.   Thus, the Russians might decide
to defeat Britain by starving it. It was therefore
mandatory, the League argued, to hold onto the
lines of communication.   Rear Admiral A. D.
Nicholl had lectured at the Annual Grand Council
of the Navy League in November 1954 and explained
the continuing need for a strong navy. He noted:

> ...quite a number of people...think that
> the Navy is out of date(because of the
> new role of aircraft)....(But aircraft)
> have not made armies or warships
> obsolete, and will not do so as far as
> we can see. Now this country needs
> about a million tons of cargo a
> week...and only a very small portion of
> that could ever be carried by air....as
> long as ships bring the cargoes, we
> shall need to protect them.[22]

The Navy League also supported the navy by
claiming that aircraft carriers were becoming
increasingly important. As had been demonstrated
in the Korean War, naval aircraft could be
effective against land targets and could support
troops effectively. Planes could be launched
swiftly. Furthermore, the League claimed that
ports and cargo more than ships were the targets
an enemy would want to destroy. Aircraft carriers
would not be considered easy targets because of
their deadly air power.

Members of the Navy League worked closely
with the Admiralty and the staff of the Admiralty.
Despite the fact that the navy was not held in as
high esteem as previously, it was influential in

the formation of military policy. The Admiralty, including Admiral Lord Louis Mountbatten, advocated that shore bases should be abandoned, and as a result, the base in the Suez Canal Zone and other bases were abandoned. The Admiralty was not particularly upset by the decision to withdraw from Suez, for it then was in a position to argue that aircraft carriers should be built as the ideal substitutes for expensive land bases to protect the shipping lanes in the future. By emphasizing the importance of the aircraft carrier, the navy had managed to find a role in the nuclear age.

The Admiralty was an effective body thanks to the civil servants who had an important part in running it. The Navy was run by civilians as well as by military personnel. There were no separate civil and military hierarchies. They were integrated in every branch of the Admiralty. Also, there was substantial contact between the civil servants and naval officers. The Admirals were admired by the civil servants and were usually in control, as E. J. Kingston-McCloughry explained:

> Even today, the Admirals often carry more prestige and influence with their Civil Servants and the Treasury than corresponds with the Generals in the War office or the Air Marshals in the Air Ministry. One reason for this is that most Civil Servants in responsible positions learned at school the traditions, glories, and power of the British Navy, and this learning still remains inherent in their minds.[23]

Although the Navy underwent a period of decline in the pre-Suez period, it managed to reassert and readjust itself to the requirements of the nuclear age.

Another influential instrument in the hands of the Royal Navy was the Board of Admiralty. It included the highest officials of the Navy, and in practice it was much more than a discussion group and an advisory council. War operations were outside its scope, but every major problem was brought to the Board for a collective determination of the Navy's position. The most influential figures in this body were the First Lord and the First Sea Lord.

Naval officers also remained influential even after their retirement. They often occupied high positions in the civil service and their sense of duty remained strong. They were usually conservative in their political outlook, and as such, had more influence on the Conservative Party. The Navy used its influence whenever it could. The correspondent of The Observer commented on the Navy's influence, saying that: "The Navy had always been the most cunning propagandist of the three (services):it has fanatically loyal ex-officers scattered through every profession."[24]

The fact that the Royal Navy mentioned the possibility of Soviet naval attack with naval units as mobile nuclear bases, reinforced the case for the establishment of a strong naval carrier force. Articles to that effect were written by the naval elite and by commentators with the deliberate effort to influence the Government's policy in a direction satisfactory to the Admiralty. The Royal Navy had exceeded its previous limitations on stating its case.

The Royal Navy was, and hoped to remain, a force with a general purpose rather than a special mission. The fact that it had a variety of uses helped its ability to adjust to the defense

requirements of the nuclear age with relative
ease. Overseas bases were discarded as a result
of their argument that these were no longer needed
when the aircraft carrier was available. Only the
Army considered the security of bases overseas as
important because its traditional role had always
been to preserve peace in distant places.

By the mid—fifties, the Royal Navy was
already based on a limited number of highly mobile
aircraft carrier task groups. The task groups
included "afloat support" ships to refuel, supply
and refit the task force at sea by what they
called a "Float Train" which was a mobile base.
"Afloat Support" was developed during the naval
warfare in the Pacific by the United States and
was subsequently adopted by the Royal Navy. The
Royal Navy had to operate 3,000 to 4,000 miles
from its
naval base at Sydney, Australia when it had been
impossible to use Singapore and Hong Kong. The
British Pacific Fleet Train had been formed and
placed under the command of Rear Admiral D.B.
Fisher to supply the ships at sea. This unit
became a floating base with factories, repair
shops, floating docks, cranes, stores, barracks,
refrigerators, fuel depots, breweries, hospitals,
offices and everything needed to keep the ships
fully repaired and supplied. This unit included a
hundred vessels which provided food and recreation
for the sailors. Swimming pools, libraries and
theaters were also part of this floating base.
This mobile base enabled the British Pacific Fleet
to carry out attacks on Japanese airfields. The
same system of supply was also followed in the
Korean War and during the nuclear testing in the
Pacific.

Those who argued in favor of building a
formidable fleet of carriers pointed to the most
recent technical advances which turned the carrier

into a viable weapon. The years 1953-1954 witnessed a revolution in the technique of operating aircraft from the decks of aircraft carriers, thanks to the improvements developed by the British. The advent of turbo-jet aircraft increased the speed of landing and take-off. The angled deck had increased the virtual length of the flying deck by forty percent. The steam-operated catapult had greatly simplified the problem of operating aircraft from fast carriers which were large enough to provide a steady platform and could be built at a reasonable cost. Thus the value of the aircraft carrier as a strategic weapon had indeed increased.[25]

The mobile base policy was accepted in Britain because it was more compatible with the requirements for mobility and flexibility of the new age. Moreover, it was more economical than maintaining bases and there was also much less danger of alienating the local population which was enimical to a base. Also it was much less likely to intimidate the Soviet Union.

Despite the emergence of nuclear weaponry, important functions still remained for the Royal Navy: first, the provision of mobile bases for launching bombs and missiles; secondly, the support of joint operations, especially in destroying coastal defenses from a range of several miles with great accuracy; thirdly, the provision of mobile bases for reconnaissance and guidance of long range striking forces of nuclear bombers and rockets; fourthly, the provision of naval assistance in construction of ports and urgent unloading of cargoes;and fifthly, the supply and assistance to nuclear submarines.[26]

After the Korean War the Government had decided to complete four of the ten light fleet carriers whose construction had been stopped at the end of the Second World War. In 1952 the fleet carrier Eagle and the two ships of the Daring class were completed. The carrier Ark Royal and the remaining six Darings were near completion. Four light fleet carriers of the Hermes class were also nearly complete.

Naval strategists assumed that aircraft carriers were essential for limited wars. There were also those who argued that in an atomic war only the fleet would manage to survive. The Navy won a position in the new armed forces because of its ability to contribute to deterrence.[27]

The proponents of the aircraft carrier argued that since the effective range of the bomber was limited, it was necessary to have advanced bases in order to reach enemy bases. Permanent airfields could be a convenient target for an enemy due to their immobility. Carriers of the Forrestal class could operate aircraft with a radius of at least 1500 miles when loaded with nuclear weapons. Carriers of the Midway, Essex, Royal Ark and Hermes classes could project medium range aircraft which were also capable of carrying nuclear weapons. A carrier task force was also capable of defending itself by radar and sonar against submarine attack. A carrier task force consisting of four to six fleet carriers, a few large cruisers, guided weapons ships and a large number of escorts was regarded as an excellent system of defense provided that it was widely dispersed.[28]

The American naval strategist, Laurence Green, explained the advantages of the aircraft carrier to an American audience. His opinion was shared by British naval strategists. He stated:

> The large ship with long-range weapons was, and still is, the very basis upon which control of the sea is built. The fact that we must add air superiority

over the sea to this basic tenet, does
not in any way nullify the tenet itself,
but valuably expands it in yet another
dimension. The attack carrier provides
those vehicles by which air power to
control the seas can be placed,
immediately and continuously, wherever
and whenever it is most urgently
needed.[29]

Green reacted to arguments about the vulnerability
of aircraft carriers by saying: "Men can be
killed...aircraft can be shot down...(but)it is
necessary to balance vulnerability against the
need for the weapon. To deny a carrier because of
its alleged vulnerability alone is a serious error
in logic."[30]

It has also been proven in previous wars that
aircraft carriers were capable of protecting
convoys against U-boats. Escort carriers were
believed to be the best way of providing local
protection to British convoys. Carriers equipped
with radar, sonar and other modern devices were
the best and the cheapest method of naval defense
and the improved performance of submarines
rendered the carrier more important than ever.[31]

Control of the sea, the strategists contended, was still necessary even in the age of nuclear
power. Mahan's philosophy was not out of date.
The side which controls the sea has a great
advantage over the other side even in the nuclear
era. The side which possesses sufficient naval
power could destroy the naval trade of the other
side and undermine his military power. The
strategic concept of the early fifties that a
future war would be completely different than wars
in the past became refined toward the mid-fifties.
Strategists began to believe that future wars

would have many points of similarity with past wars; therefore, control of the sea would remain an important pre-requisite for victory. Speaking at the 20th Communist Party Congress, Marshal Zhukov noted: "In the future war, the struggle at sea will be of immeasurably greater importance than it was in the last war."[32]

As soon as Sandys took office as Minister of Defense in Britain in 1957, he intended to eliminate the aircraft carrier from the naval forces. The Board of Admiralty bitterly objected and made strenuous attempts to justify its usefulness in limited wars and in combatting submarine attacks. The Board argued that the Korean War had proven the usefulness of the Fleet Air Arm. Its contribution to land operations and its detachment from air bases were all arguments used to enhance the value of the carrier. Efforts to develop the aircraft carrier and to turn it into the backbone of the naval fighting forces continued throughout the fifties and beyond.[33]

The navy had powerful allies who supported its fight for additional carriers: the ship builders, some trade union leaders and other conservative elements who argued that since land bases were not useful as they had been in the past, relying on carriers was the only way to secure Britain's imperial interests. The R.A.F. became a supporter of the Navy's claim for additional carriers because members of the air lobby were beginning to realize that British air power outside Europe might soon become meaningless unless a way was found to carry all the middle range bombers to within range of their target area.[34] It is remarkable that the Navy managed eventually to convince the Conservative Government in the early sixties to build a new carrier which was one of the most expensive single weapons in the nation's armory at the time.

The use of a helicopter carrier was also a possible method of bringing an effective force to quick action in distant places and overseas territories. The British had used helicopters in Malaya and Cyprus. Naval officers had argued that the helicopter carrier would be valuable in every future operation which the Navy might be called on to perform, both in a 'hot war' and in local disturbances.[35]   This argument served as an additional weapon in the hands of the Navy in its attempt to find a new role.

Despite the fact that the navy continued to be regarded as less essential than the other services in global war, the understanding that the navy was of value because it could provide mobile launching bases became widespread. All doubts regarding the future of the aircraft carrier around which all naval planning revolved were swept away. The role of the navy in future wars was established.

FOOTNOTES

CHAPTER SIX

1. A. T. Mahan, The Influence of Sea Power Upon History (Boston, 1890), p. 33. See also, Fernand Braudel, La Mediterranee et le Monde Mediterraneen a l'epoque de Philippe II (Paris, 1949), pp. ix-xv.

2. Cited in Margaret Tuttle Sprout, "Mahan: Evangelist of Sea Power," in W.M. Earle, ed., Makers of Modern Strategy (Princeton, 1971), p. 421.

3. Bernard Brodie, A Guide to Naval Strategy (Princeton, 1958), pp. 178-179.

4. Harold and Margaret Sprout, Toward a New Order of Sea Power (Princeton, 1940), p. 15.

5. Mahan, Influence of Seapower, p. 67.

6. Sprout, "Mahan: Evangelist...," loc.cit., p.24 and also, A.T. Mahan, The Problem of Asia (N.Y. and London, 1900), pp. 125-6,430-1,440.

7. Mahan's Influence of Sea Power was enthusiastically adopted by British advocates of sea power; for example, Rear Admiral P. H. Colomb, Col. Sydenham Clarke, J.K. Laughton, J.R. Thursfield and Thomas G. Bowles were under his influence, according to W.D. Puleston, The Life and Work of Captain A. T. Mahan (New Haven, 1939), pp. 108-110.

8. See the "Statement of the First Lord of the Admiralty on the Navy Estimates," 1947-1948, Cmd. 7054 1948-49, Cmd. 7337 and 1949-50, Cmd.7632. See also Pollard, British Economy, p. 406.

9. Carlo M. Cipolla, The Economic Decline of Empires (London, 1970), pp. 1-15 and Charles Owen, No More Heroes: The Royal Navy in the Twentieth Century: Anatomy of a Legend (London, 1975), p. 191.

10. Mahan, Influence of Sea Power, p. 67;H. and
    M. Sprout, "Retreat from World Power;Process
    and Consequences of Readjustment," World
    Politics 15/4(1963), pp. 665-6; Rosecrance,
    Defense of the Realm, p. 212.

11. M.M. Postan, British War Production(London,
    1952), p. 289; Anthony E. Sokol, Sea Power in
    the Nuclear Age(Washington,D.C., 1961),p.161.

12. See Michael Lewis, The History of the British
    Navy(Baltimore, 1957), pp. 213-222.

13. Sampson, Anatomy of Britain, p.346 and Lewis,
    British Navy, p. 270.

14. Slessor, The Great Deterrent, pp. 78-79.

15. Michael Howard,"Britain's Strategic Problem,"
    International Affairs 42/2(London, 1966), pp.
    179-183.

16. Liddell Hart, Memoirs, p. 327;H.G.Thursfield,
    "The Influence of Sea Power Today," in
    Brassey's Annual(1949), p. 1.

17. A. J. Youngston, The British Economy:1920-
    1957(Cambridge, Mass., 1960), p. 216; see
    also, A. T. Peacock and Jack Wiseman, The
    Growth of Public Expenditure in the United
    Kingdom(Princeton, 1961), pp. 92, 106.

18. Monroe, Britain's Moment, p. 160;and Slessor,
    The Great Deterrent, p. 79.

19. Owen, No More Heroes, p. 183.

20. Admiral Lord Louis Mountbatten was the only
    one who went to Cambridge as well as to
    Osborne and Dartmouth;see Armstrong, loc.cit.
    p. 97;Sampson, Anatomy, 347-348;and Owen, No
    More Heroes, p. 194.

21. Sampson, Anatomy, p. 344;P.E. Garbutt, Naval
    Challenge 1945-61: The Story of Britain's
    Postwar Fleet(London, 1961), p. 8.

22. Rear Admiral A.D. Nicholl, "The Naval Situ-
    ation: the Policy of the Navy League,"The
    Navy Vol. 59(Nov., 1954), pp.330-332.

23. Rear Admiral A.D. Torlesse, "The Role of the

Aircraft Carrier," Brassey's Annual(1955), p.
80;Wing Comm. P.G. Wykeham-Barnes, "The War
in Korea...,"JRUSI 97/586(May, 1952), pp.149-
163;and Air Vice Marshall E.J. Kingston-
McCloughry, Global Strategy(London, 1957),pp.
169-170.

24. The Observer(April 7, 1957; Armstrong loc.
cit., p. 105.

25. Donald Barry, "Afloat Support,"The Navy Vol.
62(Aug., 1957), p.239-240.

26. Air Vice Marshal E. J. Kingston-McCloughry,
"The Future Structure of the Armed Forces..."
in Brassey's Annual(1956), pp. 41-42.

27. Rear Admiral R.M.H. Hutton, "The Future of
Maritime Power," JRUSI 96/582(May, 1951),
p. 226.

28. A. D. Torlesse, "The Role of the Aircraft
Carrier," Brassey's Annual(1955), pp. 75-77.

29. Laurence B. Green, "A Case for the Attack
Carrier in the Missile Age," U.S. Naval
Institute Proceedings 84/7(1958), p. 49 ff.

30. Green, Ibid.

31. Air Vice Marshall W. Carter, "Air Power Confronted," Brassey's Annual(1965), p. 174.

32. Green, "Attack Carrier,"loc.cit..

33. "British Defense Policy: The Long Recessional," Adelphi Paper No. 61, p. 15.

34. Ibid., p. 17.

35. Captain T.M.P. Stevens, "The Helicopter
Carrier," The Navy Vol. 62(Oct.,1957),p. 323;
Donald Barry, "The British Navy in the Nu-
clear Age," U.S. Naval Institute Proceedings
Vol. 83(Oct., 1957), p. 1070.

CHAPTER VII

IMPERIAL REMNANTS: ADEN AND THE PERSIAN GULF

Britain's concern about the Middle East must be seen and treated as an integral part of its policy towards the entire area which lies east of Suez. In addition to its bases in southern Arabia, Britain maintained bases in Kenya, Singapore, Malaya, the Far East and some islands in the Indian Ocean. Between 1957 and 1971 economic constraints, however, forced Britain to terminate its commitments in the Middle East. Nevertheless, the importance of Britain's possessions east of Suez made the Middle East an important link to the Far East. Priority was therefore given to the defense of remaining overseas territories in both the Middle and Far East over its responsibilities to help defend Europe.

The Suez operation of 1956 had ended in a fiasco, the consequences of which were detrimental to Britain's policies in its remaining possessions. The Suez Zone not only had been a base in which British forces were stationed, but also had served as a link in a network of sea and air communications which for over a century sustained the entire fabric of the British Empire. The retreat from the Suez Canal Zone by no means concluded Britain's role in the Middle East, because Britain's role east of Suez demanded a vigilant watch over the southern part of the Arabian Peninsula.

British troops had been stationed in Aden since 1839; however, the bases there remained relatively unimportant while the Suez base was in British hands. Following the Suez debacle, the strategic emphasis shifted southward. The base in Aden assumed greater importance and the southern part of the Arabian Peninsula became an area of major concern for Britain as long as its presence east of Suez continued. By the early sixties the British had come to the realization that it was no longer safe to remain in the newly established base in East Africa when African nations were rapidly advancing towards independence. Thereupon, the British decided that their troops must be transferred to Aden at once. Consequently, the focus of Britain's attention moved away from the Suez Canal Zone and the Eastern Mediterranean to Aden and the Persian Gulf. No serious attempt had been made by successive British governments to abandon the territories east of Suez although the leaders were fully aware of Britain's inability to maintain them. It seemed as if no one had learned any lesson from the Suez experience. British politicians still clung to the traditional policy of imperial defense; therefore, the occupation of overseas bases continued until 1971.

The end of the fifties witnessed the increasing involvement of Britain, first in Malaya in 1957, then in Brunei in 1958 and as late as 1961 in Kuwait. The constant turmoil in these areas did not permit the luxury of an early and smooth withdrawal. On the contrary, it increased the importance of maintaining a presence east of Suez and extended the period of occupation. In a debate on the 1961 Defense White Paper, Defense Minister Harold Watkinson stated that the British government had no intention of abandoning important sites such as the Arabian Peninsula or Hong Kong.[1]

In the summer of 1957 a revolt had erupted in Central Oman. Also, the Aden-Yemenite conflict lasted throughout this period, and the British government deemed it necessary to interfere. It intervened in Jordan in 1958 and reinforced its strategic mobile forces in its bases east of Suez. In 1957 Britain concluded a defense agreement with

Malaya and in 1958 it assumed the responsibility of defending Singapore after its independence. In addition, Britain remained obligated to protect the Sultan of Brunei.

Whereas during the fifties the general consensus in government circles was that Europe was the area in which a conflict was most likely to erupt, throughout the sixties the overwhelming opinion was that war in Europe was a remote possibility and that limited conflicts overseas, rather than a total war, might pose a threat to peace. Whereas in the fifties British policy was aimed at defending the Middle East, the Persian Gulf and other territories east of Suez against Soviet expansion southeast, in the sixties the British outlook had changed. The British did not necessarily think about a conventional attack capable of wiping out these areas entirely. There was increasing sensitivity to Soviet subversion and involvement in local conflicts which could be used to expand Communist influence. The Jordan operation of 1958 strengthened this view.[2] The British Chiefs of Staff were convinced that the Sino-Soviet conflict had made the possibility of conflict in Europe quite remote.

The first attempt to review Britain's role east of Suez was made in 1958 by Prime Minister Harold Macmillan. He established a committee composed of members of the Foreign Office, the Commonwealth Relations Office and the Colonial Office. The Committee's task was to review Britain's role overseas. It recommended that Britain continue its active role in the Indian Ocean. The consequence of this recommendation was that possessions east of Suez assumed greater importance and that retreat was delayed. The Committee's recommendations were fully adopted by the Chiefs of Staff. In 1962 the Committee published a paper outlining Britain's defense needs.

By the beginning of the sixties, the strategic reserve concept had gained wide acceptance in Britain and army and naval forces were moved to the Arabian Peninsula, Malta and to Kenya later that year. In spite of the flurry when the National Service law expired in 1962, withdrawal was impossible because British forces were still engaged in quelling tribal revolts in both the Arabian Peninsula and the Persian Gulf. In addition, the British were fighting and facing other serious problems in Africa and Asia. According to the 1962 Defense White Paper, Britain still had to maintain over 100,000 troops and support units to maintain security in the Middle and Far East.[3]

By 1962 the Near and Middle East, Africa, Europe and the Mediterranean seemed secure. This was the opinion Lord Montgomery had expressed in the House of Lords.[4] The 1962 Defense White Paper confirmed this observation and stressed the need to maintain forces east of Suez. It stated that Britain's task was to contain Communism and to maintain peace and stability in those areas of the world whose stability was deemed vital to the West. Furthermore, it pointed out that the forces in Germany might have to be transferred to other areas as needed. British forces in Europe were increasingly regarded as a reservoir of manpower for operations east of Suez. The detente with the Soviet Union enabled the British to withdraw forces from Europe at least temporarily.

By February 1963 disturbances overseas confirmed the need to give priority to the defense of the bases east of Suez. Apart from unrest in Aden and the outbreak of hostilities in Radfan, rebellions broke out in Eat Africa, Cyprus and British Guiana. Southeast Asia was also in turmoil. Raids by Indonesian guerrillas across the border

of Sarawak and Sabah had increased. Terrorism
broke out in South Arabia in January 1963 when
Aden joined the South Arabian Federation, which
had been established by Britain in 1959 in an
effort to safeguard its bases in the area. The
republican coup d'etat which occurred in Yemen in
September, 1962 resulted in Egypt's sending troops
to San'a and Taiz to incite the tribes along the
border to resist the British occupation. In
January, 1964 the British fought against them in
the Radfan region north of Aden.[5] In May 1964 a
revolt erupted in the Radfan area and the Yemenis
attacked across the Dhala borders.

Early in the summer the carrier HMS Centaur
returned to Aden to provide air support. Simultaneously, naval reinforcements were sent to
British Guiana. By June the shortage of manpower
became acute. The British strategists understood
that Britain was no longer capable of maintaining
forces in order to crush revolts everywhere.
Occupation of bases continued, however, because
the pressures to retreat were countered by pressures to continue the occupation. The British
strategists understood that Britain was no longer
capable of maintaining forces in order to crush
revolts everywhere.

Until late in 1961 the United States was concerned primarily with Britain's contribution to
NATO. Then, the United States had become more[6]
supportive of Britain's role east of Suez.
American foreign policy had changed because the
American government became concerned that British
abandonment of positions east of Suez might invite[7]
the Soviets to step into the power vacuum.

Britain, as a member of NATO and holding a
special relationship with the United States, was
in no position to disregard American world interests; therefore, it was unable to expedite its
retreat from east of Suez. Wilson's government

was receptive to the American concern and those
Labor Party members who still believed that
Britain should maintain a presence east of Suez
continuously emphasized Britain's obligation to
the Atlantic alliance.   Although it would be
wrong to conclude that the entire cabinet was
influenced by the American position, it is
possible to state with certainty that at least
some individuals were influenced by it.[8]

When Harold Wilson, Denis Healey and Michael
Stuart visited the United States at the end of
April 1965, the American leaders insisted that
Britain's role east of Suez continue.   This
pressure had a delaying effect on Britain's
decision to leave Singapore.   In addition,
Australia encouraged Britain to maintain its
presence east of Suez. Consequently, withdrawal
from the last posts of the Middle East did not
appear imminent.[9]   Nevertheless, Britain decided,
according to Richard Crossman, to terminate its
presence east of Suez and that decision was
received with great dismay in Washington.[10]   It
was after Suez that Britain encountered great
difficulties in carrying out its strategic plans
in the Middle East.   In 1962 Israel and the Sudan
refused to allow British aircraft to fly over
their territories, therefore, British pilots
were compelled to fly from Malta to Kano in
Nigeria and across Central Africa to Nairobi.[11]
Consequently, the airlifting of great numbers of
troops to distant areas east of Suez could not be
carried out as planned. According to the military
correspondent of The Times, airlifting a brigade
to a point east of Suez via this cumbersome route
could take about eight days. African states were
rapidly approaching independence, and there was a
major concern in Whitehall that they might deny
Britain these routes as well. Moreover, the
passage of ships through the Suez Canal became

unsafe since Britain had lost its supremacy in Egypt. Contrary to these intentions, however, the Arabian Peninsula remained important in the eyes of British planners and they were reluctant to leave. In fact, the British had become even more fully engaged in the years 1958-1961. They not only reinforced their positions in Kenya and Singapore, but they also stationed the Amphibious Warfare Squadron in Aden. In addition, the Middle Eastern and East African Commands were reorganized in late 1957. The denial of air transit rights even helped delay the final retreat. The number of troops deployed in the area was difficult to reduce while rapid deployment remained impractical.[12]

Britain's attitude towards the Middle East and other areas east of Suez was also determined by the political rivalry between the Labour and the Conservative parties at home. The Labour Party was opposed to the idea of retaining colonial territories but in favor of domestic social reforms. In addition, Labour MPs believed that stationing forces overseas was dangerous at a time when priority should be given to the defense of Europe and to NATO. The Macmillan Government simply argued that bases were essential because Britain had to honor its obligations to United States regional organizations, to the Commonwealth countries and the protectorates.[13] Furthermore, the Defense Minister, Harold Watkinson, held that an incident outside Europe was more likely to develop into a global conflict. Emmanuel Shinwell was one of the first cabinet members to maintain that there was no need even to station a large number of troops in Germany.[14]

In the early sixties, Labour MPs reassessed Britain's defense needs and some of them concluded that Britain should maintain its possessions in Asia. These Labourites believed that Britain had

a solemn duty to prevent anarchy and war in Asia,
the Middle East and Central America.[15] But many
continued to disagree with this changed view
because they felt that the Labour Party might
encourage Wilson to adopt a European role if the
Labour Party came to power. Hence many in the
Labour Party still urged the government to
accelerate the process of withdrawal from overseas
territories.[16] They also criticized the
government for its intention to guarantee Indian
defense with nuclear or conventional weapons.
Again the number of Labour MPs objecting to
Britain's involvement east of Suez began to
increase.

In the beginning of August 1965, the Labour
Party reconvened and called upon the government to
reduce defense spending by 25 per cent and to
discard the "outmoded military bases abroad."[17]
By the end of 1965 the opposition to Britain's
role east of Suez had also spread to groups
outside the Labour Party. Members of the Liberal
Party stated that Britain's involvement there
caused major revolutions and wars and therefore
must be terminated. Some Conservatives also said
that the Tories should realize that their traditional stand on the east of Suez issue must
change. Members of the left wing of the Labour
Party praised the establishment of the People's
Socialist Party of Aden which was fighting for
independence.[18]

The economic situation had worsened by
November, 1967; thus, an urgent need for severe
retrenchment forced the Labour Government, then in
power, to make cutbacks in social services. These
measures were strongly attacked by some members of
the Labour Party, who felt that these proposals
meant a betrayal of socialism. The government
also announced that British forces would be
withdrawn from the Gulf by the end of 1971. The

Conservatives, in opposition, wanted to gain political profit by condemning Labour's action and by referring to it as a contemptuous betrayal. This ploy appealed to traditional emotions and feelings of imperial pride. The Tories insisted that it was essential to maintain a presence in the Gulf.[19]

Members of the Conservative opposition argued also that a withdrawal would inevitably lead to chaos in the Gulf. Although Conservatives at the time pledged to consult the leaders of the Gulf regarding their future, they failed to keep their promises once they came to power. They did not revoke Labour's decision to withdraw, and they accepted the ceilings on defense expenditure which were laid down by the Labour government in October of 1970. There was in fact no money to maintain British forces in the Gulf.

J.B. Kelly, perhaps the government's most outspoken critic, argued that Britain's retreat from the Gulf was an act of betrayal, that Douglas Home's proposals for military help to the United Arab Emirates were insincere and that Britain intended to leave the Gulf states without any defense arrangements. According to Kelly, the British were concerned about their friendship with Saudi Arabia; therefore, they did not intend to send troops to the area because such action might upset the Saudis.[20]

Some of the detailed arrangements made in the 1960s to maintain a hold on peripheral areas of Arabia seem to contradict some of Kelly's arguments. Britain really made a serious attempt to "hold on" in the sixties, but nationalism among the Arabs and world events, not to mention Britain's dire financial state, forced Britain's hand. In August, 1961, Ian Mcleod, the Secretary of State for the Colonies, stated at a meeting of Conservative MPs that Britain would soon lose its base in Kenya and that it would no longer be able to establish or retain bases in colonial or newly independent countries. Yet, the base in Aden, as a case in point, was expanded with complete disregard of this realistic appraisal.[21]

Aden had been a staging post on the air routes to Malaya, Australia and the Far East. It served as a refuelling station for British aircraft and as an area of acclimatization for the army. A garrison was stationed in Aden long before the Suez crisis, but it remained small until then. Gradually, the British increased the number of troops there and established an independent command. Between 1956 and 1959, there was a fourfold increase in the military population of Aden. When the British were about to lose the base in Kenya, a decision was made to develop Little Aden, an area approximately 20 miles away from the main town. The British had build Little Aden as an alternative refuelling station for the Royal Navy following the nationalization of the Abadan refineries by Iran in 1951. This construction project was the largest undertaken by the British government ever. It included housing for 2,500 troops, 1,000 women and children, workshops and entertainment facilities. The British believed that the independence of Aden was still quite distant. They had no intention of abandoning Aden in the near future, because the disturbances in Cyprus, which ended in its independence, did not give the British much hope that the island could still be used as a major base. The Aden Alliance, a moderate pro-Commonwealth Party, expressed its desire to advance further toward self government with an elected legislature and an elected ministry. Nonetheless, Macmillan's government did not demonstrate willingness to retreat. In a speech to the Aden legislature in May, 1956, Lord Lloyd, Under-Secretary of State

for the colonies, gave no hope to the Adenese for
independence. Hence the opposition in Aden intensified. The British attempted to tighten the
links between Aden and the Federation of Arab
Emirates, thereby hoping to maintain their influence on the Peninsula, but this tactic also proved
sterile.[22]

The gradual deterioration of relations in
Aden came at an inopportune time because the
British, with the untenability of the Kenya base
after 1962, were forced to concentrate their
defense measures for the Middle East in Aden.
Prior to Britain's withdrawal from Kenya in 1964,
she secured the right to use Kenya's naval and air
facilities. Thereupon, 6,000 British troops
evacuated the country and, within nine months, the
Headquarters 24th Infantry Brigade Group and most
of its administrative units were sent to Aden
while the remaining units returned to Britain.
This move was made in part owing to the intense
pressure exerted on the government by the military
chiefs. They were apprehensive that the Soviets
might step into the area.[23]

The British Government also developed projects for Bahrain and Sharjah. After the independence of Kuwait was declared in 1961, the
remaining Gulf posts assumed greater importance.
They assigned a battalion to Bahrain and in 1962
the British began to build permanent facilities
there. The objective was to establish an alternative base to Kuwait in the Persian Gulf.[24]

When Kuwait, which had been under British
protection since 1899, was proclaimed independent,
Iraq suddenly presented a claim to sovereignty
over Kuwait. In response to this claim, the Amir
of Kuwait, Abdullah Salem al-Sabah, asked Britain
to return its military forces. British forces had
withdrawn in October, 1961, at which time Kuwait
was accepted as a member of the Arab League. The

League then established a Pan Arab force to defend
Kuwait together with the British.

The mobilization of these forces not only
blocked any overt action by Iraq, but also the
lessons of this episode were valuable for Britain.
If Britain were to retain some role east of Suez,
she had to develop a mobile army equipped with
sophisticated weapons. The Kuwait operation
demonstrated that, in spite of some improvement,
the British forces had a long way to go to keep
abreast of new military hardware. Britain found
it difficult to handle an operation of large
magnitude without moving forces from other
theaters, especially from Germany. The
transportation of 7,000 men to Aden and then to
the Persian Gulf in the first six days of the
operation had proven that the RAF's capacity of
flying troops over long distances had substantially increased since 1958. The Iraqi army,
however, had a number of sophisticated weapons
such as Soviet T54 tanks in addition to Centurions
and American M24s. The Iraqi air force had MIG
17s, MIG 19s, Ilyushin 28 bombers, Hunters, Venoms
and Vampires. The Soviet Government had, in this
manner, been modernizing a number of Asian and
African armed forces.[25]

The costs of the operation were also staggering. According to a statement made by Harold Watkinson in the House of Commons on July 25, 1961,
the cost of the build up and partial withdrawal in
the Kuwait operation amounted to one million
pounds.[26] As the costs of maintaining forces
overseas increased, the British became more
reluctant to play the role of a Great Power.
There was mounting resistance at the Ministry of
Defense especially after 1965 when it was revealed
that the cost of the Malaysian operations amounted
to 90,000 pounds a week.[27]

The British role east of Suez demanded air

mobility. This concept had developed rapidly in
those years. The Transport Command was built and
heavy emphasis was placed on the combined operation of sea and air forces. The air lifting
capability of the RAF had constantly improved.[28]
But the Kuwait experience had proven that despite
the mobility of the Navy and the RAF, there was
still a need for bases. Bases were still essential for acclimatization and as training grounds
for the army. Those who favored the maintenance
of bases emphasized the important role of airports
and terminal facilities.[29]

Throughout the entire period the competition
between the Royal Navy and the RAF for greater
shares of the government's budget did not affect
the army. An immediate abandonment of bases would
have meant that the army would diminish in size
and the navy would expand. Such a change would
have required a rather drastic re-adjustment in
the roles of high ranking personalities. Hence,
an attempt was still made in the sixties to
maintain a delicate balance of service roles,
hardware and manpower.[30] Thus the process of
withdrawal from the bases had been delayed.

Items such as the HS681, a fifth Polaris
submarine, the F111A aircraft and the aircraft
carrier CVAOI had to be cancelled. The Navy had
insisted that the CVAOI carrier together with the
HMS Eagle and the HMS Hermes were indispensable if
Britain intended to maintain territories east of
Suez. Concurrently, the RAF had demanded 75 of
the F111A aircraft as a replacement for the
Canberra. With these aircraft, the RAF contended
that it could replace the aircraft carrier system
in the Indian Ocean. The air force plan came to
be regarded as an alternative to carrier air
power, given the need to economize. The Minister
of Defense and the Chief of Staff eventually
accepted the air force arguments regarding the

slowness and the vulnerability of the carrier; thus, the building of a new carrier was given up. Little did the British cabinets realize in the sixties how detrimental a decision this would be in the light of the Falkland Island crisis of 1981 and 1982. Thus, despite its initial success in the fifties, the Royal Navy lost its struggle for an equitable part of the budget in the mid-sixties.[31] The plan to build aircraft carriers would have decreased the need to station forces in overseas bases had it been implemented as planned. But the relative inflexibility and the high cost of the carriers had lead to the Navy's decline.[32]

All the previously mentioned factors, the increasing importance of world events east of Suez, the American insistence on the British role there, the treaty obligations to the states of the Gulf, and the persistence of tradition merely postponed the inevitable withdrawal. It seems that the most important factors regarding retreat from the east were intangible rather than the age old question of 'guns versus butter.'[33]

To balance Britain's domestic and foreign interests dictated Britain's withdrawal from distant lands, even from the Arabian Peninsula where it no longer enjoyed its former popularity. While in the immediate postwar era it was accurate to say that Britain was still respected in the Arab world, by the end of the sixties her image had changed dramatically.

The popularity and the sense of confidence which Britain enjoyed in the past had vanished not only because of Britain's eroding power and the growth of Arab nationalism, but also because the Arabs of the Gulf gained legendary wealth from their oil deposits and began to use the London money market as a casino. This was one of the most important reasons for Britain's inability to stay in Aden and the Gulf. As Harper noted:

> The irresponsible sabotage of the
> Western financial system by the Arabs
> brought the British malaise to crisis
> more rapidly. One of these factors was
> a loss of confidence, a loss of pride
> amounting to shame for the greatness of
> the past. This was the core of Britain's
> abdication of responsibility in Aden and
> the Gulf.[34]

During the sixties the British press also advocated withdrawal with greater intensity. The Times and the Observer argued that preference should be given to the defense of Europe. There were of course opposing views of Conservatives who still maintained that Britain should continue to maintain its positions east of Suez.[35]

Retreat was inevitable even though it contradicted Britain's lingering desire to occupy overseas territories. Thus, in November, 1964, a provisional decision was made to reduce the defense budget planned for 1969-70 from 2.4 billion pounds to 2 billion pounds.[36] The government decided to withdraw from Aden and to repudiate a defense agreement with the Federation of South Arabia as a first step in the process of cutting back commitments. In February, 1966, it was announced in Parliament that British troops would be withdrawn from Aden by 1968.

That the economic problems weighed more heavily than any other consideration in determining Britain's decision to retreat is demonstrated by the fact that the Treasury had set 2 billion pounds as the ceiling for defense spending. No alternative was left but to retreat.[37]

The 1966 Defense White Paper stated unequivocally that Britain would not undertake major operations except in cooperation with other allies. Also, it was made clear that Britain would no longer undertake obligations to any country, unless that country would be willing to provide appropriate facilities. Furthermore, it stated that troops would not be maintained in any country against the wishes of its inhabitants. The Aden base was to be abandoned, and South Arabia was to become independent in 1967 or 1968. Also it was emphasized that no defense agreement would be signed with the Federation. The forces in the Persian Gulf were to be increased slightly. Singapore was to be maintained as long as possible. The existing carrier force was expected to operate until the seventies, and thereafter, aircraft operating from land bases were to provide defense.

By March, 1966, it became abundantly clear that Britain could no longer hope to play an active role east of Suez. The main problem was how to withdraw and yet maintain stability in the remaining possessions. Fortunately the tension in Indonesia of that year subsided and the American pressure on Britain lessened. An agreement between Malaysia and Indonesia ending a three years conflict was signed on June 1, 1966 enabling the British to retreat from the Far East.

In July, 1966, sterling came under heavy pressure and the Prime Minister announced expedient steps to cut expenses, especially overseas. It was decided that public investment in 1967-68 would be drastically reduced and that this would include a cut in military and civil expenditure of at least 100 million pounds overseas.[38]

In April, 1967, a decision was made to withdraw British forces from the Far East between 1970 and 1975. The decision was outlined in details in the 1967 Defense White Paper. But by November, the government announced its intention to acceler-

ate the process. On January 16, 1968, Prime
Minister Wilson announced the government's
decision to withdraw from the Far East and the
Persian Gulf by the end of 1971. A strategic
reserve was to be maintained in Europe for use in
case of need.[39]

Apart from Britain's economic weakness, there
were difficulties in ruling Aden and the Gulf.
The British governors of Aden had pressed the
government to grant sovereignty to Aden and to
encourage it to join the Federation of Arab
Emirates of the South.[40]

The sense of responsibility to the Gulf
states did delay the decision to withdraw. On May
19, 1967 King Faisal of Saudi Arabia met with
Harold Wilson and expressed his concern regarding
Britain's intention to withdraw. He argued that
retreat would be detrimental to the stability in
the Gulf and that British forces should remain to
defend Saudi Arabia against the incessant attacks
by nationalist guerrilla fighters who were supported by Egypt. The British government was in an
awkward position because it had just completed the
construction and equipment of a highly expensive
air defense system for the western region of Saudi
Arabia. Also, the Israeli-Egyptian crisis over
the status of the Straits of Tiran, an issue in
which the Saudis were involved, added to the
complications. Britain had a chance to re-exert
its influence in Arabia when the Egyptian troops
were forced to evacuate Yemen following Egypt's
defeat in the Six Day War; however, Britain was
not deterred from her course. The Foreign
Secretary, George Brown, announced in the House of
Commons that Aden would be granted independence on
January 9, 1968.[41]

The British government decided to leave Aden
in the hands of the National Liberation Front for
Occupied South Yemen (NLF). The immediate result

of this decision was a bitter fight between the NFL and the Front for the Liberation of South Yemen(FLOSY). The British netotiated with the NFL at a conference held at Geneva on November 22, 1967. It was agreed that the islands of Kamran, Perim and Socotra would be given to the NLF. A sum of 3 million pounds in the Aden treasury would be granted to the NFL, and a further sum of 12 million pounds was pledged after independence. The Kuria Muria Islands which had been ruled from Aden ever since they had been bequeathed to Queen Victoria by the Sultan of Oman in the middle of the nineteenth century were returned to Omani authority, to the dismay of the NLF.

Humphrey Trevelyan commented on the British decision to quit Aden thus:

> We left without glory but without disaster. Nor was it humiliation. For our withdrawal was the result not of military or political pressure, but of our decision, right or wrong, to leave.[42]

The Shah of Iran, the rulers of the Trucial States and King Faisal of Saudi Arabia were told that financial difficulties compelled the British government to abrogate the assurances given to them concerning Britain's intention to maintain a military and naval presence in order to fulfill treaty obligations and to help maintain stability and peace in the area. The four oil producing shaikhdoms, Dubai, Abu Dhabi, Bahrain and Qatar offered to pay the cost of maintaining the British forces in the area. This sum then amounted to about 12 million pounds per annum.[43] However, for Britain to accept the offer of the Arab shaikhs to finance its presence in the Persian Gulf was even more humiliating than retreat. It was obvious that the British could not agree to such a proposal. One can readily understand Healey's remark that: "It would be a great mistake if we allowed ourselves to become mercenaries for people who like to have British troops around."[44] It is true that in the case of the retreat from the Gulf, the economic argument was hardly convincing; however, here, more than in any other case, self-pride played an important role.

The British thus planned to combine the states in the Gulf into a union under the leadership of Saudi Arabia. The border disputes between Saudi Arabia and Oman and Abu Dhabi were resolved and the creation of the United Arab Emirates(UAE) concluded Britain's responsibility in the Gulf.[45]

On March 1, 1970, Home announced in the House of Commons that the treaties with the Trucial Shaikhdoms, Qatar and Bahrain, which had been in force since 1835, would be terminated before the end of the year and that all British forces would be withdrawn by the same date. He offered a treaty of friendship to the UAE and proposed that the Trucial Scouts be maintained to provide the neucleus of a federal defense force. He added that Britain would be willing to provide military assistance and to maintain its naval presence in the area. Thus, clearly seeing her position in the world severely limited by a new set of circumstances, Great Britain closed the chapter on her "Book of Empire" to the east of Suez.

FOOTNOTES

CHAPTER SEVEN

1. House of Commons(H.C.) Debates, Vol. 635,
    Col. 1509(28 April, 1961).
2. Army League, The British Army in the Nuclear
    Age, p. 16.
3. "Britain's Defence Emphasis Shifts East," The
    Times(15 March, 1960); Command 363, para.39.
4. House of Lords(H.L.) Debates, Vol. 238, Col.
    579(21 March, 1962); Ministry of Defence(MoD)
    Statement of Defence 1962, Cmnd. 1639(1962),
    para. 15.
5. King Gillian, Imperial Outpost--Aden, pp. 67-
    73; W.P. Kirkman, Unscrambling an Empire, pp.
    149-162; Sir Charles Johnston(Gov. of Aden,
    1960-1963), The View from Streamer Point,
    passim.
6. Statements by Denis Healey and Sir Fitzroy
    Maclean, H.C. Debates, Vol. 637, Cols. 46 and
    302-303; Philip Darby, British Defence Policy
    p. 222.
7. The Times(16 Feb., 1962); Sunday Times(25
    Feb., 1962); Christian Science Monitor(Dec.
    22, 1962); also, A. Verrier, An Army for the
    Sixties, p. 262, n. 10.
8. H.C. Debates, Vol. 704, cols. 425-6(16 Dec.,
    1964) and Vol. 707, cols. 1375-6(3 Mar.,
    1965); The Times(8,9 and 10 Dec., 1964);
    Darby, pp. 294-295.
9. The Times(3 Feb., 1966).
10. Cited in Richard Crossman, The Diaries of a
    Cabinet Minister, Vol. II(New York, 1977),
    p.646.
11. C. DeWitt Armstrong III, "The Strategy of the
    British Bases," Unpubl.Ph.D.Thesis, Princeton
    University, 1960, p. 37; Army League, p. 37.
12. The Times(15 Mar. and 28 July, 1960);Sir

Peter Gretton(Vice Adm.), Maritime Strategy, London, 1965), p. 50;Darby, British Defence Policy, p. 163.

13. Army League, p. 16; also, Alastaire Buchan, "Commonwealth Military Relations," in W. B. Hamilton and others, eds, A Decade of the Commonwealth 1955-64(London, 1966), p.203.

14. H.C. Debates, Vol.635, Col. 1202(Feb., 1961).

15. Darby, op.cit., p. 215: H.C. Debates, Vol. 655, Colls. 70 and 324(5 and 6 March, 1962) and Vol. 690, Cols. 469-70(27 Feb., 1964).

16. A. Verrier, "British Defense Policy under Labour, " Foreign Affairs, Vol. 42/2(Jan., 1964), pp. 282-292;The Times(3 March, 1965).

17. H. C. Debates, Vol. 707, Cols. 1369-70(3 Mar. 1965);The Guardian(19 March and 3 Aug.,1965); The Times(3 Aug., 1965); and The Report of the Sixty Fourth Annual Labour Conference (Sept.-Oct., 1965), pp. 186-201.

18. The Guardian(29 Sept. and 15 Oct., 1965); The Times(15 Oct., 1965); J.B. Kelly, Arabia, the Gulf and the West(N.Y., 1980), pp. 14 and 49.

19. Ibid., pp. 57-58.

20. H.C. Debates,Vol. 803, Col. 348(6 July,1970); Kelly, p. 91.

21. The Sunday Telegraph(3 Sept., 1961).

22. The Daily Telegraph(17 Dec., 1959): War Office Memorandum on the Army Estimates,1961-1962, Cmnd. 1280, para. 66; and The Times(21 May, 1956).

23. The Times(7 March, 1964).

24. The Guardian(12 Dec., 1962); The Daily Telegraph(28 Feb., 1962 and 20 Mar., 1963); MoD Statement on Defense for 1963, Cmnd 1936, p. 57, para. 68;W.O. Memo. on Army Estimates, 1962-63, Cmnd. 1631, para. 80.

25. The Times(11 July, 1962); for figures on number of troops transported, see H.C.Debates Vol. 644, Col. 1244(19 July, 1961); see also

N. Brown, Strategic Mobility(London, 1963), pp. 91-92.

26. N. Brown, "Disengaging in South East Asia," Survival, Vol. 8/no. 8(Aug., 1966), p. 256.

27. Statement by Dennis Healey, H.C. Debates, Vol. 705, Xol. 200(1 Feb., 1965).

28. MoD Statement on Defense for 1963, Cmnd. 1936 p. 71, para. 38-39; the same for 1964, Cmnd. 2270, para. 191 and Sir Kenneth Cross(Air Marshall), "Transport Command 1943-1964," RAF Quarterly, Vol. 4/2(Summer, 1964), p. 91.

29. A. Verrier, "Strategically Mobile Forces-- U.S. Theory and British Practice," Journal of the Royal United Service Institution(JRUSI), Vol. 106, No. 624(Nov., 1961), p. 484; Army League, "The Army Britain Needs," pp.28-29; and J. L. Moulton(Maj. Gen.), "The Real Cost: A Study on the Effectiveness of Overseas Forces," The Navy, Vol. 69, No. 11(Nov., 1964), p. 360.

30. Darby, British Defense Policy, p. 276.

31. The total cost of the three-carrier force was estimated to be 1.4 billion pounds over a ten year period, MoD Statement on Defense Est. for 1966, part 1; Defense Review Cmnd 2901, p. 10, para. 5; Liddell Hart, Deterrent or Defense, p. 127.

32. J. William Crowe(Cdr., U.S. Navy), "The Policy Roots of the Modern Royal Navy 1946- 63" (Unpubl. Ph.D. Thesis, Princeton, 1965).

33. Stephen Harper, Last Sunset(London, 1978), p. 54.

34. Ibid., p. 185.

35. The Times(27 Oct., 1961 and Jan. 3, 1964); The Observer(17 Sept., 1961); The Daily Telegraph(15 Nov., 1961).

36. Christopher Mayhew, Britain's Role Tomorrow, pp. 131 and 134.

37. Darby, British Defense Policy, p. 298.
38. H.C. Debates, Vol. 732, Cols. 632-633(July 20 1966).
39. The Sunday Times(23 April, 1967); MoD Suppl. Statement of Defense Policy for 1967, Cmnd 3357, 1967, p. 12, para. 1; H.C. Debates, Vol. 756, Cols. 1580-1585(16 Jan., 1968).
40. Kelly, Arabia, The Gulf and the West, pp. 12, 19, 41, 43.
41. Kelly, Ibid., p. 31.
42. Kelly, p. 43; H.C. Debates, Vol. 750, Col. 2494(20 July, 1967).
43. D. C. Watt, "The Decision to Withdraw...," Political Quarterly, Vol. 34, No. 3, p. 310.
44. Kelly, p. 50.
45. Ibid., p. 82.

CONCLUSION

A thorough review of Britain's withdrawal
from the Middle East and from other areas east of
Suez leads to a major conclusion, namely, that the
weakness of the British economy in the postwar era
weighed heavily in the recessional process. The
severe winter of 1947 made the crises even worse
and caused the Attlee government to withdraw from
Palestine even though the old rationale for maintaining bases in the Middle East had been the need
to safeguard the lifeline of the British Empire to
India. When India gained its independence, Middle
East bases no longer were essential to the
British. Nevertheless, British defense policy did
not follow such logic. Successive British governments continued to act as if the British Empire
remained intact and between 1945 and 1971 they
demonstrated extreme reluctance to liquidate the
empire. Strategists, expecially those in high
positions, managed to influence the Government to
change the deployment pattern of British forces
overseas. In the mid-fifties, the military
intellectuals assumed a great importance in the
formation of defense policy. For instance, Liddell
Hart said at that time: " Experience should have
taught us by now the folly of 'standing' on
crumbling sand castles all over the world."
Defense Minister Sandys became convinced. Thus,
his White Paper of 1957 ended a period of readjustment in defense policy which had begun in the
immediate postwar years.

The process of withdrawal from imperial bases
did not follow an uninterrupted course. As
Britain abandoned one base, the search for the
location of another had been begun. This was done
because the basic concepts at the heart of British
defense policy remained basically unchanged until
the mid-fifties. Successive British governments

felt obliged to defend sea communications and to safeguard the flow of oil from the Middle East. They believed that there was a need for airfields, repair facilities and training grounds for the army, as well as a strategic reserve even though the Cyprus base which they developed as a substitute for Suez was useless due to its long distance from the Canal Zone.

The ascendency of air power produced a crucial effect on defense thinking. It provided the government with the hope that the pattern of deployment could be altered without in any way jeopardizing the security of the British Empire. The emergence of air power was responsible for the relative neglect of the navy. For the first time in its history, the Royal Navy was deprived of funds which it deemed essential for its survival. The decrease in its budget made the Royal Navy a service of secondary importance at best.

Air power appeared to be capable of offering an alternative to troop dispersal throughout the Empire. Although the experience of the Second World War had proven that strategic bombing was rather ineffective, the belief that air power could provide a more efficient and a more economical way of dealing with local disturbances in overseas territories was adhered to throughout the entire period. The effect of changes in military deployment and the capabilities of atomic weapons made overseas bases more vulnerable and encouraged the belief that it was useless to continue to occupy them. The Royal Navy responded that it was capable of fulfilling an essential role in the nuclear age with the aircraft carrier which would replace stationary bases and could transport the strategic reserve rapidly from one theater of war to another. British strategists finally agreed that the strategic reserve, the strategic nuclear force and the aircraft carrier would make a quick, economical and efficient deployment of forces from the United Kingdom possible and thereby eliminate the need to maintain permanent bases overseas. Also, as the Admiralty argued, political problems inherent in fixed bases would be eliminated.

The Admiralty's proposals were eventually adopted by the Government not only because they were convincing, but also because the Navy enjoyed wide support in the Ministry of Defense. The pressure exerted by the Admiralty led the Foreign Office and the Colonial Office to review Britain's overseas responsibilities and to favor withdrawal. These arguments were accepted by the Cabinet in 1957.

The Suez debacle confirmed the Navy's claim regarding the role of the aircraft carrier because most Arab airfields could not be used for an invasion of Egypt. During the operation, aircraft had to operate from Cyprus; consequently, they were unable to stay longer than 15 minutes over the target areas before their dwindling fuel supplies forced them to return. Whereas the effectiveness of the Fleet Air Arm in the Suez operation exceeeded all expectations, land bases and airfields proved useless.

The Sandys White Paper on Defense of 1957 integrated the main concepts of defense into a coherent form. Its basic assumptions were that Britain was indefensible against nuclear attack, that the aim of British strategy was to prevent war rather than to win it and that the strategic deployment must be affected by the technological innovations. The White Paper also pointed out that Britain's influence in the world depended upon the stability of its economy and on its export trade. It stated that military expenditures must be determined in conjunction with the need to maintain the country's financial and

economic strength. It recognized that overseas
commitments constituted a very heavy burden and
that large bases should be abandoned. Also,
emphasis was laid on the need to abolish conscription.

Following the invasion of 1956, the Suez
Canal Zone was evacuated. What happened to the
claim made by British governments that oil was the
most important reason for maintaining a presence
in the Middle East? The argument that the Suez
was needed in order to safeguard the flow of oil
into the United Kingdom was invalid. Most Middle
Eastern oil was located in the Persian Gulf, the
Trucial Coast, Saudi Arabia and Iran. How could a
base in Suez safeguard the supplies of oil located
in such distant places? A massive base in the
Persian Gulf from which tankers could be sent to
the United Kingdom with escort ships could be much
more effective in safeguarding the flow of oil.
Furthermore, the oil resources were never under
serious threat until October 1973, and even then,
the threat was more political than military. Yet
it seems that the myth regarding the bases's role
in safeguarding the oil supplies was ingrained in
the minds of successive British leaders and played
a great part in defense policy formulation.

Oil became the preoccupation of strategic
thinking regarding the role of a Middle East
presence. Only a few people suggested that oil
could be better secured by agreements with states
in the area rather than by occupying forces. But
old habits of thought die hard. One could still
hear Eden saying as late as 1956 how important
Cyprus was in safeguarding the flow of oil from
the Middle East. It was true that the lack of oil
could have meant hunger in Britain, but it was a
mistake to argue that Cyprus guaranteed the
protection of that commodity.

The persistence of traditional values in

British society delayed withdrawal from Middle
East bases for two decades. No imperial power is
ready to admit that the hour of its demise has
arrived. For those British leaders raised on
imperial tradition, it was a painful readjustment
and a crushing defeat to realize this fact. Nevertheless, some historians have indicated that in
the mid-sixties the British public had become unwilling to pay the economic price of maintaining a
world role. It is difficult to find written evi-
dence, but, on the issue of withdrawal, public
opinion played a limited role at best. Had the
British government been adequately sensitive to
public opinion, the withdrawal process might have
been completed much earlier.

Historians who have dealt with the issue of
nationalism in Asia and Africa have argued that
even after Britain's withdrawal from colonial
areas the newly independent states preferred to
stay under British protection. However, with the
possible exception of some sheikhdoms in the
Persian Gulf, the inhabitants of the Middle East
did not demonstrate any desire to have ties with
Britain. Britain lost bases and training facilities in the Arab World. Also she was denied the
right to fly over certain countries of the Middle
East, a factor which further complicated matters
and compelled her to consider retreat.

Events which followed the decision made in
1954 to abandon the Suez base seem contradictory
to the arguments discussed in this study. One
might wonder why Eden's Government decided to
invade Egypt in 1956 when, barely two years
earlier, the Churchill Government had decided to
abandon the Suez Canal Zone. The explanation is
to be found in the domestic developments in Britain between those two events.

The Agreement of 1954 was the result of a
partial readjustment in defense policy. It

triggered conservative pressures to reinstate
British authority in the Middle East. The British
were critical of the conditions created by
Nasser's nationalization of the Suez Canal in
July, 1956. In 1954, Eden, then Foreign Minister
in Churchill's Government, had to defend the
Anglo-Egyptian Agreement against Conservative
critics. In 1956, as Prime Minister, he had to
yield to pressures demanding a punitive action
against Egypt. The main pressure came from a
substantial minority of Conservative M.P.'s, known
as the Suez Group, who insisted upon immediate
action against Nasser following his nationalization of the Canal. The Suez Group became more
influential because the Conservatives were in
power and had advocated strong action against
Nasser. Also, Eden was sensitive to charges of
appeasement. The memory of Munich made it
impossible for Eden to adopt such a policy. In
addition, the nationali- zation of the Canal and
Egypt's alignment with the Soviet Union generated
fear of a Soviet advance in the Middle East and
concern that the Soviets might induce the
Egyptians to deny Britain the use of the Canal.

The military reasons given for the Suez
operation were that the Suez Canal had to be kept
open, Nasser's power had to be undermined and the
Soviet Union had to be contained. In addition,
the oil supplies had to be safeguarded. Some of
these problems had been resolved in 1954 when the
agreement was signed. The Suez Canal was open
then and there was no fear that it might be closed
in the future. Furthermore, the Suez Agreement of
1954 guaranteed Britain's right to re-enter the
base in wartime. Churchill saw no danger to the
flow of oil supplies in 1954. In 1954 the new
Egyptian regime seemed cooperative. The British
Government believed that no danger was imminent in
the Middle East. The act of nationalization

dramatically changed that belief. From that moment on, there was a danger that the Canal might be closed at any time. As Eden saw it, the inability to use the Canal route meant that Britain might suddenly be compelled to shift all trade to the Cape route, an expensive and most inconvenient undertaking which Britain could not afford to assume.

After the Suez War, the British continued to maintain their presence in Aden, the Persian Gulf and other areas east of Suez throughout the sixties. The British remained in the Gulf region despite the worsening economic crisis at home until they finally realized that it was no longer possible to maintain these remnants of the Empire and that the Army was no longer capable of intervening in the affairs of Asian and African nations without a steady increase of its arsenal and manpower. Basically, as long as Britain's leaders had the confidence that financial and military means were at their disposal, they maintained a strong will to rule over foreign subjects, but when it became obvious that the means were no longer available, the desire to rule was undermined and withdrawal from Middle EAst bases became inevitable.

Government Publications*

Command 6743. "Statement Relating to Defense 1946." February 1946.

Command 7042. "Statement Relating to Defense 1947." February 1947.

Command 7327. "Statement Relating to Defense 1948." February 1948.

Command 7631. "Statement on Defense 1949." February 1949.

Command 7895. "Statement on Defense 1950." March 1950.

Command 8146 "Defense Program." January 1951.

Command 8475. "Statement on Defense 1952." February 1952.

Command 8768. "Statement on Defense 1953." February 1953.

Command 9075. "Statement on Defense 1954-55." February 1954.

Command 9391. "Statement on Defense 1955." February 1955.

Command 9691. "Statement on Defense, 1956-57." February 1956.

Command 124. "Defense Outline of Future Policy." April 1957.

Command 7054. "Statement of the First Lord of the Admiralty
        Explanatory of the Navy Estimates 1947-48." March 1947.

Command 7337. "Statement of the First Lord of the Admiralty
        Explanatory of the Navy Estimates 1948-49." February 1948.

Command 7632. "Statement of the First Lord of the Admiralty
        Explanatory of the Navy Estimates 1949-50." February 1949.

Command 7897. "Statement of the First Lord of the Admiralty
        Explanatory of the Navy Estimates 1950-51." February 1950.

Command 8160. "Statement of the First Lord of the Admiralty
        Explanatory of the Navy Estimates 1951-52." January 1951."

* All the items listed in this section were published by
Her Majesty's Stationary Office (H.M.S.O.), London.

Command 8476. "Statement of the First Lord of the Admiralty
        Explanatory of the Navy Estimates 1952-53." February 1952.

Command 8769. "Statement of the First Lord of the Admiralty
        Explanatory of the Navy Estimates 1953-54." February 1953.

Command 9079. "Statement of the First Lord of the Admiralty
        Explanatory of the Navy Estimates 1954-55." February 1954.

Command 9396. Statement of the First Lord of the Admiralty
        Explanatory of the Navy Estimates 1955-56." February 1955.

Command 9697. "Statement of the First Lord of the Admiralty
        Explanatory of the Navy Estimates 1956-57." February 1956.

Command 151. "Statement of the First Lord of the Admiralty
        Explanatory of the Navy Estimates 1957-58." April 1957.

Command 7053. "Memorandum by the Secretary of State for Air
        to Accompany Air Estimates 1947-48." 1947.

Command 7329. "Memorandum by the Secretary of State for Air
        to Accompany Air Estimates. 1948-49." 1948.

Command 7634. "Memorandum by the Secretary of State for Air
        to Accompany Air Estimates 1949-50." 1949.

Command 7898. "Memorandum by the Secretary of State for Air
        to Accompany Air Estimates 1950-51." 1950.

Command 8162. "Memorandum by the Secretary of State for Air
        to Accompany Air Estimates 1951-52." 1951.

Command 8474. "Memorandum by the Secretary of State for Air
        to Accompany Air Estimates 1952-53." 1952.

Command 8771. "Memorandum by the Secretary of State for Air
        to Accompany Air Estimates 1953-54." 1953.

Command 9076. "Memorandum by the Secretary of State for Air
        to Accompany Air Estimates 1954-55." 1954.

Command 9397. "Memorandum by the Secretary of State for Air
        to Accompany Air Estimates 1955-56." 1955.

Command 9696. "Memorandum by the Secretary of State for Air
        to Accompany Air Estimates 1956-57." 1956.

Command 149. "Memorandum by the Secretary of State for Air
        to Accompany Air Estimates 1957-58." 1957.

Command 7052. "Memorandum of the Secretary of State for
        War relating to the Army Estimates 1947-48," 1947.

Command 7332 "Memorandum of the Secretary of State for
        War relating to the Army Estimates 1948-49," 1948.

Command 7633 "Memorandum of the Secretary of State for
        War relating to the Army Estimates 1949-50," 1949.

Command 7896. "Memorandum of the Secretary of State for
        War relating to the Army Estimates 1950-51," 1950.

Command 8161 "Memorandum of the Secretary of State for
        War relating to the Army Estimates 1951-52," 1951.

Command 8477 "Memorandum of the Secretary of State for
        War relating to the Army Estimates 1952-53," 1952.

Command 8770 "Memorandum of the Secretary of State for
        War relating to the Army Estimates 1953-54," 1953.

Command 9072 "Memorandum of the Secretary of State for
        War relating to the Army Estimates 1954-55, 1954.

Command 9395 "Memorandum of the Secretary of State for
        War relating to the Army Estimates 1955-56, 1955.

Command 9688 "Memorandum of the Secretary of State for
        War relating to the Army Estimates 1956-57," 1956.

Command 150 "Memorandum of the Secretary of State for
        War relating to the Army Estimates 1957-58," 1957.

Command 6923 "Central Organization for Defence" December 1946.

Command 8146 "Defence Programme: Statement made by the
        Prime Minister in the House of Commons on Monday
        29 January 1951", 1951.

Command 9388. "The Supply of Military Aircraft." February 1955.

Command 9389. "A Program of Nuclear Power." February 1955.

Command 9789. "Agreement between United Kingdom and United
        States for Cooperation on Civil Uses of Atomic Energy
        for Mutual Defense." June 1955.

Command 363. "Report on Defence: Britain's Contribution to
        Peace and Security," 1958.

Great Britain, Ministry of Supply, Division of Atomic Energy
        and Central Office of Information, Britain's Atomic
        Factories: The Story of Atomic Energy Production in
        Britain by K.E.B. Jay, H.M.S.O., 1954.

_____ Ministry of Supply and Central Office of Information
        Harwell; The British Atomic Energy Research Establishment
        H.M.S.O. 1952.

House of Commons Debates (Hansard: 5th Series)

House of Lords Debates (Hansard; 5th Series)

Reports from Select Committees on Estimates
        House of Commons, Select Committee on Estimate.

Second Report . . . Session 1948-9: the defence estimates, 1950.

Seventeenth Report . . . Session 1948-9; the defence estimates,
        1950.

Third Report . . . Session 1952-53; call up posting and move-
        ment of national service men.

Books and Pamphlets

Adams, Michael. Suez and After. Boston; Beacon Pres , 1958.

Allen, H.R.. The Legacy of Lord Trenchard. London; Cassel,
    1972.

Army League. The Army in the Nuclear Age. Barnet, Herts Stellar
    Press, 1955.

Asbell, Bernard. The F.D.R. Memoirs. Garden City, New York;
    Doubleday, 1973.

Attlee, C.R. As It Happened. London; Heinemann, 1954.

_____ Purpose and Policy: Selected Speeches. New York;
    Hutchinson, 1947.

Barclay, C.N. (Brig). The First Commonwealth Division: The Story
    of the British Commonwealth land forces in Korea; 1950-
    1953. Aldershot; Gale and Polden, 1954.

Barker, A.J. Suez: The Seven Day War. London; Faber and
    Faber, 1964.

Barker, Elizabeth. Britain in a Divided Europe 1945-70. London;
    Weidenfeld and Nicholson, 1971.

Barnett, Correlli. Britain and Her Army: 1509-1970. New York;
    W. Morrow, 1970.

_____ The Collapse of British Power. New York; Morrow,
    1972.

Bartlett, C.J. The Long Retreat; A History of British Defense
    Policy 1940-1970. New York; St. Martin Press, 1972.

Baylis, John and Others. Contemporary Strategy: Theories
    and Politics. New York; Holmes and Meir, 1975.

Beaufre, Andre (General d'Armée). Deterrence and Strategy.
    New York; Praeger, 1966.

Bell, Coral. The Debatable Alliance: An Essay in Anglo American
     Relations. London; Oxford University Press, 1964.

Beloff, Max. Imperial Sunset. London; Methuen, 1969.

_____ The Future of British Foreign Policy. London;
     Secker and Warburg, 1969.

_____ New Dimension in Foreign Policy: A Study in British
     Administrative Experience; 1947-59. New York; The Mac-
     millan Co., 1961.

Bentwich, Norman and Helen. Mandate Memoirs; 1918-1948. New
     York; Schocken Books, 1965.

"Biographical Summary" in The Theory and Practice of War.
     Michael Howard (ed.) London; Cassell, 1965.

Blackett, P.M.S. Atomic Weapons and East-West Relations. New
     York; Cambridge University Press, 1956.

_____ Fear War, and the Bomb. New York; McGraw Hill, 1949.

_____ Studies of War: Nuclear and Conventional. London;
     Oliver and Boyd, 1962.

Blaxland,,Gregory. The Regiments Depart: A History of the Brit-
     ish Army 1945-1970. London; Kimber, 1971.

Booth, Ken. Navies and Foreign Policy. London; Croom Helm, 1977.

Borden,L. William. There Will be No Time: The Revolution in
     Strategy. New York; The Macmillan Co., 1946.

Bowie, R. Suez 1956: International Crises and the Role of Law.
     London; Oxford University Press, 1974.

Bowman,G. War in the Air. London; Evans, 1956.

Boyle, Andrew. Trenchard. London; Collins, 1962.

Brady, A. Robert. Crisis in Britain. London; Cambridge Univ-
     ersity Press, 1950.

Braudel, Fernand. La Mediterranée et le Monde Mediterrnéen
     a l'epocque de Phillipe II. Paris; Librairie Armand
     Colin, 1949.

Broad, Lewis. Winston Churchill: The Years of Achievement:
    A Biography. New York; Hawthorne Books, 1958.

Brodie, Bernard. A Guide to Naval Strategy. Princeton;
    Princeton University Press, 1958.

_____ Sea Power in the Machine Age. Princeton; Princeton
    University Press, 1941.

_____ Strategy in the Missile Age. Princeton; Princeton
    University Press, 1958.

_____ "Technological Change, Strategic Doctrine and Political
    Outcomes" in Historical Dimensions of National Secur-
    ity Problems. Klaus Knorr (ed.) Kansas; University
    Press of Kansas, 1976.

Brogan, Colm. Suez: Who Was Right? London; Coram Publishers,
    1957.

Brogan, D.W. The English People. New York; Knopf, 1943.

Bromberger, Merry and Serge. Secrets of Suez. London; Pan
    Books; Sigwick and Jackson, 1957.

Brown, Neville. Arms Without Empire. Harmondsworth; Penguin
    Books, 1967.

_____ Britain and World Security. London; Fabian Society 1966.
    (Fabian Research Series No. 258)

_____ Strategic Mobility. London; Chatto and Windus, 1963.

Bryant, Sir Arthur. Triumph in the West 1943-1946. London;
    Collins, 1959.

_____ The Turn of the Tide. New York; Doubleday, 1957.

Bullard, Sir Reader. Britain and the Middle East. London;
    Hutchinson, 1964.

Burns, A.L. "Military Technology and International Politics"
    in Yearbook of World Affairs, 1961.

Bushby, John. Air Defence of Great Britain. London; Allan,
    1973.

Buzzard, Sir Anthony W. (R.A.) and Others. On Limiting Atomic
    War. London; RIIA, 1956.

Campbell, John C. Defense of the Middle East. New York; Harper,
    1960.

Carrington, C.E. The British Overseas. Cambridge; Cambridge
    University Press, 1950.

_____ The Liquidation of the British Empire. London;
    Harrap, 1961.

Chatfield, A.E.M. The Navy and Defence, The Autobiography II:
    It Might Happen Again. London; Heinemann, 1947.

Childers, B. Erskine. The Road to Suez. London; MacGibbon
    and Kee, 1962.

Christoph B. James (ed.) "The Suez Crisis" in Cases in Compar-
    ative Politics. Boston; Little, Brown, 1969.

Churchill, Sir Winston. The Second World War. London; Cassell
    1948-54 vol. III.

Cippola M. Carlo. The Economic Decline of Empires. London;
    Methuen, 1970.

Clark, R.W. Tizard. London; Methuen, 1965.

Cole, G.D.H. Political and Economic Planning: Growth in the
    British Economy. London; Allen & Unwin, 1960.

_____ The Postwar Condition of Britain. London; Routledge and
    Kegan Paul., 1956.

Collier, Basil. The Defence of the United Kingdom. London;
    H.M.S.O., 1957.

_____ The Lion and the Eagle: British and Anglo-American
    Strategy 1900-1950. New York; Capricorn Books, 1973.

Cooke, Colin. The Life of Richard Stafford Cripps. London;
    Hodder and Stoughton, 1957.

Council on Foreign Relations, New York and RIIA. Britain and
    the United States: Problem in Cooperation. London;
    RIIA, 1953.

Courte, W.H.B. A Concise Economic History of Britain. London;
    Cambridge University Press, 1954.

Creswell, John (Cap.) Generals and Admirals. London; Longmans
    and Green, 1952.

Crosland, C.A.R. Britain's Economic Problem. London; Cape,
    1953.

Crossman, R.S. Palestine Mission: A Personal Record. New
    York and London; Harper and Brothers, 1947.

Dalton, Hugh. High Tide and After: Memoirs, III 1945-1960.
    London; Muller, 1962.

Darby, Philip. British Defense Policy East of Suez: 1947-1968.
    London; Oxford University Press, 1973.

Day, A.C.L. The Future of the Sterling. London; Oxford University
    Press, 1954.

De Kadt J. Emannel. British Defence Policy and Nuclear War.
    London; Frank Cass, 1964.

Dikens, Sir Gerald (Ad) Bombing and Strategy. London; Sampson
    Low, 1946.

Domvill-Fife Charles W. (ed.) Evolution of Sea Power. London;
    Rich and Cowen, 1939.

Dow, J.C.R. The Management of the British Economy 1940-60.
    London; Cambridge University Press, 1964.

Earle M. Edward. Makers of Modern Strategy: Military Thought
    from Machiavelli to Hitler. Princeton, Princeton
    University Press, 1943.

Eden, Sir Anthony. The Memoirs III: Full Circle. London;
    Cassell, 1960.

Epstein, L.D. Britain-Uneasy Ally. Chicago; University of
    Chicago Press, 1954.

_____ British Politics in the Suez Crisis. University of
    Illinois Press, 1964.

Esotric, Eric. Stafford Cripps: Master Statesman. London;
     Heinemann, 1949.

Feiling, Keith. The Life of Nevill Chamberlain. London;
     Macmillan And Co., Ltd., 1946.

Finer, Herman. Dulles over Suez. London; Heinemann, 1954.

Finer, S.E. and Others. Backbench Opinion in the House of
     Commons: 1955-59. Oxford; Pergamon Press, 1961.

Fitzsimons, M.A. Empire By Treaty: Britain and the Middle East
     in the Twentieth Century. Indiana, Indiana University
     Press, 1964.

_____ The Foreign Policy of the British Labour Government
     1945-51. Notre Dame, Indiana; University of Notre Dame
     Press, 1953.

Fletcher, Raymond. £60 a Second on Defense. London; MacGibbon
     and Kee, 1963.

Foot, Michael. Aneurin Bevan: A Biography. New York; Atheneum,
     1963.

Foot, M.R.D. Men in Uniform: Military Manpower in Modern
     Industrial Societies. London; Weidenfeld and Nicolson,
     1961.

Frankel, Joseph. British Foreign Policy: 1945-1973. London;
     Oxford University Press, 1975.

_____ The Making of Foreign Policy. London; Oxford Univer-
     sity Press, 1963.

Franks, Sir Oliver. Britain and the Tide of World Affairs.
     London; Oxford University Press, 1955.

Fuller, J.F.C. (Maj. Gen.) The Conduct of War. London; Eyre
     and Spottiswood, 1961.

_____ The Reformation of War. London; Hutchinson, 1923.

_____ The Second World War. New York; Duell, Sloan and
     Pearce, 1949.

Gaitskell, Hugh. The Politics of Western Defense. New York;
        Praeger, 1962.

Garbutt E. Paul. Naval Challenge 1945-1961. London; Mac-
        donald, 1961.

Gelber, Lionel. America in Britain's Place: The Leadership
        of the West and Anglo-American Unity. New York;
        Praeger, 1961.

Gibbs, N.H. "British Strategic Doctrine 1918-1939" in Michael
        Howard (ed.) The Theory and Practice of War. London;
        Cassell, 1965.

Gibson M. Irving, "Maginot and Liddell Hart" in Earle E. Mead
        The Makers of Modern Strategy. Princeton; Princeton
        University Press, 1971.

Gilbert B. Bently. Britain Since 1918. New York; Harper &
        Row, 1967.

Goldstein, Walter. The Dilemma of British Defense: The Imbal-
        ance Between Commitments and Resources. Columbus:
        Ohio State University Press, 1966. (Hershon Center
        for Education in National Security, Pamphlet series No. 3)

Goldsworthy, D. Colonial Issues in British Politics 1945-
        1961: From Colonial Development to 'Wind of Change'
        Oxford; Clarendon Press, 1971.

Goodwin, L. Geoffrey. Britain and the United States. New York;
        Mahatten Publ. Co., 1957.

Goold-Adams Richard. The British Army in the Nuclear Age.
        Barnett Herts, The Stellar Press, 1959.

Goold-Adams Richard; Buzzard, Anthony; Blackett, P.M.S. and
        Healey, Denis. "On Limiting Atomic War" R.I.I.A. Lon-
        don; R.I.I.A., 1956.

Gowing, Margaret. Britain and Atomic Energy. London; The
        Macmillan Company, 1964.

Graham G. Gerald. The Politics of Naval Supremacy. Cambridge;
        Cambridge University Press, 1965.

Gregg, Pauline. Modern Britain; A Social and Economic History
    Since 1760. New York; Pagasus, 1966.

Gretton, Sir Peter (V.A.) Maritime Strategy: A Study of British
    Defense Problems. London; Praeger,. 1965.

Green, William and Fricker, John. The Air Forces of the
    World. London; Macdonald, 1950.

Groom, A.J.R. British Thinking About Nuclear Weapons. London;
    F. Pinter, 1974.

Groom, A.J.R. and Edmonds, Martin. "British Defense Policy Since
    1945" in A Guide to the Sources of British Military
    History, Higham Robin (ed.) Berkeley: University of
    California Press, 1971.

Gupta, S. Partha. Imperialism and British Labour Government
    1914-1964. New York; Holmes and Meier, 1975.

Gutteridge, William. Armed Forces in New States. London;
    Oxford University Press, 1962.

Guttsman, W. The British Political Elite. London; MacGibbon
    and Kee, 1963.

Gwynn W. Charles (Maj. Gen.) Imperial Policy. London; Macmillan,
    1939.

Gwynne, A. Jones. "The British Army Since 1945" in The Theory
    and Practice of War, Michael Howard (ed.) London; Cas-
    sell, 1965.

_____ "Training and Doctrine in the British Army Since 1945"
    Ibid.

Hacket, John and Anne-Marie. The British Economy. London;
    Allen and Unwin, 1967.

Hailsham Q. Hogg. The Case for Conservatism. West Drayton,
    Middlesex: Penguin,1948.

Halle J. Lewis. The Cold War as History. London; Chatto
    and Windus, 1967.

Hampshire A. Cecil. The Royal Navy: Its Transition to
        Nuclear Age. London; Kimber, 1975.

Hancock, W.K. British War Economy. London; H.M.S.O., 1949.

_____ Survey of British Commonwealth Affairs Vol. 2 Part I,
        London; Oxford University Press, 1940.

Harris, Sir Arthur (MRAF) Bomber Offensive, London; Collins,
        1947.

Harris, C.F. (ACM) "Marshal of the Royal Air Force Lord Tedder"
        in The War Lords: Military Commanders in the Twentieth
        Century. F.M. Carver Michael (ed.) Bonston; Little
        Brown and Company, 1976.

Harrod, Sir Roy. The British Economy. New York; McGraw
        Hill, 1963.

Hartley, Anthony. A State of England. London; Hutchinson and Co.
        Ltd., 1963.

Healey, Denis, "Britain and NATO" in NATO and the American Se-
        curity. Klaus Knorr (ed.) Princeton; Princeton
        University Press, 1959.

Higham Robin. The Military Intellectuals in Britain 1918-
        1939. New Brunswick; Rutgers University Press, 1966.

Hinsley, F.H. Command of the Sea. London; Christopher, 1950.

Hobsbawm, E.J. Industry and Empire. Bungay Suffolk;
        The Chaucher Press, 1975.

Howard, Michael. Disengagement in Europe. London; Penguin, 1958.

_____ Soldiers and Government. London; Eyre and Spottiswoode,
        1957.

_____ Strategy and Policy in Twentieth Century Warfare.
        Colorado Springs; U.S. Air Force Academy, 1967.

_____ (ed.) Studies in International Security in Problems
        of Modern Strategy. New York, 1970.

_____ (ed.) The Theory and Practice of War, Essays Presented to Captain B.H. Liddell Hart. London; Cassell, 1965.

Huntington, S.P. The Common Defense: Strategic Programs in National Politics. New York; Columbia University Press, 1961.

Hurewitz, J.C. The Struggle for Palestine. New York; Greenwood Press, 1968.

Jacob, Sir Ian (Maj. Gen.) "The United Kingdom's Strategic Interests" in United Kingdom Policy; Foreign Strategic, Economic. London/ R.I.I.A., 1950.

James R. Rhodes. Winston S. Churchill: His Complete Speeches 1897-1960. New York and London; Chelsea House Publishers and R.R. Bowker Co., 1974.

James, Sir William (Ad) The Influence of Sea Power Upon the History of the British People. Cambridge; Cambridge University Press, 1948.

Jane's Fighting Ships (Annual). New York, McGraw Hill Book G. Inc.

Jensen, L. "Postwar Democratic Politics: National, International Linkages in Defense Policies of the Defeated States" in Linkages Politics, J. Rosenau (ed.) New York; Free Press, 1969.

Johnson, Paul. The Suez War. London; MacGibbon and Kee, 1957.

Kahn, A.E. Great Britain in the World Economy. New York; Columbia University Press, 1950.

Kelsall, R.K. The Higher Civil Servant in Britain From 1870 to the Present Day. London; Routledge and Kegan Paul Ltd., 1955.

Kemp, P.K. (Lt. Cdr.) Key to Victory. Boston; Little, Brown; 1957.

Kennan F. George. Russia, the Atom and the West. London; Oxford University Press, 1958.

Kennedy, John (Maj. Gen.) The Business of War. London; Hutchinson, 1957.

Kimche, Jon. Seven Fallen Pillars: The Middle East 1945-1952.
      New York; De Capo Press, 1976.

King Hall, Stephen. Defense in the Nuclear Age. London;
      Gollancz, 1958.

Kingston-McCloughry, E.J. (A.V.M.) Defence. London; Stevens,
      1960.

_____ Defence Policy and Strategy. London; Stevens, 1960.

_____ The Direction of War. New York; Praeger, 1955.

_____ Global Strategy. London; Cape, 1957.

_____ Winged Warfare. London; Cape, 1937.

Kirby, Stephen. "Britain's Defense Policy and N.A.T.O." in
      Constraints and Adjustments in British Foreign Policy,
      Michael Leifer (ed.) London; Allen & Unwin, 1972.

Kissinger, A. Henry. Nuclear Weapons and Foreign Policy. New
      York; Council on Foreign Relations, 1957.

Knorr, Klaus. Military Power and Potential. Lexington; Heath
      Lexington Books, 1970.

Koestler, Arthur (ed.) Suicide of a Nation? An Enquiry into
      the State of Britain Today. New York; Macmillan, 1964.

Laqueur, Walter. History of Zionism. New York; Holt Reinhart &
      Winston, 1972.

Leifer, Michael (ed.) Constraints and Adjustments in British
      Foreign Policy. London; Allen and Unwin, 1972.

Leruez, Jacques. Economic Planning and Politics in Britain.
      New York; Barnes and Noble, 1976.

Lewis, Michael. The History of the British Navy. Fair Lawn;
      New Jersey, 1959.

Lewis, Roy and Maude, Angus. The English Middle Class. New
      York; Knopf, 1950.

Leyland, John. The Royal Navy: Its Influence in English
     History and the Growth of Empire. London; Cambridge
     University Press, 1914.

Liddell Hart B.H. The British Way in Warfare. London; Faber and
     Faber, 1933.

_____ The Defence of Britain. New York; Random House, 1939.

_____ Defence of the West. London; Cassell, 1950.

_____ Deterrent or Defence. London; Stevens, 1960.

_____ Dynamic Defence. London; Faber and Faber, 1940.

_____ Memoirs: 1895-1938. New York; Putnam, 1965.

_____ Paris or the Future of War. London; E.P. Dutton &
     Co., 1925.

_____ Revolution in Warfare. London; Faber and Faber, 1946.

_____ Strategy. New York; Praeger, 1955.

Lloyd, T.O. Empire To Welfare State: English History 1906-1967.
     New York and Oxford; Oxford University Press, 1970.

Lloyd, Christopher. The Nation and the Navy: A History of Naval
     Life and Policy. London; Casset Press, 1954.

Luuvas, Jay. The Education of An Army: British Military Thought
     1815-1940. Chicago: University of Chicago Press, 1964.

Macmillan, Harold. Memoirs III, Tides of Fortune 1945-1955.
     London; Macmillan, 1969.

Mahan, Alfred Thayer. The Influence of Sea Power Upon History:
     1660-1783. Boston; Little, Brown & Co., 1890.

_____ The Influence of Sea Power Upon The French Revolution.
     Boston; Little, Brown & Co., 1892.

_____ Problems of Asia. New York & London; Kennikat Press, 1900.

Mansergh, Nicholas. Survey of British Commonwealth Affairs IV:
     Problems of Wartime Cooperation and Postwar Change 1939-
     1952. London; Oxford University Press, 1958.

Marder, A.J. The Anatomy of British Sea Power: A History of
    British Naval Policy in the Pre Dreadnought Era 1880-
    1905. London; Frank Cass, 1964.

Marlowe, John. Arab Nationalism and British Imperialism. Lon-
    don; Cresset Press, 1961.

_____ A History of Modern Egypt and Anglo Egyptian Relations:
    1800-1956. Hamden, Conn.; Archon Books, 1965.

Martin, L.W. "British Defense Policy; The Long Recessional",
    London Institute of Strategic Studies, 1969. (Also;
    in Adelphi Papers No. 61, Nov. 1969)

_____ The Sea Power in Modern Strategy. London; Chatto and
    Windus, 1967.

Marwick, Arthur. Britain in the Century of Total War. Boston,
    Little, Brown, 1968.

Mayer, J. Arno. "Domestic Causes of the First World War" in
    The Responsibility of Power. L. Krieger (ed.) Garden
    City, New York; Doubleday, 1967, pp. 286-300.

McClintock, R.M. The Meaning of Limited War. Boston; Houghton
    Mifflin, 1967.

McDermot, Geoffrey. Leader Lost: A Biography of Hugh Gaitskell.
    Princeton, Vertex Books, 1971.

Medlicott, W.N. British Foreign Policy Since Versailles 1919-63.
    London; Methuen, 1968.

Meehan, Eugene. The British Left Wing and Foreign Policy.
    New Brunswick, N.J.; Rutgers University Press, 1961.

Millis, Walter (ed.) The Forestal Diaries. New York; Viking
    Press, 1951.

Minney, R.J. The Private Papers of Hore-Belisha. London;
    Collins, 1960.

Monroe, Elizabeth. Britain's Moment in the Middle East 1914-
    1956. London; Methuen, 1965.

_____ "Mr. Bevin's 'Arab policy'" in Middle Eastern Affairs.
    A. Hourani (ed.) London; Chatto and Windus, 1961.

Montgomery, B.L. (Field Marshal Lord Montgomery of Alamein)
     Memoirs. London; Collins, 1958.

Morgenthau, J. Hans. Politics Among Nations: The Struggle for
     Peace and Power. New York; Praeger, 1973.

Morrison, S. Herbert. An Autobiography. London; Odhams Press,
     1960.

_____ Government and Parliament: A Survey from the Inside.
     New York; Oxford University Press, 1954.

Moulton, J.L. Defence in a Changing World. London; Eyre and
     Spottiswoode, 1954.

Murphy, J.T. Labour Big Three. London; Bodley Head, 1948.

Murphy, Robert. Diplomats Among Warriors. London; Collins, 1954.

Murray, Sir Oswyn. The Admiralty. London; Putnam's, 1939.

Nicholas, H.G. Britain and the United States. London; Chatto
     and Windus, 1963.

Northedge, F.S. British Foreign Policy: The Process of
     Readjustment 1945-1961. London; Allen and Enwin, 1962.

Nutting, Anthony. No End of a Lesson: The Story of Suez. London;
     Constable, 1967.

O'Ballance, E. Malaya: The Communist Insurgence War. London;
     London; Faber, 1966.

_____ The Sinai Campaign: 1956. London; Faber and Faber, 1956.

Own, Charles. No More Heroes: The Royal Navy in the Twentieth
     Century: Anatomy of a Legend. London; Allen and Unwin,
     1975.

Palestine: Termination of the Mandate (May 15, 1948). London;
     H.S.M.O., 1948.

Peacock, T. Allen and Wiseman, J. The Growth of Public Ex-
     penditure in the United Kingdom. Princeton; Princeton
     University Press, 1961.

Pierre J. Andrew. Nuclear Politics: The British Experience With
    An Independent Strategic Force 1939-1970. London;
    Oxford University Press, 1972.

Pile, Sir Frederick. "Liddell Hart and the British Army" in
    Theory and Practice of War. Michael Howard (ed.)
    London; Cassell, 1965.

Pollard, Sidney. The Development of the British Economy 1914-
    1967. London; Edward Arnold, 1969.

Polmar, Norman. Aircraft Carrier: A Graphic History of Carrier
    Aviation and Its Influence on World Events. Garden City,
    New York; Doubleday, 1969.

Postan, M.M. British War Production. London; H.M.S.O., 1952.

Potter, Allen. Organized Groups in British National Politics.
    London; Faber, 1961.

Pratt, Fletcher. Empire and the Sea. New York; H. Holt and
    Co., 1946.

_____ Sea Power and Today's War. New York; Harrison-Hilton
    Books, Inc., 1939.

Puleston, W.D. (Cap.) The Life and Work of Captain Alfred Thayer
    Mahan. New Haven; Yale University Press, 1939.

Rees, David. Korea: The Limited War. Macmillan and Co., Ltd.,
    1964.

Report of the Annual Conference of the Labour Party, 1947.

Reynolds, G. Clark. Command of the Sea: The History and Strategy
    of Maritime Empires. New York; Morrow and Co., Inc., 1974.

Richmond, Sir Herbert (Ad). Statesmen and Sea Power. Oxford;
    Clarendon, 1946.

R.I.I.A. Atomic Energy, Its International Implications.
    London, New York, 1948.

_____ British Interests in the Mediterranean and the Middle
    East. London, Oxford University Press, 1958.

_____ British Security: A Report by a Chatham House Study
Group. London, 1946.

_____ Defence in the Cold War. London, 1950.

_____ Documents on European Recovery and Defence: 1947-9.
London; New York, 1949.

_____ Political and Strategic Interests of the United Kingdom.
Oxford University Press, 1939.

_____ United Kingdom Policy: Foreign, Strategic, Economic.
Appreciations by Professor Sir Charles Webster, Major
General Sir Ian Jacob and E.A.G. Robinson. London, 1950.

_____ The United Kingdom Strategic Interests. London; 1950.

Robertson, Terence. Crisis: The Inside Story of the Suez
Conspiracy. London; Hutchinson, 1965.

Rosecrance, R.N. Defense of the Realm: British Strategy in
the Nuclear Epoch. New York; Columbia University Press.
1968.

Rosenau, N. James (ed.) Domestic Sources of Foreign Policy.
New York; Free Press, 1967.

Roskill, S.W. (Cap. R.N.) The Strategy of Sea Power. London;
Collins, 1962.

_____ The War at Sea, vol. I-III. London, H.M.S.O., 1959-60.

_____ White Ensign: The British Navy at War 1939-1945.
Annapolis; U.S. Naval Institute, 1960.

Russel, S. Donald. The Empire and Commonwealth Yearbook. London;
1953.

Sabine, J. British Defence Policy. London; Allen and Unwin,
1969.

Sacher, M. Howard. Europe Leaves the Middle East 1936-1954.
New York; Knopf, 1972.

Sampson, Anthony. Anatomy of Britain. New York; Harper and
        Row, 1962.

_____ Anatomy of Britain Today. New York; Harper and Row,
        1965.

_____ The New Anatomy of Britain. New York; Stein and Day,
        1971.

Shanks, Michael. The Stagnant Society: A Warning. London;
        Penguin, 1961.

Shinwell, Emanuel. Conflict Without Malice. London; Odhams,
        1955.

_____ I've Lived Through It All. London; Gollancz, 1973.

_____ The Labour Story. London; Macdonald, 1963.

Shofield, B.B. (V.A.) The Royal Navy Today. London; Oxford
        University Press, 1960.

Shonfield, Andrew. British Economic Policy Since The War.
        London; Penguin, 1958.

Shwadran, Benjamin. The Middle East: Oil and the Great Powers.
        New York; Praeger, 1955.

Slessor, Sir John (M.R.A.F.) Strategy for the West. London;
        Cassell, 1954.

_____ The Central Blue. London; Cassell, 1956.

_____ The Great Deterrent. New York; Praeger, 1957.

Snow, C.P. Science and Government. Cambridge; Harvard University
        Press, 1961.

Snyder, P. William. The Politics of British Defense Policy 1945-
        -1962. Columbus; Ohio State University Press, 1964.

Sprout, T. Margaret. "Mahan: Evangelist of Sea Power" in Makers
        of Modern Strategy. Earle Mead (ed.) Princeton;
        Princeton University Press, 1971.

Stewart, J.D. British Pressure Groups: Their Role in Relation to the House of Commons. Oxford; Clarendon Press, 1958.

Stewart, Michael. Policy and Weapons in the Nuclear Age. London; Fabian Society. 1955.

Strachey, John. The End of Empire. London; Victor Gollanz, 1959.

Strang, Lord William. Home and Abroad. London; Deutsch, 1956.

_____ Britain in World Affairs. New York; Praeger, 1961.

Straus, Eric. European Reckoning. London; Allen and Unwin, 1962.

Sykes, Christopher. Crossroads to Israel. Ohio; World Pub., Co., 1965.

Tedder, Lord A.V. (M.R.A.F.) Air Power in War. Westport, Conn.; Greenwood Press, 1975.

_____ With Prejudice: The War Memoirs. London; Cassell, 1966.

Templewood, Viscount (Sir Samuel Hoare). Empire of the Air: The Advent of the Air Age 1922-1929. London; Collins, 1957.

Terrain, John. The Life and Times of Lord Mountbatten. London; Hutchinson, 1968.

Thayer, George. The British Political Fringe. London; A. Blond, 1965.

Thetford, Owen. Aircraft of the Royal Air Force Since 1918. London; Putnam, 1968.

Thornton, A.P. The Imperial Idea and Its Enemies. London; Macmillan, 1959.

Truman, S. Harry. Memoirs II: Years of Trial and Hope. Garden City, New York; Doubleday, 1956.

Tuker, Sir Francis (Lt. Gen.) While Memory Serves. London; Cassell, 1950.

_____ The Pattern of War. London; Cassell, 1948.

Turner, B. Gordon (ed.) A History of Military Affairs in Western
     Society Since the Eighteenth Century. New York; Harcourt,
     Brace and Co., 1952, 1953.

Vaizy. John. The Cost of Social Services. London; Fabian
     Research Series No. 166, 1954.

Verrier, Anthony. An Army for the Sixties. London; Secker &
     Warburg, 1966.

Vital, David. The Making of British Foreign Policy. London;
     Allen and Unwin, 1958.

Walters, E. Robert. Sea Power and the Nuclear Fallacy. New
     York; Holmes and Meier, 1975.

Warburg, P. James. Crosscurrent in the Middle East. New York;
     Atheneum, 1968.

Ward, Barbara. "Despite Austerity Britain Still Faces a Crisis"
     in Britain 1919-1970. John F. Naylor (ed.) New York
     Times Books, Chicago, 1971.

Warner, Edward. "Douchet, Mitchell, Seversky's Theories of
     Air Warfare" in Makers of Modern Strategy. E.M. Earle
     (ed.). Princeton; Princeton University Press, 1943.

Watt, D.C. "Britain and the Suez Canal." London; R.I.I.A.,
     August 1956.

Williams, Francis. Ernest Bevin: Portraing of a Great English-
     man. London; Hutchinson, 1952.

_____ Press, Parliament and People. London; Heinemann,
     1946.

_____ A Prime Minister Remembers; The War and Postwar Memoirs
     of the Rt. Hon. Earl Attlee . . . London; Heinemann,
     1961.

_____ Socialist Britain. New York; Viking Press, 1949.

_____ Twilight of Empire: Memoirs of Prime Minister Clement
     Attlee. New York; A.S. Barnes and Co., 1962.

Windrich, Elaine. British Labour's Foreign Policy. Stamford;
    Stanford University Press, 1952.

Woodcock, George. Who Killed The British Empire?
    An Inquest. New York; Quadrangle, 1974.

Woodhouse, C.M. British Foreign Policy Since the Second World
    War. London; Hutchinson, 1961.

Worcester, Richard. The Roots of British Air Policy. London,
    Hodder and Stoughton, 1966.

Worswick, G.D.N. and Ady, P.H. (eds.) The British Economy in
    The Nineteen Fifties. London; Oxford University Press,
    1962.

_____ The British Economy 1945-1950. New York; McGraw-
    Hill, 1963.

Younger, Kenneth. Changing Perspectives in British Foreign
    Policy. London; Oxford University Press, 1964.

Youngton, A.J. The British Economy 1920-1957. Cambridge;
    Harvard University Press, 1960.

Zasloff, J. Jermiah. Great Britain and Palestine. Muncheun;
    Verlagshaus der Amerikanischen Hochkommission, 1952.

Zinkin, Maurice and Taya. Britain and India: Requiem for Empire.
    London; Chatto and Windus, 1964.

Articles

Air Power. "The Air Forces in Parliament: Defence Policy" vol. 4 (April 1957) pp. 231-4.

Alanbrooke (Alan Francis Brook, Lord) "Empire Defense", JRUSI 92/566 (May 1947) pp. 182-6.

Amery, Julian. "Hold on to Suez," Time and Tide vol. 35 (24 July 1954) pp. 981-3.

The 76th Annual Report of the Conservative Conference, 1956.

Armstrong C. DeWitt. "The British Re-Value their Strategic Bases" JRUSI 104/616 (Nov. 1959) pp. 423-32.

Army Quarterly, "Commonwealth Manpower-A Plea for a Colonial Army" 61/1 (Oct. 1950) pp. 53-61.

Atkinson, D. James. "Liddell Hart and the Warfare of the Future," Military Affairs 29/4 (1966) pp. 161-163.

Barber, A. James (Cdr. U.S. Navy) "Mahan and Naval Strategy in the Nuclear Age: A Lecture delivered at the Naval War College," Naval War College Review vol. 24 (March 1972) pp. 78-87.

Barclay, C.N. (Brig.) "Atomic Warfare," Brassey's Annual (1952) pp. 59-70.
_____ "Historical Background, General Policy, and Tasks of the Army," Brassey's Annual, (1950) pp. 135-44.

_____ "The Imperial Army; Composition, Organization and Distribution," Brassey's Annual (1950) pp. 145-159.

_____ "Lessons of the Korean Campaign," Brassey's Annual, (1954) pp. 122-33.

_____ "The Problems of the Arab World," Brassey's Annual (1959) pp. 137-47.

Barnes, B.H.P. (Maj.) "Future Strategic Importance of the Middle East to the British Commonwealth of Nations," Army Quarterly 57/1 (Oct. 1948) pp. 161-77.

Barrett, G.G. (Gp. Capt.) "The Role of the R.A.F. in the Pre-
    Servation of Peace," JRUSI 91/561 (Feb. 1946) pp. 77-82.

Barry, Donald, "Afloat Support," The Navy (Aug. 1957)
        vol. 69, pp. 239-40.

_____ "The British Navy in the Nuclear Age", United States
        Naval Institute Proceedings vol. 83 (Oct. 1957) pp. 1069-
        77.

_____ "The Navy Today," The Navy vol. 68 (May 1958) pp. 106-
        12.

_____ "The Navy Today and Tomorrow," The Navy 59/5 (May 1954)
        pp. 114-118.

Baylis, John. "Defense Policy Analysis and the Study of
        Changes in Postwar British Defense Policy," International
        Relations 4:4 (November 1973) pp. 383-399.

Beer, H. Samuel. "Pressure Groups and Parties in Britain,"
        American Political Science Review 50/1 (March 1956)
        pp. 1-23.

Beloff, Max. "Suez and the British Conscience," Commentary vol.
        23 (April 1957) pp. 309-15.

Bennet, G.M. (Cdr.) "Imperial Defence", JRUSI 91/562 (May 1946)
        pp. 165-175.

Bertram, Christoph. "Internal Pressures Behind Defence Policies
        in Western Europe," Survival (Jan, 1971) pp. 13-16.

Beytagh, W. (W. Cdr.) "Air Power and Air Transport," RAF Quar-
        terly 17/1 (Dec. 1945) pp. 16-21.

Blackett, P.M.S. "British Policy and the H-Bomb, I, III,"
        New Statesman and Nation vol. 48 (14, 28 Aug. 1954)
        pp. 172-3, 226-7.

_____ "Tizard and the Science of War," Nature 185/4714
        (March 5, 1960) pp. 647-53.

Bond, Brian, "Nuclear Age Theories of Sir Basil Liddell Hart",
        Military Review 50/8 (Aug. 1970) pp. 10-20.

Bower, R.H. (Maj. Gen.) "Air Support for the Army," Brassey's
    Annual (1954) pp. 180-8.

Bowles, Geoffrey. Letter to the Editor, "An Absence of Bases"
    Time and Tide vol. 38 (12 January 1957) p. 44.

_____ Letter to the Editor, "An Absence of Bases," Time
    and Tide vol. 38 (26 January 1957) p. 99.

Boyle, Sir Dermot (A.C.M.) "The Air in Peace and War," United
    Empire vol. 48 (Apr-Mar 1957) pp. 60-3.

Brazier-Creagh K.R. (Brig.) "Anti-Terrorist Operations in Malaya
    1953-54," Brassey's Annual (1954) pp. 327-39.

_____ "The Local Defense of Overseas Territories," Brassey's
    Annual (1956) pp. 219-31.

_____ "Limited War," Brassey's Annual (1957) pp. 35-45.

Brodie, Bernard. "Some Notes on the Evolution of Air Doctrine,"
    World Politics 7:3 (April 1955) pp. 48-62.

Bronowski, J. "The Real Responsibilities of the Scientist,"
    Bulletin of the Atomic Scientist 12/1 (Jan. 1956)
    pp. 10-13, 20.

Brook, C. Philip. "Some Antecedents of British Defense Policy,"
    The Army Quarterly vol. 102 (Oct. 1971) pp. 70-80.

Buchan, Alastir. "P.M.S. Blackett and War," Encounter (Aug. 1961)

_____ "Britain and the Nuclear Deterrent," Political Quar-
    terly 31/1 (Jan.-Mar. 1960) pp. 36-45.

Buzzard, Anthony. "The Crux of Defence Policy," International
    Relations 1/5 (April 1956) pp. 195-206.

_____ "The H-Bomb: Massive Retaliation or Graduated Deterrence"
    International Affairs vol. 32 (April 1956) pp. 148-58.

_____ "Massive Retaliation and Graduated Deterrence," World
    Politics 8/2 (Jan. 1956) pp. 228-37.

Buzzard, Anthony, Slessor John and Lowenthal, Richard. "The
        H-Bomb, Massive Retaliation of Graduated Deterrence-
        A Discussion," International Affairs 32/2 (April 1956)
        pp. 148-165.

Campbell (Campbell) D.R.F. (Cap.) "The Philosophy of Naval Air
        Warfare," Flight (22 March, 1957) vol. 71 pp. 377-8.

Carey, Roger. "The British Nuclear Force: Deterrent or Economy
        Measure," Military Affairs 36/4 (Dec. 1972) pp. 133-8.

Carter, W. (A.V.M.) "Air Power Confronted," Brassey's Annual
        (1965) pp. 169-176.

_____ "The Middle East in Modern Strategy," Brassey's Annual
        (1961) pp. 115-24.

Cartmel, B.S. (Gp. Cap.) "Maintenance of the R.A.F. Overseas,"
        JRUSI 92/565 (February 1947) pp. 100-5.

Castle, Barbara. "A Co-operative Commonwealth," New Statesman
        and Nation vol. 53 (8 June 1957) pp. 724-5.

Chamier, J.A. (Wg. Cdr.) "The Use of the Air Force for Re-
        placing Military Garrisons," JRUSI 66/462 (May 1921)
        pp. 205-16.

Chappell, John. "Trooping by Air," The Navy 61/9 (Sept. 1956)
        pp. 270-4.

Chassin, L.M. (General) "Un Grand Pensuer Militaire Britannique:
        B.H. Liddell Hart," Revue de Defence National Tome II,
        (Année 6) pp. 334-46.

Cockburn, R. "Science in War," JRUSI 101-601 (Feb. 1956)
        pp. 23-35.

Cohen, Israel. "The Partition of Palestine," The Contemporary
        Review vol. 173 (Jan. 1948) pp. 7-10.

Collier, A.C. (A.V.M.) "Air Transport," JRUSI 90/557 (Feb. 1945)
        pp. 36-51.

Colville, R.F. (Lt. Cmd.) "Russia's Foreign Policy: The Lessons of History," JRUSI vol. 95 (Aug. 1950) pp. 477-8.

Colyer, Douglas. "Air Warfare," Fortnightly Review vol. 170 (1948) pp. 168-73.

Commercial and Financial Chronicle, "The Financial Situation," N.Y. 151/3937 (Dec. 7, 1940) pp. 3281-3.

Condor, H.R.R. (Lt. Col.) "Future Development in Imperial Defense," JRUSI 92/567 (August 1947) pp. 374-82.

Connell, John, "Decline and Fall," Time and Tide vol. 36 (31 July 1954) p. 1026.

Cox, Donald. "A Dynamic Philosophy of Air Power," Military Affairs 21/3 (Fall 1957) pp. 132-138.

Craig, T.S. "Trooping Today," Army Quarterly 76/2 (July 1958) pp. 214-23.

Cross, Sir Kenneth (Air Marshal) "Transport Command 1943-64" R.A.F. Quarterly 4/2 (Summer 1964) pp. 85-92.

_____ "Transport Command Royal Air Force," Brassey's Annual, pp. 184-187.

Crossman, R.H.S., "The Role Britain Hopes to Play," Commentary vol. 5 (June 1948) pp. 493-497.

David, J.G. (Gp. Cap.) "The Employment of Air Forces in Im-perial Defence," R.A.F. Quarterly 17/2 (March 1946) pp. 77-82.

Deane-Drummond, A.J. (Lt. Col.) "The Army in the Transport Age: A Look into the Future," Army Quarterly 70/2 (July 1955) pp. 186-91.

Desoutter, D.M., "The Royal Air Force in Time of Change and Growth," Brassey's Annual (1957) pp. 299-306.

De Weerd, H.A., "Britain's Changing Military Policy," Foreign Affairs 34/1 (Oct. 1955) pp. 102-16.

_____ "Britain's Defence, New Look Five Years Later," RAND Corporation Document p 2562 (March 1962).

_____ "British Defense Policy: An American View" RAND Corporation Document p 2390, 3 (Aug. 1961)

Dinerstein, S. Herbert. "The Impact of Air Power on the International Scene: 1933-1940," Military Affairs 19/2 (Summer 1955) pp. 65-70.

Earle, E. Mead, "The Influence of Air Power Upon History," Yale Review 35/4 (Summer 1946) pp. 573-93.

The Economist. "Rebellion in Palestine" 151/5367 (July 6, 1946) p. 8-9.

_____ "Palestine Dilemma" 151/5368 (July 13, 1946) pp. 45-6.

_____ "Defence in Two Worlds" 152/5398 (Feb. 8, 1947) pp. 227-8.

_____ "Crisis as Usual" 152/5400 (Feb. 22, 1947) pp. 305-6.

_____ "Russia's Strength" 152/5412 (May 17, 1947) pp. 745-7.

_____ "Palestine Parley" 152/5412 (May 17, 1947) p. 754.

_____ "The Price of Admiralty" 156/5519 (June 4, 1949) pp. 1028-30.

_____ "Defence Orders and Aircraft Employment" 158/5560 (March 18, 1950) pp. 612-3.

_____ "Third Appropriation 158/5560 (March 18, 1950) pp. 569-71.

_____ "The Cost of Welfare" 158/5562 (April 1, 1950) pp. 694-6.

_____ "Forward in Europe" 158/5562 (April 1, 1950) pp. 691-2.

_____ "The Strategic Emphasis" 158/5562 (April 1, 1950) pp. 692-4.

_____ "Balanced Forces" 158/5563 (April 8, 1950) pp. 755-7.

_____ "Priorities for Containment" 159/5578 (July 22, 1950) pp. 153-5.

_____ "Middle East Vacuum" 159/5598 (Dec. 9, 1950) pp. 984-5.

_____ "Affair of Admiralty" 160/5610 (March 3, 1951) pp. 467-8.

_____ "The British Colonial Army" 160/5616 (April 14, 1951) pp. 844-5.

_____ "South of the Soviets" 160/5625 (June 16, 1951) pp. 1413-4.

_____ "Oil and Bases in Iraq" 161/5644 (Oct. 27, 1951) pp. 984-5.

_____ "The Anglo Egyptian Treaty" 161/5649 (Dec. 1, 1951) pp. 1314-5.

_____ "Security in the Canal Zone" 161/5650 (Dec. 8, 1951) p. 1384.

_____ "Darkness in Egypt" 162/5658 (Feb. 2, 1952) pp. 258-9.

_____ "Precedence in Defence" 162/5664 (March 15, 1952) pp. 627-9.

_____ "Canal Defence and Regional Defence" 166/5714 (Feb. 28, 1953) p. 544.

_____ "Tory Reform for Defence" 166/5714 (Feb. 28, 1953) pp. 547-9.

_____ "What Price Convertibility" 166/5714 (Feb. 28, 1953) pp. 549-50.

_____ "New Outlook for Middle East Defence" 167/5720 (April 11, 1953) pp. 96-7.

_____ "Defence Without a Date" 167/5725 (May 16, 1953) pp. 419-21.

_____ "Middle Eastern Alternatives" 169/5752 (Nov. 21, 1953) pp. 561-2.

_____ "An Army Extended" 170/5766 (Feb. 27, 1954) pp. 660-3.

_____ "Waiting for a New Fleet" 170/5766 (Feb. 27, 1954) pp. 663-4.

_____ "Agreement on Suez" 172/5788 (July 31, 1954) pp. 343-4.

_____ "Defender of Defence" 172/5792 (Aug. 28, 1954) pp. 639-40.

_____ "Do We need a Navy?" 173/5809 (Dec. 25, 1954) pp. 1061-2.

_____ "Labour and Defence"174/5818 (Feb. 26, 1955) p. 691.

_____ "The Unconventional Armament" 174/5818 (Feb. 26, 1955) pp. 727-9.

_____ "What Price Oil" 174/5818 (Feb. 26, 1955) pp. 739-40.

_____ "From Defence to Deterrence" 174/5818 (Feb. 26, 1955) pp. 723-7.

_____ "The Military Consequences of Mr. Sandys" 184/5946 (Aug. 10, 1957) pp. 439-40.

_____ "Kenya Looking for a Base" 183/5940 (June 29, 1957) p. 1145.

_____ "Baghdad Pact: Defence Without Iraq" 188/5997 (Aug. 2, 1958) pp. 358-9.

Eden, Anthony. "Britain in World Strategy" Foreign Affairs 29/3 (April 1951) pp. 341/50.

Eldridge, W.J. (Maj. Gen.) "The Technical Training of Army Officers" JRUSI vol. 95 (Aug. 1950) pp. 399-404.

E.M.E.L. "The Start of Guided Weapons in the United Kingdom" Naval Review 42/1 (Feb. 1954) pp. 9-10.

Emme, M. Eugene. "Technical Change and Western Military Thought 1914-45" Military Affairs vol. 24 (Spring 1960) p. 6-19.

Falls, Cyril. "Obscurities of Defense" The Illustrated London News (Aug. 11, 1956) p. 218.

_____ "The Reshaping of Defense" Ibid., (Feb. 23, 1957) p. 292.

_____ "The Biggest Change in Military Policy Ever Made"
        Ibid. (April 13, 1957) p. 576.

Flight. "Defence: The New Shape" vol. 71 (12 April 1957) p. 461.

_____ "Middle East Air Force" vol. 71 (28 June 1957)
        pp. 878-80.

Foley, C.J. "Army Equipment" Brassey's Annual (1950) pp. 171-8.

Ford, Sir Denys (V.A.)"The Technical Training of the Naval Officer
        To-day" JRUSI vol. 95 (Aug. 1950) pp. 377-98.

Foxley, Norris. "Aircraft for Small-Scale Operations Overseas"
        Brassey's Annual (1965) pp. 177-187.

Frankland, Noble. "Britain's Changing Strategic Position"
        International Affairs (London) 33/4 (October 1957)
        pp. 416-26.

Franks, Sir Oliver. "Britain and the Tide of World Affairs,"
        The Listener vol. 52 (1954) pp. 2341-6.

Fuller, J.F.C. "The Pattern of Future War" Brassey's Annual
        (1951) pp. 130-9.

Garton, James. "Air Control of Dependent Territories" Time and
        Tide vol. 39 (4 Jan. 1958) p. 67.

Glasgow, George "Foreign Affairs" The Contemporary Review vol.
        171 (April 1947) pp. 247-253.

Glubs, J.B. (Capt.) "Air and Ground Forces in Punitive Ex-
        peditions" JRUSI 71/484 (Nov. 1926) pp. 777-84.

Goldberg, Alfred. "The Atomic Origins of the British Nuclear
        Deterrent," International Affairs (London) 40/3 (July
        1964) pp. 409-29.

_____ "The Military Origins of the British Nuclear Deterrent"
        International Affairs (London) 40/4 (Oct. 1964) pp. 600-18.

Goldsmith, R.F.K. (Maj. Gen.) "The Development of Air Power in
        Joing Operations," Part I, Army Quarterly 94/2 (July
        1967) pp. 192-201.

_____ "The Development of Air Power in Joint Operations," Part II, _Army Quarterly_ 95/1 (Oct. 1967) pp. 59-69.

Goodhart, H.C.N. "Development of the Aircraft Carrier," _Flight_ (22 March 1957) pp. 379-80.

Green, A. (Lt. Col.) "Military Air Transport-Everybody's Darling; Nobody's Baby" _Air Power_ 4/2 (Jan.1957) pp. 109-15.

Green, B. Laurence, "A Case for the Attack Carrier in the Missile Age," _U.S. Naval Institute Proceedings_ (July 1958) 84/7 pp. 46-53.

Gwynne, Jones (Lt. Col.) "British Commitments Overseas: Modern Strategic Concepts" _JRUSI_ 108/629 (Feb. 1963) pp. 4-13.

Hall, Nowell, "The Problems of Naval Bases: Are Fleet Trains the Answer?" _The Navy_ 61/8 (Aug. 1956) pp. 231-2.

Hartley, Anthony. "The British Bomb," _Encounter_ (May 1954).

Higham, Robin. "The Dangerously Neglected; The British Military Intellectuals 1918-1939," _Military Affairs_ 29/2 (Summer 1965) pp. 73-87.

Hill Sir Roderic (Air Mar.) "The Air Defence of Great Britain," _JRUSI_ 91/562 (1946) pp. 153-64.

Hodgson, P.E., "The British Atomic Scientists Association 1946-1959" _Bulletin of the Atomic Scientists_ 15/9) pp. 393-4.

Howard, Michael. "Bombing and the Bomb," _Encounter_ 18/4 (April 1962) pp. 20-6.

_____ "Britain's Defenses: Commitments and Capabilities," _Foreign Affairs_ 39/1 (Oct. 1960) pp. 81-91.

_____ "British Strategic Problems East of Suez," _International Affairs_ (London) 42/2 (April 1966) pp. 179-83.

_____ "Organization for Defense in the United Kingdom and the United States 1945-1958" _Brassey's Annual_ (1959) pp. 69-77.

_____ "Strategy in the Nuclear Age," JRUSI 102/608 (Nov. 1957) pp. 473-82.

Hudson, C.F. "Will Britain and America Split in Asia?" Foreign Affairs 31/4 (July 1953) pp. 536-47.

_____ "The Great Catastrophe," Twentieth Century vol. 161 (January 1957) pp. 5-14.

Hughes, Hallet C. (Ad) "Naval Logistics in a Future War," JRUSI 95/578 (May 1950) pp. 232-45.

Hughes, Hallet J. "Thoughts on the New British Defense Policy," Brassey's Annual (1957) pp. 263-74.

Hutton, R.M.J. (R.A.) "The Future of Maritime Power," JRUSI 96/582 (May 1951) pp. 222-233.

Imlah, A.H. "The Pax Britannica," South Atlantic Quarterly vol. 50 (Jan. 1951) pp. 12-24.

International Review of Defence. "The Carrier Controversey in Britain," 3/2 (1970) pp. 208-10.

Jacob, Sir Ian (Maj. Gen.) "Principles of British Military Thought," Foreign Affairs 29/2 (Jan. 1951) pp. 219-28.

James, Sir William M. (Ad) Letter to the Editor, "An Absence of Bases," Time and Tide vol. 38 (19 January 1957) p. 72.

_____ A Letter to the Editor, "An Absence of Bases," Time and Tide vol. 38 (2 Feb. 1957) p. 125.

Johnson, J.E. (A.V.M.) "The Role of the Air Forces Middle East," R.A.F. Quarterly 5/3 (Autumn 1965) pp. 169-75.

Joubert, Sir Philip (A.C.M.) "Air Power," Time and Tide vol. 35 (17 July 1954) pp. 965-6.

_____ "The H-Bomb-The Impact on Military Strategy," The Listener (3 June 1954) pp. 953-5.

Kendall, A.J.V. (Cap.) "Air Mobility for the Soldier," Air Power 7/3 (Spring 1960) pp. 179-85.

Kimche, Jon. "Can the British Hold the Middle East?" The Nine-
    teen Century and After 173/886 (Dec. 1950) pp. 358-369.

Kingston-McCloughry E.J. (A.V.M.) "The Future Structure of
    Armed Forces-The Effect of the New Weapons," Brassey's
    Annual (1956) pp. 36-47.

"L'Aiglon," "The Fleet Air Arm," The Navy vol. 62 (Sept. 1957)
    pp. 270, 272, 274.

Lamb, C.B. (Cdr.) "Land/Air Warfare (Some Thoughts on the
    Navy's Part)"Air Power vol. 4 (July 1957) pp. 257-63.

Lewin, Ronald. "Sir Basil Liddell Hart: The Captain Who
        Taught Generals," International Affairs 47/1 (Jan. 1971)
        pp. 79-86.

"Liason," "Some Reflections on the Conduct of War," The Navy
        vol. 59 (Aug. 1954) pp. 225-6.

_____ "British Defence Policy," The Navy vol. 59 (Feb. 1954)
        pp. 33-4.

Liddell Hart, B.H. "Small Atomics . . . A Big Problem," Marine
        Corps Gazzette (Dec. 1959) 43/12 pp. 10-2.

Lindsell, Sir Wilfrid, "The Development of India as a Base for
        Military Operations," JRUSI 92/566 (May 1947) pp. 223-31.

London Times "Facts for Trade Policy: Britian Overseas
        Supplies Before the War" (Dec. 19, 1945) p. 5 cols. 6-7.

_____ "Need for the Navy Will Remain: First Sea Lord and
        the Atom Bomb" (Dec. 19, 1945) p. 5 col. 2.

_____ "The Atomic Bomb: Defence Against New Weapons" (March
        8, 1946) p. 7 col. 6.

_____ "Canadian Loan for Britain £281 million at 2%"
        (March 8, 1946) p. 4 col. 4.

_____ "Future of Naval Warfare: First Lord on Defence Against
        Atomic Bomb" (March 8, 1946) p. 6 col. 1-2.

_____ "The Naval Future" (March 8, 1946) p. 5 col. 2.

_____ "Size of the Navy Reduced: Release Figures" (March 8, 1946) p. 6. col. 6.

_____ "Empire Defence" (An Address by Field Marshal Lord Allanbrooke given to the Royal Empire Society on Nov. 6, 1946) (Nov. 7, 1946) p. 5. col. 4.

_____ "Commonwealth Defence: Lord Alanbrooke's Proposal" (Nov. 7, 1946) p. 2. col. 2.

_____ "Releases from the Forces: Programme for the First Part of 1946" (Nov. 7, 1946) p. 2. col. 2.

_____ "Royal Navy in Peace Time: First Sea Lord on Its Needs" (Nov. 7, 1946) p. 2 col. 4.

_____ "Egypt and Britain: High Feelings in Cairo" (Sept. 13, 1947) p. 3 col. 4.

_____ "Every Industry Given Its Target: Sir S. Cripps Explains Basis of Export Campaign" (Sept. 13, 1947) p. 4 cols. 1-2.

_____ "Military Stores from India and Egypt: Huge Depot in East Africa" (Sept. 13, 1947) p. 3 col. 7.

_____ "Kenya Stores Depot" (Sept. 16, 1947) p. 3 col. 3.

_____ "Putting Export Plan Into Force: Conferences with Leaders of Industry" (Sept. 16, 1947) p. 4 cols. 1-2.

_____ "Future of Gurkhas: Tripartite Agreement" (Dec. 2, 1947) p. 3 col. 2.

_____ "British Policy in Palestine:30 Years Reviewed" (May 14, 1948) p. 5 col. 5.

_____ "British Rule in Palestine: The Striving for Reconciliation" (May 14, 1948) p. 4 col. 6.

_____ "Iraq in Ferment: The Suspicion of British Policy in the Middle East" (May 14, 1948) p. 5 col. 6-7.

_____ "The Palestine Mandate: Britain's Major Task" (May 14, 1948) p. 3 col. 2.

_____ "Britain and Zionism: Jewish War Recorded" (May 22, 1948) p. 5 col. 5.

_____ "Burden of Public Spending: Cost of Social Services in Welfare State" (July 17, 1953) p. 5 col. 5.

_____ "Mr. Sandys Back from Tour: Early Decision on Mid-East Base" (June 24, 1954) p. 6 col. 6.

_____ "Airlines to be Diverted: Avoiding Zone in East Mediterranean" (Nov. 1, 1956) p. 9 col. 6.

_____ "Labour Censure Move To-Day: Campaign Against Government" (Nov. 1, 1956) p. 10 col. 6.

_____ "Labour to Oppose Policy of Intervention" (Nov. 1, 1956) p. 4. cols. 1-7.

_____ "Suez Traffic Flow Dwindles: British Liners Turn West for Cape" (Nov. 1, 1956) p. 9 cols. 7-8.

_____ "Impact of Suez on Sterling Prospects" (Nov. 5, 1956) p. 15 col. 1-2.

MacFadyean (McFadyean) Sir Andrew "Economic Survey for 1947" The Contemporary Review vol. 171 (April 1947) pp. 197-202.

Martel, Sir Gifford (Lt. Col.) "The Pattern of a Future War: The Land Aspect" JRUSI 95/578 (May 1950) pp. 221-31.

_____ "The Trend of Future Warfare" JRUSI 92/567 (August 1947) pp. 370-3.

Martin, H.G. (Lt. Gen.) "The Eastern Mediterranean and the Middle East" Brassey's Annual (1955) pp. 95-109.

Martin, L.W. "British Maritime Policy in Transition," International Journal 23/4 (Autumn 1968) pp. 541-50.

_____ "The Market for Strategic Ideas in Britain; The Sandys Era," American Political Science Review 56/1 (March 1962) pp. 23-41.

Mayer, J. Arno. "Internal Causes and Purposes in War in Europe
      1870-1956; A Research Assignment," Journal of Modern
      History 41/3 (Sept. 1969) pp. 291-304.

Mayhew, Christopher. "British Foreign Policy Since 1945,"
      International Affairs (London) 26/4 (Oct. 1950) pp.
      477-86.

McKitterick, T.E.M. "What Are British Interests?" Political
      Quarterly 31/1 (Jan-Mar 1960) pp. 7-16.

Menken, Jules. "Problems of Middle Eastern Strategy," Brassey's
      Annual (1956) pp. 129-39.

Monroe, Elizabeth. "British Bases in the Middle East: Assets or
      Liabilities?" International Affairs 42/1 (Jan. 1966)
      pp. 24-34.

Montgomery, B.L..(Lord Montgomery of Alamein) "A Look Through
      A Window at World War Three," JRUSI 99/596 (Nov. 1954)
      pp. 507-23.

_____ "Organizing for War in Modern Times," 100/600 JRUSI
      (Nov. 1955) pp. 509-31.

_____ "The Panorama of Warfare in a Nuclear Age," JRUSI
      101/604 (Nov. 1956) pp. 503-20.

Moulton, J.L. (Maj. Gen.) "The Real Cost: A Study of the
      Effectiveness of Overseas Forces," The Navy 69/111
      (Nov. 1964) pp. 359-61.

_____ "Bases or Fighting Forces?" Brassey's Annual (1964)
      pp. 143-51.

_____ "The Role of British Forces in a Strategy of Flexible
      Response," Brassey's Annual (1965) pp. 23-32.

Mountbatten Lord Louis (Adm.)"The Royal Navy and Its Future,"
      The Listener (May 14, 1959) pp. 825-8.

_____ "The Role of the Royal Navy: A Speech by Admiral Earl
      Mountbatten of Burma," Brassey's Annual (Jan. 18, 1954)
      pp. 29-34.

Murphy, Charles J.V.,"A New Strategy for N.A.T.O.", Fortune
    (Jan. 1953) pp. 80-5, 166-70.

_____ "Defense and Strategy," Ibid. (Dec. 1953) pp. 73-84.

 The National and English Review, "Wild Thinking About Defence"
    vol. 148 (April 1957) pp. 170-1.

The Navy. "Britain to Build Big Aircraft Carrier: Decision on
    Royal Navy's New Flattop Confirms Mobile Base Policy,"
    6/10 (Oct. 1963) pp. 15-17.

'Ned', "The Fleet Train," Brassey's Annual (1953) pp. 213-21.

New Statesman and Nation, "British Defense Budget: The Real Cost"
    (27 Feb. 1954) pp. 255-58.

_____ "Belated Wisdom in Suez" vol. 48 (17 July 1954) p. 61.

_____ "The Agreement in Suez" vol. 48 (31 July 1954) p. 119.

_____ "Colonial Defence" vol. 53 (13 April 1957) p. 462.

New York Times, "British Renew Bid of Palestine Aid" (May 14,
    1948) p. 1 col. 6.

_____ "British Renew Offer to Palestine" (May 14, 1948)
    p. 4 col. 4-6.

_____   "Text on the British Statement on Palestine Chronicling
    History and Policy of the Mandate," (Statement by the
    Foreign Office and the Colonial Office on the Termin-
    ation of the British Mandate in Palestine)(May 14, 1948)

_____ "British to Expand Military Aircraft" (Feb. 9, 1956)
    p. 3 col. 2-3.

Newsweek, "Palestine: Between Whips and Bayonets" (Jan. 13, 1947)
    p. 32.

_____ "Britain: Blitz by General Winter" (Feb. 17, 1947)
    p. 36.

_____ "Britain: God Save the People" (Apr. 28, 1947) p. 40.

Nicholl, A.D. (R.A.) "The Naval Situation: The Policy of the
    Navy League" The Navy vol. 59 (Nov. 1954) pp. 330-3.

_____ "World Strategy and Suez" The Navy (January 1957)
    pp. 2-4.

_____ "The Danger by Sea" The Navy (April 1957) pp. 81-2.

Nicholl, Angus, "The Navy in the Push-Button Age," The Listener
    (2 Sept. 1954) pp. 345-6.

_____ "The Potentialities of Guided Missiles" Brassey's
    Annual (1954) pp. 234-40.

Nicholl, G.W.R. "The Future of the Aircraft Carrier," Brassey's
    Annual (1952) pp. 101-6.

Owen, Sir Leonard. "Nuclear Engineering in the United Kingdom-
    The First Ten Years," Journal of British Nuclear
    Energy Society 2/1 (Jan. 1963) pp. 23-32.

Panikkar, K.M. "The Defence of India and Indo-British Obligations"
    International Affairs (London) 22/1 (Jan 1946) pp. 85-90.

Pelly, P.H.D. (R.N.) "The Pattern of Future War: The Sea Aspect"
    JRUSI 95/578 (May 1950) pp. 221-31.

Portal, C.F.A. (Air Cdr.) "Air Force Cooperation in Policing
    the Empire" JRUSI (May 1937) pp. 343-58.

Powell, Enoch, "A Policy for Britain," The Twentieth Century
    155/923 (Jan. 1954) pp. 10-21.

Power, Manley (V.A. R.N.) "The Fleet Air Arm: A Superb Poten-
    tiality," The Aeroplane (Nov. 28, 1958) pp. 787-94.

Rau, S.M. (V.A.) "The Fleet Train," JRUSI vol. 99 (Feb. 1954)
    pp. 16-34.

Ropp, Theodore. "A Theorist in Power: (B.H. Liddell Hart)"
    Air University Review 18/3 (March-April 1967) pp. 105-9.

Rosinki, Herbert. "The Role of Sea Power in Global Warfare of
    the Future," Brassey's Naval Annual (1947) pp. 102-116.

Round Table, "The Empire and the Middle East" 47/188 (Sept. 1957) pp. 327-41.

_____ "The Empire and the Middle East" 37/146 (March 1947) pp. 103-111.

_____ "Manpower and Defence" 39/156 (Sept. 1949) pp. 323-8.

_____ "Manning the Defences" 41/161 (Dec. 1950) pp. 44-51.

_____ "Three Questions on Defence" 47/188 (Sept. 1957) pp. 327-41.

Salter, K. (Wng. Comd.) "Communion and Its Counteraction," JRUSI vol. 95 (Aug. 1950) pp. 479-485.

Saundby, Sir Robert (Air Marshal). "Air Power in Limited War," JRUSI 103/611 (Aug. 1958) pp. 378-83.

_____ "Air Transport and the Strategic Reserve," The Aeroplane vol. 95 (26 Sept. 1958) pp. 492-3.

_____ "Defence in the Nuclear Age," Brassey's Annual (1957) pp. 25-34.

_____ "The Royal Air Force in the Atomic Age," Brassey's Annual (1958) pp. 22-32.

_____ "The Royal Navy in the Atomic Age," Brassey's Annual (1955) pp. 149-157.

_____ "Sea Power and the Aircraft Carrier," Brassey's Annual (1953) pp.114-21.

Schofield, B.B. (V.A.) "Britain's Postwar Naval Policy," The Navy 63/8 (Aug. 1958) pp. 217-19, 63/9 (Sept. 1959) pp. 267-72.

"Securus", "Influence of Air Power Upon the Control of Sea Communications," Brassey's Naval Annual (1938) pp. 181-7.

Seversky de Alexander (Maj.) "A Lecture on Air Power," Air University Quarterly Review vol. I (Fall 1947) p. 32.

Shepherd E. Colston, "The Carrier as a Strategic Weapon,"
        The Navy 60/9 (Sept. 1955) pp. 272-6.

_____ "Air Power and the Land Battle," Brassey's Annual (1954)
        pp. 189-197.

Shepherd, F.C. "The Deterrent Force," Brassey's Annual (1956)
        pp. 121-8.

Shipley, A.O. (Cap.) "Imperial Defense and the Rise of Nat-
        ionalism in Colonial Territories," Journal of the Royal
        Artillery vol. 84 (Oct. 1957) pp. 242-5.

Shwadran, Benjamin. "The Beginning of the End," Palestine Affairs
        4/1 (Jan. 1949) pp. 1-7.

Skloot, Edward. "Labour East of Suez," Orbis 10/3 (Fall 1966)
        pp. 947-57.

Slessor, Sir John (M.R.A.F.) "Air Power and the Future of War,"
        JRUSI 99/595 (Aug. 1954) pp. 343-58.

_____ "Air Power and World Strategy," Foreign Affairs (Oct.
        1954) 33/1 pp. 43-53.

_____ "British Defense Policy," Foreign Affairs 35/4 (July
        1957)pp. 551-63.

_____ "The Great Deterrent and its Limits," Bulletin of the
        Atomic Scientist 12/5 (May 1956) pp. 140-6.

_____ "A New Look at Strategy for the West," Orbis 2 (Fall 1958)
        pp. 320-26.

_____ "Some Reflections on Airborne Forces," Army Quarterly
        56/2 (July 1948) pp. 161-6.

_____ "Western Strategy in the Nuclear Age", Orbis 1/3 (Fall
        1957)pp. 357-64.

Smedley, W.M. (Sq. Ld.) "R.A.F. Strategic Mobility in a Guided
        Weapon Era," Air Power (5 October 1957) pp. 25-30.

Smith, O. Dale (Brig. Gen. U.S.A.F.)"The Role of Air Power
        Since World War II", Military Affairs 19/2 (Summer 1955)
        pp. 71-76.

Spaatz, Carl (Gen.) "Evolution of Air Power," Military Review
    vol. 27 (June 1947) pp. 3-13.

Sprout, Harold. "Britain's Defense Program," Britain Today:
    Economic, Defense and Foreign Policy, pp. 65-71.

    (Papers delivered at a meeting of Princeton University
    Conference, May 12-13, 1959)

_____ "Retreat from World Power," World Politics 15/4 (July
    1963) pp. 665-88.

Stevens, T.M.P. (Cap.)"The Helicopter Carrier," The Navy (Oct.
    1957) pp. 322-3.

Stewart, James (Lt. Cdr.) "The Suez Operation," U.S. Naval
    Institute Proceedings (April 1964) pp. 37-47.

Stewart, Oliver (Maj.) "The Air War at Sea, Brassey's Annual
    (1946) pp. 81-8.

_____ "Unsinkable Carrier," The Navy vol. 58 (March 1953)

Suckerman, Sir Solly "Liberty in the Age of Science," Nature
    184/4681 (July 18, 1959) 135-8.

Survival, "British Defence Policy" 6/6 (Nov.-Dec. 1964) pp. 256-7.

Swain, S.L. "How can the lessons learnt from the development of
    the Services in organization and technique since 1939
    be applied to the solution of Imperial Defense Problems?"
    JRUSI vol. 92/566 (May 1947) pp. 165-185.

"Tarbrook," "Britain's Future Strategic Reserve," Brassey's
    Annual (1958) pp. 71-84.

Taylor, J.W.R. "Give the Army Wings," R.A.F. Quarterly 4/1
    (Jan. 1952) pp. 13-18.

_____ "Military Air Transport in a Nuclear Age," Air Power 4/3
    (Apr. 1957) pp. 174-84.

_____ "The Future of Air Power," Air Power vol. 4 (July 1957)
    pp. 265-267.

Tedder, Lord, A.V. (M.R.A.F.) "A Defense Warning to Britain,"
    Sunday Express (Oct. 19, 1947)

Thomson, G.P. (R.A.)"Look-Out at Westminster" The Navy vol. 59
        (April 1954) pp. 96-7.

_____ "A New Look at the Defence Plan," The Navy vol. 62
        (Nov. 1957) pp. 346, 361.

Thursfield, H.G. (R.A.)"Lessons of the War," Brassey's Naval
        Annual, (1946) pp. 1-12.

_____ "The Naval Prospect," Brassey's Naval Annual (1947)
        pp. 1-10.

_____ "A Naval Survey," Brassey's Naval Annual(1948) pp. 1-13.

_____ "The Influence of Sea Power Today," Brassey's Naval
        Annual (1949) pp. 1-9.

_____ "The Disposition of British Sea Forces," Brassey's
        Annual (1954) pp. 320-6.

Time and Tide, "Abandoning Suez" vol. 35 (31 July 1954) pp.
        1011-1012.

_____ "The Problems of Cyprus" vol. 35 (14 Aug. 1954) p. 1068.

_____ "An Absence of Bases" vol. 38 (5 Jan. 1957) p. 6.

_____ "The Battle of Storey's Gate" vol. 39 (1 March, 1958)
        pp. 246-7.

Tizard, Sir. T. Henry, "The Influence of Science On Strategy,"
        Brassey's Annual (1951) pp. 112-5.

Torlesse, A.D. (V.A.) "The Role of the Aircraft Carrier,"
        Brassey's Annual (1955) pp. 72-82.

Tuker, Sir Francis (Lt. Gen.) "Pacts, Bases and the Common-
        wealth," Twentieth Century vol. 161 (Feb. 1957) pp. 111-
        115.

Varga, E. "The Marshall Plan and the British Economic Crisis,"
        New Times: A Soviet Weekly Journal No. 42 (Oct. 15, 1947)
        pp. 3-7.

Verrier, Anthony. "Strategically Mobile Forces--United States
        Theory and British Practice," JRUSI 106/624 (Nov. 1961)
        pp. 479-85.

Vivekandan, B. "Britain's Defense Policy East of Suez," In-
      ternational Studies 14/1 (Jan-March 1975) pp. 53-67.

"Volage," "The Future of Naval Aviation," Brassey's Naval
      Annual (1947) pp. 68-87.

_____"The Development of Carriers and their Aircraft,"
      Brassey's Annual (1950) pp. 105-17.

Wansborough-Jones, J. "Present Science and Future Strategy," JRUSI
      95 (Aug. 1950) pp. 405-423.

Wells, W.T. "Defense and the Imperial Conference," Fortnightly
      Review vol. 170 (1948) pp. 90-5.

Williams, G.R.R. "Atomic Weapons and Army Training," JRUSI
      99/596 (Nov. 1954) pp. 570-3.

Wilson, A.D. (Lt. Col.) "The Relevance of Air Mobility to the
      Middle East," Army Quarterly 69/2.

The World Today, "The Palestine Problem" 3/10 (Oct. 1947) pp.
      458-9.

_____ "Britain, Egypt and the Canal Zone Since July 1952,"
      The World Today: Chatham House Review 10/5 (May 1954)
      pp. 186-197.

Wright, Esmond. "Defence and the Baghdad Pact," Political
      Quarterly 28/2 (Apr.-June 1957) pp. 185-97.

Wykeham-Barnes, P.G. (Wg. Cdr.) "The War in Korea With Special
      Reference to the Difficulties of Using Our Air Power,"
      JRUSI 97/586 (May 1952) pp. 149-69.

Wyndham, E.H. (Col.) "The Influence of New Weapons Upon the
      Conduct of War," Brassey's Annual (1950) pp. 84-9.

_____ "The Near and Middle East in Relation to Western
      Defence," Brassey's Annual (1952) pp. 40-46.

Yool, W.M. (A.V.M.) "Air Action in Korea," R.A.F. Quarterly 3/2
      (April 1951) pp. 111-114.

_____ "Air Lessons from Korea," Brassey's Annual (1951)
      pp. 397-404.

Unpublished Material

Armstrong, C. DeWitt III (Lt. Col. U.S. Army) The Changing
    Strategy of British Bases , Unpublished Ph.D.
    Dissertation, Princeton University, 1960.

Crowe, J. William (Cdr. U.S. Navy) The Policy Roots of the
    Modern Royal Navy 1946-63, Unpublished Ph.D. Disser-
    tation, Princeton University, 1965.

Davis, Vincent. Admirals, Politics and Post-War Defense Policy:
    The Origins of Post-War U.S. Navy 1943: 46 and After,
    Unpublished Ph.D. Dissertation, Princeton University,
    1961.

Fletcher, E. Max, Suez and Britain: A Historical Study of the
    Effects of the Suez Canal on the British Economy, Un-
    published Ph.D. Dissertation, University of Wisconsin,
    1957.

Goldstein, Walter. The Labour Party and the Middle East Crisis;
    1956, Unpublished Ph.D. Dissertation, University of
    Chicago, 1961.

Levy, Morris, Alfred Thayer, Mahan and United States Foreign
    Policy, Unpublished Ph.D. Dissertation, New York Univ-
    ersity, 1965.

Lutrin C. Edward, The Trident in Politics: The Royal Navy As
    Interest Group, Unpublished Ph.D. Dissertation, University
    of Missouri-Columbia, 1972.

Rose C. Richard, The Relation of Socialist Principles to British
    Labour Foreign Policy 1945-51, Unpublished Ph.D. Disser-
    tation, University of Oxford, 1961.

_____ "The Changing Pattern of the R.A.F.," Brassey's Annual (1953) pp. 327-53.

_____ "Defense Trends in Britain," Brassey's Annual (1964) pp. 32-40.

_____ "The Royal Air Force: Fifty Years of Service," The Army Quarterly 96/1 (April 1968) pp. 38/42.

_____ "Royal Air Force Problems," Brassey's Annual (1955) pp. 169-84.

SUPPLEMENTAL BIBLIOGRAPHY

Abadi, Jacob, "Oil Protection in Britain's Middle Eastern Defense Policy--Rationalization or Necessity?" The American Journal for the Study of Middle Eastern Civilization, Vol. I(Spring, 1980), pp. 10-21.

Crossman, R. S., The Diaries of a Cabinet Minister, 2 vols., New York; Holt, Rinehart and Winston, 1967.

Verrier, Anthony, "British Defense Policy under Labour,"Foreign Affairs, Vol. 42, No. 2(Jan., 1964), pp. 282-292.

Watt, D. C., "The Decision to Withdraw from the Gulf," Political Quarterly, Vol. 39, No. 3, p.310.

INDEX

Abdulla Salem al Saba, 206
Aden, 23, 96, 135-6, 196-7, 200, 202, 205-7,
    210-13
Aden Alliance Party, 205
Admiralty, Board of the, 186, 191
Air Ministry, 50
Airfields, 72, 85-7, 91, 96, 101, 134-5, 137-8
Aqaba, 84
Alexander, A.V., Field Marshal, 70, 98
Alexand, H., Field Marshal, 16
Alexandria, 90
Allanbrook, Lord F., 12, 45, 65, 124
Anglo-American Committee, 26
Anglo-Iranian Oil Dispute, 78, 104
Arab League, 64, 86, 90, 206
Arab Legion, 9, 28, 85
Arabian Peninsula, 196-7, 202, 209
Attlee, Clement, Prime Minister, 3, 6, 10-11, 13,
    21, 23, 25, 27, 42, 63, 65-6, 68, 70-1, 76,
    78, 89, 96, 102, 118, 123, 132, 155-6, 164

Baghdad, 185
Baghdad Pact, 12, 77, 87-8
Bahrein, 96
Baldwin-Chamberlain, Program of, 136
Balfour Declaration, 2
Barnes, B.H.D., 94-95
Bartlett, C.J., 11
Basra, 85
Beaufre, Andre, 153
Belisha, Sir Lesslie Hore, 46-7, 49
Beloff, Max, 38
Ben Smith, 7
Bentwich, N. and H., 21-22
Berlin, Siege of, 69-70
Bevin, Aneurin, 17
Bevin, Ernest, 10, 12, 14, 16, 21, 23, 26, 29, 70,
    91, 155

Black Sea 77. 84
Blackett, P.M.S., 160-63
Bond, Brian, 50
Borden, W.L., 79
Brassey's Annual, 179
British Guiana, 104
Brodie, Bernard, 51, 120
Brown, George, 212
Brussels Pact, 71
Burma, 68
Butler, R.A., 97
Buzzard, Sir Anthony, 42, 52
Bywater, H.C., 46

Cape Route, 12, 65, 79, 81, 84
Carter, W., 136
Castle, Barbara, 17
Central Treaty Organization(CENTO), 87
Ceylon, 68
Chassin, L.M., 51
Churchill, Sir Winston, 18, 38, 45, 57, 61-2, 73,
        77-8, 80-1, 84, 91-3, 100-102, 105, 120, 125,
        140, 143, 151, 156, 158-61, 163, 165-67, 180
Cold War, 38, 59, 96
Commonwealth of Nations, 75-6
Condor, H.A.R., 62, 95, 149
Conningham, Leigh Mallory, 122
Cripps, Sir Arthur, 13, 21, 27
Crossman, Richard, 14, 17, 94, 97, 201
Cyprus, 5, 23, 62-3, 66, 86, 88, 90, 92-3, 96,138
Cyrenaica, 80, 90

D'Arcy, W.K., 26
Dalton, Hugh, 10, 12-3, 20-1, 27, 65, 89
Defense Committee, 17
Delargy, Hugh, 17
Dhahran, 92
Douhet, G., 72, 119-22
Dunkirk Treaty, 71

Earle, E.D., 129
East Africa Base, 61, 66, 90, 94-5
Economist, 19, 26-7, 47-8, 61, 76, 82, 97
Eden, Sir Anthony, 22-3, 62, 93, 103
Egypt, 5, 8, 12, 14, 23-4, 28, 63, 65, 80-3, 87,
    100, 138
Eniwetok, 166
Ethiopia, Invasion of(by Italy), 79-80
Europe, Defense of, 20, 60, 69-73
Europe, Financial Assistance, 29, 105

Falkland Islands, 94, 104
Faisal, King of Saudi Arabia, 212-13
Fisher, R.B., Rear Admiral, 187
Fitzsimons, M.A., 21, 66, 90
FLOSY(Front for the Liberation of South Yemen),213
Foot, Michael, 17
Fuller, J.F.C., 45-8, 52

Gaza, 90
Germany, 7, 71, 73
Germany(Troop Maintenance Costs), 7, 17, 69
Gibraltar, 80
Goldsmith, R.F.K., 138-9
Greece, 5, 11, 22, 58, 65, 73, 80, 83-85
Green, Laurence, 189
Gregg, Pauline, 14
Groves, P.R.C., 48, 125
Guderian, Heinz(General), 51
Gurka, 97

Habbaniya, 88,91
Haifa, 63, 66, 81, 92
Hailsham, Q.H., 19
Hallet, Hugh C.C., 151
Harper, Steven, 210
Hart, Liddell, H.B., 13, 20, 45, 47-52, 56-8, 61,
    68, 75, 78, 79, 81, 94, 97-8, 100, 104, 120,
    123, 139, 150-1, 157, 163
Head, Sir Anthony, 85, 98

Healey, Denis, 201, 214
Henderson, Arthur, 132, 141
Higham, R., 40, 44-6, 53
Hill, A.V., 142, 160
Home, Sir Douglas, 204, 214
Hong Kong, 59, 104, 149
Howard, M., 51, 126, 151-2
Hurd, Sir A., 46
Hurewitz, J.C., 8
Hussein, Sharif of Mecca, 2, 31

Imperial Defense College, 44
India, 1, 7, 22, 63-9, 81, 86, 88-9, 97, 154
Indian Ocean, 19, 66-7, 75, 198, 208
Inskip, Sir T., 49
Institute for Strategic Studies, 45
Iran, 65, 74, 82, 85-7, 95
Iran (Nationalization of Oil) 181, 205
Iraq, 1, 8, 14, 24, 28, 65, 82, 84, 86, 88, 92,
     207
Israel, 22, 82, 92
Israeli Army, 85

Jewish National Home, 1
Jomini, A.H., 121
Jones, Creech, 18
Jordan, 1, 26, 77, 86-7, 90, 92, 96
Jordan(Operation), 197-8
Journal of the Royal Air Force College, 46
Journal of the Royal United Service Institution
(JRUSI), 46

'Keep Left' Group, 94
Kelly, J.B., 204
Kennedy, Sir J., 33, 124
Kenya, 12-3, 89-90, 95
Keynes, Lord Meynard, 10
Korea, 73, 75
Kuria Muria, 213
Kuwait (Operation), 197, 207

Kuwait (Independence of), 206

Lagos, 13, 89
Latin America, 4
Leahy, W., 27
Lebanon, 77
Lee, Jennie, 17
Lend Lease, 4-5, 9-10, 31
Lewin, R., 50
Libya, 88, 91
Lindbergh, Charles A., 33
Lindemann, F. A., 142, 161, 163
Lindsay, J.(Colonel), 54
Little Aden, 205
Lloyd, Lord, 205
Lyne, Lo(Major General), 100

Mackson, H.R., 97
MacKay, Charles, 122
Macmillan, Harold, 61, 104, 142-3, 155, 158-9,
      198, 202, 205
Mafraq, 88, 91
Mahan, A.T.(Admiral), 173-4, 190
Malaya, 5, 59
Malta, 23, 62, 64, 79-80, 90
Marshall, General George C., 29
Martin, H.G., 70, 93
Mayhew, Christopher, 76
McLeod, Ian, 204
McKinnon Road, 89-90
McLoughry, E.J. Kingston-, 42, 52, 163
McMahon, Sir Henry, 2
Mediterranean, 16, 19, 23, 50, 62, 65, 67, 69-70,
      72, 77, 79, 81, 83, 87, 90-1, 94-5, 100, 103,
      104, 138, 173, 197
Menken, J. 158-9
Middle East, 1-2, 8, 10, 12-17, 20, 22, 27, 38-9,
      49, 56, 60, 62, 65-7, 71-4, 77-9, 81, 84-6,
      89-96, 100, 102-5, 133-4, 137-140, 149, 154,
      158-9, 164, 167, 180-1, 196, 198-202, 206

Mikardo, Ian, 14, 94
Milne, Lord G., 47
Mitchell, Billy, 120, 122
Mombassa, 89
Monroe, Elizabeth, 6, 65
Montgomery, Lord B.L.(Field Marshal), 42, 64, 70,
    102, 130, 179, 199
Montreux Convention, 84
Mosul, 85
Mountbatten, Lord Louis, 42, 185
Muhammad, Ali, 178

NATO(North Atlantic Treaty Organization), 59,
    69-72, 74, 83, 85, 87-8, 96, 152, 200, 202
Naval Review, 46
Navy League, 183-4
New Zealand, 65, 104
Nicholl, A.D.(Rear Admiral), 184
NLF(National Liberation Front for Occupied South
    Yemen), 212-3
Norris, C.F.(Air Chief Marshal), 81, 184
Northern Tier, 82-3, 85, 86, 87-8

Oil, 3, 8, 14, 16-7, 23, 59, 66, 77, 80, 90, 92-3,
    101, 103
Oilfields, 71, 73-4, 77, 81-2, 84, 159
Ottoman Empire: See Turkey

Pakistan, 67-8, 82, 85, 87, 92
Palestine, 1-2, 5, 7, 19, 60, 63-4, 82, 90, 92,
    134; Government, 9;Strategic Importance, 8
Palestine(Costs) 7, 13, 17-8, 24, 26, 27-8
Palestine(Revolt) and Troop Numbers, 3, 7-9, 60
Palestine(Withdrawal), 3, 11-2, 19-20, 22-25, 38,
    58, 66, 70, 89, 99, 164
People-s Socialist Party of Aden, 203
Persian Gulf, 1, 16, 64, 82, 84, 90, 92, 197-9,
    203-4, 206-7, 209, 210-4
Petain, Marshal Henri, 120
Petroleum: See Oil

Pile, Sir F., 51
Portal, C.F.A., 122, 135-7
Pound Sterling, Its Convertibility, 11, 17

R.A.F.(The Royal Air Force), 63, 86, 88, 91-96,
    118, 121-128, 130, 134, 136-7, 140, 155, 182,
    191, 207-8
Radfan, 199
Raschid Ali(Revolt in Iraq), 82
Richmond, Sir Herbert, 45-6
Roosevelt, President Franklin D,, 32-3
Rowe, A.P., 160
Royal Institute of International Affairs, 43
Royal Flying Corps, 45
Royal Navy, 130, 166, and Chapter VI
Royal United Service Institute (RUSI), 54, 58, 151
Sandys, Duncan, 90, 120, 142-3, 163, 191; Sandys'
    White Paper, 57, 143
Saudi Arabia, 1, 28, 204, 212, 214
Saundby, Sir Robert, 120, 130, 163
SEATO(Southeast Asia Treaty Organization), 104
Seversky, Alexander de, 128-9
Shaiba, 91
Shinwell, Emanuel, 9-10, 42, 202
Sidky, Ismail, 11
Simonstown, 90
Singapore, 104, 137, 149
Six Day War, 212
Slessor, Air Marshal John, 42, 61, 70-1, 92, 96,
    104-5, 117, 122, 125, 132-3, 139, 142, 151,
    155, 157, 163, 179
Snow, C.P., 160
Socony Vacuum, 77
Somaliland, 95
South Arabian Federation, 200, 210-=11
Soviet Union, 17, 69, 72-74, 76, 78, 83-4, 86, 96,
    105
Speed, Sir Eric, 99
Standard Oil of New Jersey, 77
Statement on the Termination of the Mandate, 29-30

Sterling Bloc, 11
Strachey, Sir John, 25
Strang, Lord William, 10-11
Strategic Reserve, 49-50, 57-63, 93, 95, 98,
    101-2, 104, 138, 152
Stuart, Michael, 201
Sudan, 88, 90, 95
Suez Canal(Zone), 1, 3, 16, 23, 38, 58, 61-66, 69,
    76, 78-95, 99, 100, 102, 104, 116-7, 132,
    141, 154, 162-8, 185, 196-7
    (Convention), 102
Suez Operation, 93, 103, 158, 180, 196, 205
Suez(East of), 66-7, 102, 196-203, 207, 209-11,
    214
Swain, S.L., 57, 107
Sykes, Sir Frederick, 45, 48, 52, 125-6

Tedder, Lord A.V., 128
Templeton, Viscount, 72, 122
Ten Year Rule, 69, 72, 105, 150
Thursfield, Captain H.G., 46, 179
Tiran, Straits of, 212
Tizard, Henry, 142, 159, 160-1
Tranchard, Viscount H., 45-6, 48, 72, 97, 120,
    122-5
Transjordan: See Jordan
Transport Command, 63
Trevelyan, Humphrey, 213
Tripolitania, 91, 95
Truman Doctrine, 78
Tuker, Sir Francis(Lt. General), 117
Turkey, 22, 58, 65, 73-4, 77-8, 80, 82-5, 87
Turkish Petroleum Company, 77

United States of America, 4, 9, 11-2, 20,22, 27,
    69, 71, 75-8, 85, 92
United Nations, The, 11, 22, 29
United Arab Emirates, 214

V-Bomber, 132

Valetta, 140
Valiant, 132
Vampire, 132
Van Fleet, General James A., 75
Varga, E. 7
Venezia Gulia, 7
Venom, 132
Vicker Victoria, 138
Victor, 132
Viking, 140
Vulcan, 131

Walsh, D.I., 33
War Office, 24, 50
Warburg, J.P., 20
Watkinson, Harold, 197, 202 207
Wavell, A.P., 45
Wayfarer, 140
Welfare State Project 15, 21
West Africa Base, 94
West Coast Route, 79
White Papers on Defense:(1946) 155; (1948) 11, 21,
     (1952) 156; (1954) 62, 179, 183; (1957) 49,
     50, 90, 103, 163, 168; (1961) 197; (1962)
     199; (1966) 210; (1967) 211
Wilkes, L., 28
Wilson, A.D., 80, 138
Wilson, Harold (Prime Minister), 200-1, 203, 212
Wimperis, H.E., 160
Woodcock, George, 3
Woodhouse, C.M., 2

Yugoslavia, 83
York, 140

Zarqa, 88
Zhukov, Marshal Georgi, 191